Labor and the Course of American Democracy

THE HAYMARKET SERIES

Editors: Mike Davis and Michael Sprinker

The Haymarket Series offers original studies in politics, history and culture, with a focus on North America. Representing views across the American left on a wide range of subjects, the series will be of interest to socialists both in the USA and throughout the world. A century after the first May Day, the American left remains in the shadow of those martyrs whom the Haymarket Series honors and commemorates. These studies testify to the living legacy of political activism and commitment for which they gave their lives.

Forthcoming titles:

Millennial Dreams: Contemporary Culture and Capital in the North
by Paul Smith

*The Invention of the White Race, Volume 2: The Origin of
Racial Oppression in Anglo-America* by Theodore Allen

Miami by John Beverley and David Houston

*The Cultural Front: The Laboring of American Culture in the
Twentieth Century* by Michael Denning

Power Misses: Essays Across (Un)Popular Culture by David James

*Messing with the Machine: Modernism, Postmodernism
and African-American Fiction* by Wahneema Lubiano

Public Transport by Eric Mann

Black Avant-Garde Film by Ntongela Masilela

Weekend in Silverlake by Kevin McMahon

*Dancing on the Brink: The San Francisco Bay Area at the End
of the Twentieth Century* by Richard Walker

Labor and the Course of American Democracy

US History in Latin American Perspective

CHARLES BERGQUIST

VERSO

London • New York

"Five Easy Pieces"
for Joel and Andrea

First published by Verso 1996
© Charles Bergquist 1996
All rights reserved

The right of Charles Bergquist to be identified as
the author of this work has been asserted by him in accordance
with the Copyright, Designs and Patents Act 1988

Verso
UK: 6 Meard Street, London W1V 3HR
USA: 180 Varick Street, New York NY 10014–4606

Verso is the imprint of New Left Books

ISBN 1–85984–865–6
ISBN 1–85984–126–0 (pbk)

British Library Cataloguing in Publication Data
A catalogue record for this book is available from the British Library

Library of Congress Cataloging-in-Publication Data
A catalog record for this book is available from the Library of Congress

Typeset by M Rules
. Printed in Great Britain by Biddles Ltd,
Guildford and King's Lynn

Contents

List of Tables   vi

List of Illustrations   vii

Preface and Acknowledgements   viii

Introduction   1

1   The Paradox of American Development   9

2   The Social Origins of US Expansionism   45

3   Latin American Revolution, US Response   81

4   Popular Culture and Democratic Values   117

5   Envisioning a History and a Politics Democratic   161

Tables

1   Imports of Slaves to America, 1600–1781   18

2   Population of the British Colonies in America excluding
    Canada, 1640–1775   22

3   British Trade with British America and Africa, 1714–73,
    and as a Percentage of All British Foreign Trade   31

4   US Direct Foreign Investments, 1919 and 1929   68

5   Reform Governments: Social and Economic
    Measures   91

6   Revolutionary Governments: Social and Economic
    Measures   93

Illustrations

1   "Europe Supported by Africa and America," engraving by
    William Blake in J.G. Stedman, *Narrative of a five years'*
    expedition, against the Revolted Negroes of Surinam
    (London 1796)   8

2   A cartoon depicting the colonial dependencies of Cuba
    and Puerto Rico, acquired by the United States after the
    War of 1898 with Spain   44

3   A view, by US political cartoonist John T. McCutcheon,
    of the Mexican Revolution   80

4   Cover of the second English-language edition of *How to*
    Read Donald Duck, by Ariel Dorfman and Armand Mattelart   116

5   Photographs of two key 1930s strikes, the San Francisco
    General Strike of 1934, and the 1937 Flint Sit-down Strike
    at General Motors   160

Preface and
Acknowledgements

Any claim to originality and political utility in this little book lies in its perspective and its form. Except for a portion of a chapter on popular culture, this is not a book of original research. Rather, it is a reinterpretation of United States and Latin American history, and of the relationship between the two, based on the published work of others.

The book does look at the history of the Americas from an unusual perspective, however. It focuses on the role of working people in the divergent histories of Latin America and the United States. It examines, in particular, the influence of labor in the evolving relationship between these two parts of the Americas. The goal of the book is to contribute through historical understanding to a new, more democratic,* labor politics in the hemisphere today.

I like to think of these essays as "Five Easy Pieces." That is not because they are especially easy or fun to read, at least not in any conventional sense. The essays are exercises in logic and interpretation that address the complex problem of how historians and others have understood the American past. The essays try to figure out what meanings people find in our history, and why. They try to show how these historical meanings have changed over time, and why. And they try to decide whether, on the basis of the historical information we have on the table, some meanings of the American past are "more accurate" and in some sense "better" than others. Involving oneself in these interpretive endeavors entails hard intellectual work. But the rewards can be illuminating. Reinterpretation of the past, I hope to show in these essays, has important political implications for all of us. That is why everyone, not just historians, should be concerned with how the past is understood.

---

* I use the term "democratic" here in the conventional sense of "government by the people." I define the term more carefully in the Introduction and explore its deeper meanings in each of the chapters that follow.

All historians worth their salt realize that their work is based on assumptions. These reflect their personal experience and the concepts, methods, and sources they rely on. Generally, however, historians discuss these critical issues in esoteric scholarly books and articles written for fellow specialists. In contrast, when historians try to reach out to a general audience, in textbooks, for example, or in popular accounts, they produce narratives chock-full of concrete evidence that give the impression that history really happened the way they say it did. In fact, however, the history they tell reflects what they have chosen to emphasize. And the interpretations they draw from their material are based on their assumptions.

The historian's practice of separating critical analysis from accounts for general readers can be justified in a variety of intellectual and professional ways. But it is fundamentally undemocratic. It assumes that critical discourse (about assumptions, concepts, methods, and sources) is appropriate for elite specialists, and that unexamined narrative (which is akin to propaganda) is sufficient for the rest of the people. It is also an ironic practice, since, as these essays attempt to show, the assumptions historians employ in their narratives (and other academics dress up as abstract theory) are often in fact widely shared by the public at large.

The essays in this book attempt to bridge the chasm historians and other academics have created between what they talk about among themselves and what they tell their general readers. Finding effective ways to do this has not been easy. In fact, I found writing this book much harder than doing the historians' histories I have written in the past. I have tried not to assume any specialized knowledge and have avoided (or explained) concepts and terms academics customarily use as a kind of shorthand in their conversations among themselves. Doing that has itself been an eye-opening experience. I often found that in trying to translate academic terms and concepts into plain English I discovered I had not appreciated fully what they meant or what they assumed.

The sense in which these essays are "Five Easy Pieces" is implied by the analogy to learning to read music. Looking at US and Latin American history together, and focusing one's concerns on labor, suggests simple, powerful explanations of some of the most important and complex problems in American history. The elementary concepts outlined here are conceived as stepping stones toward a democratic history and politics for the Americas. Mastering these simple ideas, I contend, allows one to make better sense of the intricate and interrelated histories of the American nations and to think more democratically about their future. What makes the elementary notions in these essays "hard" to assimilate is that they challenge the conventional wisdom of many historians and other academics and the common sense of many in the public at large.

If these claims for the perspective and form of this book are as valid as I hope they are, they are not the result of any special talent or insight on my part. Rather, they are largely the product of the way struggle for democratic reform in Latin America has affected my life as a citizen of the United States.

I was first forcefully made aware of the central problems discussed in this book when I went to Latin America as a young Peace Corps volunteer in the early 1960s. I was assigned to a small town in rural Colombia, in a coffee-growing region some four hours by bus from Bogotá. The Peace Corps, created by the US government in the wake of the Cuban Revolution of 1959, was designed to promote economic development, democratic social and political reform, and, perhaps most importantly, goodwill toward the United States in the underdeveloped or "third" world. At that time, in Washington's eyes, the whole of Latin America was threatened by the prospect of socialist revolution.

Sent by the US government to teach dirt-poor Colombian coffee farmers about development and democracy, I ended up learning far more from them about those subjects than they ever did from me. The hard-working, highly inventive Colombian working people I encountered did not fit the stereotypes about Latin Americans I had learned growing up in the United States. The obstacles to economic development and democratic practice they and other Colombians faced were not, in the first instance, the result of traditional cultural values and deficient individual motivation and attitudes (that was how historians and social scientists in the United States, people who called themselves "modernization theorists," explained underdevelopment at the time). I learned instead through daily experience that the problems Colombians faced were social, and that they were historical in origin and systemic in nature. They had to do with things like the concentration of land ownership and wealth, and the travesty both made of the nation's formally democratic institutions.

Experience in Latin America in the Peace Corps was the start of a Latin American learning process that over the last thirty years has taught me as much about my own society as it has about Latin America. Upon my return to the United States I was able to attend graduate school and specialize in Latin American history thanks to a National Defense Foreign Language Fellowship. That scholarship program was another US government response to the threat of socialist revolution in the underdeveloped world. Afterwards, in my university teaching and research, I continued to grapple with the question of Latin American development and democratic reform. My studies began with the history of Colombia, but as time went on they focused more and more on labor issues and more generally on Latin America as a whole. Eventually they included comparative study of my own society and the history of its relationship with Latin America.

In this book I try to distill what I have learned as a Latin American historian for a US readership. Readers will find that the range of historical issues addressed is broad. The volume of published material on these subjects is large and, as a non-specialist on most of the subjects addressed in this study, I have had to be very selective in my reading and in the choice of topics for discussion. I have focused on slices of American history that I believe help reveal the essence of the whole and have depended on specialists on each subject to guide my reading and criticize the drafts of the essays I have written.

The essays are built around critiques of a handful of classic and influential books on the subjects addressed. Some were written a long time ago, and my critique and appreciation of them depends on the research of many scholars, Latin American and US specialists alike, whose work has appeared in the decades since they were written. (Many of these important studies appear in the selection of readings included at the end of each chapter.)

The assumptions imbedded in these classic works, liberal in some cases, Marxist in others, informed historical debate and political action in the Americas during the half-century that has elapsed since the end of World War II and the end of the Cold War in our own time. In a broader sense, these crucial assumptions undergird the entire twentieth-century history of conflict in US–Latin American relations. For these reasons, I argue, coming to terms with these classic works and their fundamental assumptions now, at a time when the people of the Americas (and the world as a whole) are called upon to fashion a new, post-Cold War order, is especially fruitful. It allows us to frame an elementary understanding of American history that can contribute to fresh democratic thinking about the future of the Americas and the role of labor within it.

Critical review of these classic texts allows me and the reader, as non-specialists, entry into a range of scholarly debate on subjects as diverse as economic development theory and cultural criticism. It also enables me to outline large chunks of the history of the Americas in relatively few pages, and make connections between fields and specialized literatures that are customarily considered in isolation. It is this linking of material from US and Latin American studies and across historical sub-specialties that is, I believe, the main strength of the study as a whole.

This book, then, is not a conventional narrative history, but a study in the construction of historical meaning. It addresses interpretive issues

xii   LABOR AND THE COURSE OF AMERICAN DEMOCRACY

that customarily concern historians and other scholars and challenges the way many academics (particularly US academics) understand and convey the American past. But because I believe questions of historical interpretation are too important to leave exclusively in the hands of historians I have tried to write about them in a language accessible to a broader reading public. It is my hope that any reader seriously concerned with how the past—and our readings of it—defines the future will find these essays useful.

Finally, although this is a labor-centered interpretation of aspects of the whole of American history, it focuses particularly on US history and addresses primarily a US readership. It is, as I have indicated, my effort as a long-time student of Latin American history to come to terms with the history of my own society in the Americas. If there is any truth in the notion that the oppressed see things more clearly than do their oppressors, then perhaps both the perspective and the form of these essays may be vindicated.

This book, more than most, is built on the contributions of others and I have tried to acknowledge many of these in the text and suggested readings. Latin American scholars who do not figure there, but whose intellectual, political, and professional example and whose friendship have deeply affected me over the years include Colombian historians Hermes Tovar, Medófilo Medina, and Gonzalo Sánchez, all of whom teach at the National University in Bogotá. The central ideas in the book evolved over a long period in dialogue with students, fellow academics, and friends outside the academy who reacted to successive versions of them. Some of the specific questions addressed emerged in embryonic form in a course on hemispheric history organized with the support of the Center for International Studies at Duke University in the mid-1980s. I co-taught the course with US labor historian Leon Fink of the University of North Carolina, Chapel Hill, and we invited labor historian Bryan Palmer of Queen's University, Ontario, to provide a Canadian perspective in the course. US historians and Latin Americanists from Duke who participated in the teaching of the course included William Chafe, Lawrence Goodwyn, Carol Smith, Gary Gereffi, and Ariel Dorfman. Those from UNC included Lars Schoultz, Enrique Baloyra, and Peter Coclanis. I learned a lot from these people, including where we disagreed.

In early 1989, thanks to the History Department at the National University in Bogotá (whose chair at the time was Bernardo Tovar) and the Fulbright Commission in Colombia (directed by Agustín Lombana), I had the opportunity to pursue some of these same questions in a semester-long course on labor in the Americas with a lively group of Colombian labor leaders, university teachers, and graduate students. The experience brought home to me not only the high level of commitment among these activists and scholars to understanding American labor's past and to democratizing their own society, but the extent to which democratic aspects of North American labor struggles and labor scholarship were unknown to them.

Since joining the faculty of the University of Washington in late 1989, I have continued to try out aspects of the arguments of the book in my teaching, especially in courses on the history of US–Latin American relations and comparative labor history. The labor courses were enhanced by the establishment at the University of the Harry Bridges Endowed Professorship in Labor Studies and the Center for Labor Studies in 1992. Financing from those institutions has enabled me to invite outstanding labor scholars to campus each summer to help teach (and to teach me) about comparative labor history. US labor historians who have participated in these jointly taught courses include David Brody, Elizabeth Faue, Melvyn Dubofsky, and Mike Honey.

Listing all the people who suggested leads, loaned materials, criticized successive drafts of the chapters, or provided other kinds of support (including moral support) would probably tax the patience of even those acknowledged. But I would like to thank especially the following: among colleagues at the University of Washington, Dick Kirkendall, Richard Johnson, Richard White, John Findlay, Wilton Fowler, Laurie Sears, Jim Palais, Dauril Alden, Joan Ullman, Carlos Gil, Charles Hale (now at the University of Texas), Elizabeth Perry (now at the University of California, Berkeley), Phil Brock, Gigi Peterson, Ken Lang, and Whasook Nam; among labor historians at Duke, Andy Gordon (now at Harvard University), Alex Keyssar, and Danny James; among Latin Americanists at other US institutions, Carol Smith (University of California, Davis), Paul Drake (University of California, San Diego), and Sandra McGee Deutsch (University of Texas, El Paso); and among the Seattle-area unionists who discussed the project with me, or read the manuscript in its entirety, Dick Moork, Virginia Roberts, and my old, increasingly radical, friend Curt Pearson.

I wish to thank Liliana Porter for her generosity in granting me permission to reproduce a photograph of her original collage *The Simulacrum* (1991) as the cover illustration for the book. To my mind, her extraordinary image conveys the essence of the book's major themes: the tall blonde female figure, symbolic of Liberty and Justice, also recalls Miss Columbia, used historically to represent American democracy; the Mickey Mouse-like figure suggests the pervasiveness of

US popular culture (historically, Mickey has also been associated with the projection of US military power abroad); Che Guevara, represented here as fine (antique?) china, is widely revered in Latin America as a martyr in the struggle for social revolution; while Donald Duck (suggested by the yellow-green figure) is commonly perceived as "Everyman."

The image by William Blake, which illustrates chapter 1, is reproduced with the permission of The British Library (shelfmark 566H24). The political cartoons used to illustrate chapters 2 and 3 are reproduced from John J. Johnson, *Latin America in Caricature* (Austin, TX, 1980), and are used with the permission, respectively, of The New York Public Library and the *Chicago Tribune*. The photograph of the cover of *How to Read Donald Duck*, which illustrates chapter 4, is used with the permission of International General. The two photographs that appear at the beginning of chapter 5 are reproduced from *Who Built America?*, vol. 2 (New York 1992). The top photograph is used with the permission of the San Francisco Public Library; efforts to secure permission from the original source of the bottom photograph are ongoing.

Parts of the second and third sections of chapter 5 originally appeared in "In the Name of History: A Disciplinary Critique of Orlando Fals Borda's *Historia doble de la Costa*," and "Labor History and Its Challenges: Confessions of a Latin Americanist" in the *Latin American Research Review*, vol. 25, no. 3, 1990, pp. 156–76, and the *American Historical Review*, vol. 98, no. 3, 1993, pp. 757–64. They are published here with the permission of those journals.

Finally, I would like to thank all the people at Verso who transformed the manuscript into a book, including North American editors Mike Davis and Michael Sprinker, who oversaw the evaluation process; Jane Hindle, who handled production "briskly," as she once put it; and Helen Simpson, whose care, speed, and sensitivity made the copy-editing of this book easy, at least for me.

The book is dedicated to my children, Americans of Colombian and US descent. Their struggles, in private life and public art, to combine the democratic best in their dual heritage inspire their old father's heart.

Charles Bergquist
Seattle, May 1996

Introduction

As outlined in the Preface, this is a book about the role of labor in the history of the Americas. It looks especially at the ways working people in the United States influenced the relationship between their country and Latin America. Focus on the historical links between the United States and Latin America is especially important today. As everybody knows, the American hemisphere is now more tightly interconnected than ever before, and the trend toward greater economic, social, and cultural integration seems certain to continue. Issues such as trade, immigration, and drug trafficking preoccupy the people of all the American nations, including Canada. But the most difficult aspects of issues like these involve the relationship between the United States and Latin America, the richest and the poorest parts of the hemisphere. Study of labor in these societies, I believe, provides an important perspective on how these problems came about, and how we might think about dealing with them.

The book rests on the simple proposition that if Americans better understood the past, we could collectively create a better future. That sounds straightforward enough. The rub comes in defining what is "better." By better I mean throughout this book "more democratic." But since democracy is a word that means different things to different people, let me try to define my sense of it before I introduce the five essays that form the core of the book.

The conventional definition of democracy is "government by the people." As generally understood in the United States today, that means that all adults enjoy the right to vote in elections to decide issues of public policy, or to elect government officials to decide those issues for them. To be effective, these electoral rights depend on basic civil liberties, such as the freedom of speech, assembly, and association, on protection from arbitrary actions of the state, and on electoral processes that are free of corruption.

These conditions are fundamental to democracy, but in practice they may not lead to very effective participation in and control over public decision-making by the majority of people. Current debates in the United States over the proper financing of electoral campaigns, over the cost of access to the mass media for political purposes, over the ways special-interest groups influence Congress, and over low rates of voter registration and voting among the poor are examples of the problems involved in making equal political rights effective. These examples point to the ways private economic power and the unequal distribution of wealth undermine the ideal operation of democratic political rights, even in nations, like the United States, which are generally considered to have reached a high level of democracy.

[Private economic power not only undermines democratic ideals in the realm of electoral politics and public decision-making, however. It also influences our lives in more intimate and fundamental ways.] For example, our control over decision-making in the workplace is extremely limited. Except where strong unions are in place, and within certain limits set by the government, employers decide when and how we work, or whether we work at all. Within these same constraints, they decide how much and when we get paid, whether we get vacations or unpaid leave, what kind of health benefits or retirement plans we have, if any. Unchecked power of employers in the workplace can lead to discrimination by race, gender, ethnicity, and age; more generally, it routinely violates our elemental civil liberties, such as freedom of speech.

The unequal distribution of private property and wealth in our society deeply affects our private and family lives in other ways as well. It influences our decisions about forming families and having children. It affects the way we feed, clothe, and house ourselves. It structures our access to medical care and recreation and the ways we educate ourselves and our offspring. These matters are often referred to by labor historians as "reproductive" issues, because they pertain to how the labor force is maintained and reproduced. They are of special importance to women in societies like ours where men have greater access to wealth and power than women do and women traditionally have taken primary responsibility for the care and nurturing of the family. Reproductive issues thus defined go far beyond contemporary debate over the fundamental right of women to decide about giving birth to children.

[The concept of democracy used in this book addresses the ways private economic power affects the politics of the family, the workplace, the community, and the nation.] I define democracy as effective participation in, and control over, decisions about production, reproduction, and distribution by the majority of people in society. This definition encompasses the emphasis on fundamental individual political rights outlined above. But it includes as well the problem of economic and social inequality and the issue of control over decision-making in the workplace and in the family. It thus recognizes the limits on freedom and equality in the theory and practice of both existing socialist and capitalist societies.

By "society," I mean in this book all of the social groups, of ascending size, that humans have created to fulfill their individual and collective needs. I therefore use the term to encompass not only the family, the work group, the local community, and the nation-state, but the modern world social order as well. We are all increasingly conscious of the ways movements of capital, people, and culture across national boundaries intimately affect our lives. When the Ford Motor Company locates a production plant in Mexico or a Peruvian woman migrates illegally to the United States and takes a job caring for the children of a middle-class family, jobs within these nations are created and lost, income between and within them is transferred, and the experience and perception (and potentially, the politics) of all the people directly or indirectly involved in these transactions are modified. As these examples illustrate, the international movement of capital and people is powerfully shaped by the fact that the world is sharply differentiated into rich, high-wage societies and poor, low-wage ones.

Measured in historical time, this modern world of ours—closely linked yet sharply divided into rich and poor nations—is a relatively recent creation. It began some five hundred years ago with the expansion of Europe and the origins of capitalism. Capitalist organization of production has vastly extended our technical ability to transform the natural environment. Expanded production of material commodities—from food and fuel to machines and medicines—has greatly increased the physical power, life expectancy, numbers, and global interdependence of human beings. These achievements have been won, however, at great cost. Under capitalism we have inflicted great ecological damage on the planet. And we have created the highly unequal division of wealth and power—among nations and along lines of race, class, gender, and ethnicity—that we experience in the societies of the world today.

It is not social inequality in itself that defines our modern world, however, but the unique form and potentially transformative expression that social inequality has acquired. Over time, capitalism produced a novel system of production based on free wage labor. That system developed within the growing economic integration of the parts of the world that became industrialized and rich (beginning with Western Europe) and those that have remained agriculturally based, only partly industrialized, and poor (Latin America, Africa, much of Asia). Out of the new forms of class, racial, gender, and ethnic inequality that developed within this global capitalist system emerged the most striking philosophical and political characteristic of our modern world: an expanding democratic consciousness and escalating social struggle to overcome inequality.

The focus of this book on the history of working people in the United States and Latin America throws this complex global process into sharp relief. It also reveals how labor's struggle in each part of the hemisphere has influenced the course of capitalist development and democracy in the other part. These mutual influences, as noted above, have become ever more powerful and direct over time. Understanding them more fully, I argue in these five essays, can contribute to democratic thought and politics in the hemisphere today.

The first essay, "The Paradox of American Development," seeks to explain how the richest European colonies in the New World became the poorest independent nations of the Americas, and, conversely, how the poorest colonies became the core of the richest nation in the hemisphere and the world. The essay challenges the deep and often unconscious cultural and racial assumptions that most Americans, including many US historians, rely on to explain these outcomes. It argues instead that the United States developed into a powerful industrial democracy, while Latin American societies have not, primarily because of the legacy, established during three centuries of European colonialism, of free versus slave (or coerced) labor. In the United States the triumph of a system of free labor launched the nation on the path toward vigorous industrial development and stable democratic politics. In Latin America the legacy of forced labor gravely compromised both developments. The struggle to overcome the legacy of colonialism through democratic reform is the central thread of the history of Latin America throughout the nineteenth and twentieth centuries. Understanding the paradox of colonial American development is fundamental to democratic thinking about every aspect of US–Latin American relations. It is the basis for all the essays that follow.

The second essay, "The Social Origins of US Expansionism," analyzes the relationship between workers' struggles and the first of two phases of US expansion into Latin America and the world beyond. This first phase, which followed the dramatic mobilization of US rural and urban workers during the last decades of the nineteenth century, was primarily targeted at Latin America. It was formally inaugurated in the war with Spain in 1898 and lasted until the start of the Great Depression in 1930. During this period the government sought access to foreign markets and promoted private lending to governments and direct investments abroad in utilities, in communications and transportation, and, most significantly, in the production of raw materials for export.

The second phase of US expansionism followed the spectacular organizational gains of US industrial workers during the 1930s and World War
II and is still in progress today. It is analyzed in detail in chapter 5.
Although the initial forms of investment abroad continued, what distinguishes this phase from the first is its increasingly global nature and the
tendency to locate industrial production facilities abroad through the
vehicle of US-based multinational manufacturing corporations.

This second essay argues that students of US history, particularly labor
historians, have systematically ignored or misread the role of labor during
both periods of expansionism. It contends that they have also failed to
assess fully the contradictory ways expanding economic and political
interests abroad affected the potential for democratic progress at home,
particularly within the labor movement.

The third essay, "Latin American Revolution, US Response," examines the consequences of US expansionism in Latin America. It analyzes
the emergence in this century of movements in Latin America bent on
fundamental social reform and greater control over US investments and
influence. Spearheaded by workers, these movements have occurred
most often and most intensely in precisely those areas where US economic and/or political penetration has been greatest. The essay
compares revolutionary reform movements in Mexico after 1910, in
Cuba in 1933 and 1959, in Bolivia and Guatemala in the early 1950s, in
Chile, 1970–73, and in Nicaragua and El Salvador in the 1970s and 1980s.

From the outset, the US government consistently opposed these Latin
American reform movements, although in the end it came to an accommodation with some of them. It claimed that all of them were inspired by
Communism, or otherwise threatened US security, and that its policies
toward them promoted American democracy. The essay challenges these
ideological justifications of US policy and the mainstream scholarship
that supports them. It shows how US opposition to these struggles for
reform in Latin America reflects the "security interests" of privileged
elites in the hemisphere, who have benefited most from the social status
quo. Rather than promoting democracy, the essay argues, US policy has
historically subverted it, both at home and abroad.

Essay four, "Popular Culture and Democratic Values," explores the
role of what is conventionally called the "mass media" in influencing the
ways we think about the social system that binds the United States and
Latin America together. Mass media like comic books, film, and television
are not the only, nor even the most important, of the influences that
affect how we learn to make sense of the world around us. But unlike
other influences, the role of the mass media is relatively new and it is
growing. The mass media have also become highly centralized and

increasingly global in their influence. And, precisely because forms of mass entertainment are "popular," that is, avidly consumed by large numbers of people, they are of special relevance to study of the experience and attitudes of the working people who are the majority in society.

The essay focuses on the content and appeal of the Disney comic, one of the most popular examples of mass culture in the Americas and the wider world. It contends that, contrary to widespread belief and the Disney Corporation's formal avowals, these comics involve much more than simple entertainment. It also challenges the opposing view, common among early Marxist critics of mass culture, that the Disney comic is some kind of elite conspiracy designed to reinforce the social status quo. The essay argues that forms of popular culture like the Disney comic are theaters of contested cultural meaning, in which decidedly undemocratic messages are entwined with basic democratic ones. Understanding what makes something popular, the essay contends, helps us think about what a democratic politics for the future might entail.

Essay five, "Envisioning a History and a Politics Democratic," applies the concepts advanced in the first four chapters to the questions of writing democratic history and making democratic political choices in the here and now. It begins with an analysis of the fate of labor in the contemporary era, the period since World War II. In the United States, the essay contends, the crisis of labor today is in part a paradoxical result of the organizational victories working people won during the Great Depression and World War II and of the compromises organized labor made with government and corporations in the postwar period. The second part of the essay illustrates how labor historians writing since the war have revolutionized the study of labor and how they provide democratic concepts that can help revitalize labor and democratic politics today. The essay's final section argues that historians have a democratic method, however unrealized it is in practice, and that our biggest problem lies in breaking out of our narrow specializations and reaching a general audience. The chapter as a whole places narrow contemporary debates in the hemisphere over issues like trade, immigration, and human rights within the broad historical perspective of the book. Emphasizing the interests of working people, it suggests ways to rethink more general issues of productivity and international competitiveness, environmental policy, and the definition of democracy itself.

Taken together, these essays illustrate the importance of labor to the course of American democracy. They emphasize the persistent efforts of working people in the United States and Latin America to democratize their own societies and the way social elites and governments, particularly in the United States, have undermined, deflected, or subverted labor's democratic goals. What emerges with great clarity is the way struggles over democratic reform in the United States and Latin America are intertwined and interdependent. If nothing else, I hope this study suggests how better understanding of the history and promise of American democracy depends on a labor scholarship that transcends the sacrosanct boundaries of the nation-state.

William Blake, "Europe Supported by Africa and America," in J.G. Stedman, *Narrative of a five years' expedition, against the Revolted Negroes of Surinam* (London 1796). For Latin-American scholars of the mid-twentieth century, the triangular economic relationships between these three "partners" after 1500 held the key to understanding industrialization and underdevelopment in the modern world.

1

The Paradox of American Development

Most US citizens, if pressed to explain why their country developed into a powerful industrial democracy while Latin American countries remain weak, unstable, and poor, would probably respond with vague references to different cultural values, including attitudes toward work. Remembering our history textbooks, many of us would go on to contrast the predominantly Protestant English settlers who peopled the British colonies along the Atlantic seaboard of North America with the Catholic Spanish conquerors who colonized the southern part of North America, the islands of the Caribbean Sea, and, along with the Portuguese, the whole of South America.

These observations would be made in the context of some understanding of the racial geography of the Americas. Most of us are aware of the fact that the British colonies of North America (once most of the indigenous people had been exterminated or pushed west, and despite the existence of slavery) were predominantly of white, European descent. And most of us know that the majority of people in the Spanish and Portuguese colonies (despite drastic decline of a vastly more numerous indigenous population than existed in British America, and because of even greater reliance than the British colonies on slaves from Africa) were of mixed Indian, African, and European ancestry. These days most of us would not explicitly use race to explain the different historical evolution of the United States and Latin America. But behind the cultural explanations we depend on to explain this question lurks the issue of race nonetheless.

These ideas about the development of the Americas are not "wrong" in themselves. In fact, they point to some of the central elements in any explanation of the divergent histories of the American colonies. But the way these ideas are generally used to explain the different historical fates of the British and Iberian colonies in the Americas is fundamentally misleading.

This essay tests the logic of our commonsensical understanding of these matters and posits an alternative explanation for the divergent development of the Americas. It begins by challenging the climatic and racial determinism of what is still the single most important work on the history of US–Latin American relations, Samuel Flagg Bemis's 1943 publication, *The Latin American Policy of the United States*. It then explores the paradox of American development, how the richest European colonies became the poorest independent states, and vice versa. Comparison of the different roles played by the British and Iberian colonies in an evolving world economy provides one key to understanding the paradox of their historical development. Another key lies in the interconnections between the American colonies, especially their relationship within the famous "triangular trade" between Europe, Africa, and the Americas. This part of the essay draws on a classic work by Trinidadian historian Eric Williams, *Capitalism and Slavery*, which was published in 1944, just a year after the appearance of Bemis's book. The final section of the essay assesses the legacies of colonialism in the Americas in the post-independence era. The essay as a whole contends that the labor systems of the American colonies, not the independent action of climate, race, or culture, best explain the paradoxes of their historical development.

I

Serious study of US–Latin American relations must begin with the work of Samuel Flagg Bemis. Although now half a century old, *The Latin American Policy of the United States* remains the most comprehensive and detailed treatment of US diplomacy in the region from the era of independence to World War II. The book is even more important, however, for what it reveals about the assumptions behind that diplomacy. As we shall see in subsequent chapters, Bemis's interpretation prefigures all subsequent academic justifications of US policy toward Latin America. It also reveals the deep cultural and racial attitudes that undergird that policy.

At the time he published the book, Bemis was well on his way to becoming the preeminent US diplomatic historian of his generation. After receiving a PhD in history at Harvard in 1916, and publishing half a dozen books, he was honored in 1935 with a chaired professorship in diplomatic history at Yale. In 1937–38, thanks to a major award from the Carnegie Endowment for International Peace, he travelled extensively in Latin America, giving lectures and doing research. This experience, complemented by intensive research in US archives, resulted in his book on US policy toward Latin America, which was published in 1943, at the height of World War II. Among his subsequent publications, the most famous was *John Quincy Adams and the Foundations of American Foreign Policy* (1949), which won him the Pulitzer Prize for biography in 1950.

The Latin American Policy of the United States is a remarkable blend of powerful historical analysis and passionate political commitment. Its thesis is best conveyed in Bemis's own words.

> Historically the Latin American policy of the United States has been based on the nation's own independence under a republican form of government, on its Manifest Destiny (i.e., freedom for expansion through an empty continent to the other ocean), and on security for the Continental Republic which is the greatest single achievement of American nationalism. These fundamentals naturally favored independence for the whole New World, republican self-government for the new states, opposition to European intervention in their affairs, termination as soon as possible of remaining European sovereignties in the Western Hemisphere, and political solidarity of the nations of the New World against the imperialist powers of the Old World. (Preface, unpaginated)

In short, Bemis argued that what was good historically for the United States was good for Latin America as well.

Bemis developed his argument through cogent, chronological analysis of the traditional themes of US–Latin American diplomatic history. Although subsequent research on these subjects has increased our knowledge of them, Bemis's treatment is still the best introduction to the subject as a whole. He analyzed the limited role of the United States in the Latin American struggle for independence, which began in 1810 and had virtually freed the whole region (Cuba being the most important exception) from Spanish and Portuguese rule by 1825. He detailed the origins of the Monroe Doctrine of 1823, which declared "hands off" to any territorial designs in America by the Old World powers. Although unenforced by the United States until the end of the century, the Doctrine provides the basis for all subsequent US policy in the hemisphere. Bemis then carefully reviewed the march of US territorial expansion across North America during the nineteenth century. In the remainder of the book he reviewed the history of twentieth-century US–Latin American relations up to the start of World War II.

Bemis's interpretation of these themes is consistently pro-United States. In fact, it is no exaggeration to say that he unconditionally enlisted his scholarship in the service of the historic and contemporary aims of US policy in the hemisphere. So patriotic was he that his more progressive students and academic colleagues nicknamed him Samuel "Wave the Flagg" Bemis. He celebrated the acquisition by the United States during the nineteenth century of vast new territories at the expense of native Americans, the European powers, and Mexico. Indians were not despoiled, because they were "uncivilized." Before the arrival of Europeans the continent was essentially "empty." The European powers were "civilized," but they were "imperialist." "The United States," Bemis concluded, "acquired the whole western territory from the Mississippi River to the Pacific Ocean without unjustly despoiling any civilized nation, and this statement holds good for the war with Mexico presently to be discussed" (p. 74). His discussion of that war, in which Mexico lost roughly half of its territory, justifies it by contending that, although Mexico was a republic, it was not fit to govern itself. Mexico was a "feudal" land, ruled by a "narrow creole minority" and subject to "political anarchy" (p. 75).

Bemis had only a little more difficulty rationalizing the advent of US imperialism in 1898 and US interventions in Latin America in this century. At the end of the nineteenth century, he argued, the threat to the "security of the Continental Republic" posed by European powers prompted the United States to engage in a "short-lived benevolent imperialism" toward parts of Latin America. Fortunately, once that threat receded after World War I, this "ill-fitting imperialism" was liquidated and the resulting "Good Neighbor" policy of the 1930s came "just in time" to assure inter-American solidarity in the face of the Axis threat that culminated in World War II (Preface, unpaginated).

Underlying Bemis's formal thesis, and his interpretation of US expansionism and interventions in Latin America, lie deep cultural assumptions. To his credit, Bemis is explicit about these. He lays them out for the reader in his introductory chapter, entitled "Latitude and Altitude." There he succinctly reviews the geography of the Americas to stress the fact that the part that became the United States is located almost exclusively in the temperate zone, while Latin America lies primarily in the tropics. (The concept of altitude is important to Bemis because in the highlands of Latin America the climate is cool, and thus moderates the worst social effects of the tropics.)

Bemis then introduces his concept of "climatic energy" and reproduces a map of its distribution around the globe. The areas of "optimal" and "high" climatic energy are confined to Europe, the United States, New Zealand, Canada, bits of Australia and South Africa, a narrow swathe across central Chile and Argentina, and Japan. Bemis comments:

It is a scientific fact of political, economic, and social geography, that the areas of best and of second-best climatic energy coincide geographically with the more impressive evidence of human civilization, such as maximum wheat yield, maximum of professional occupations, maximum of industrial production, greatest number of schools and colleges, of automobiles and of telephones per capita, maximum of railway networks, and best human health. All these imply social progress and political stability. [F]avorable climate is a necessary basis of modern civilization. (p. 6)

Climate, for Bemis, also explains the racial geography of the Americas. The most populous indigenous societies of the New World were located in the highlands of Central and South America. The tropical lowlands "still present a barrier to white populations"; the lowlands of South America "may be expected to develop, if at all, on some other than a pure Caucasian basis" (p. 7). Bemis calculated that, at the time of his writing, the United States was about 90 per cent white. In contrast, Central and South America—except for the "overwhelmingly" white populations of southern Brazil, Uruguay, and Argentina—were predominantly of mixed and non-white blood. "This racial mixture," he asserted, "has been a key factor in the central theme of Latin American history, the struggle for social and political order, and it is a volatile element in the amalgam of inter-American solidarity" (p. 9).

Climate thus explained the unequal development of the Americas. Or, in Bemis's terms, it determined the degree of modern civilization attained by the United States and Latin America by the twentieth century. Climate also dictated the racial geography of the Americas, which in turn influenced the relative orderliness of American societies and the character of their relations with each other. These differences of climate and race, Bemis emphasized at the beginning of his book, were the root cause of conflict in US–Latin American relations. They tended to "separate what the human spirit tries to bring together in a common front of liberty." "They are the mountains that faith must move" (p. 3).

The book thus reveals explicitly the cultural and racial assumptions that governed the thought of a preeminent member of the US academic elite as late as the 1940s. These days, US academics, like policy-makers and the general public itself, rarely express these assumptions publicly. The rise of powerful nationalist movements in the Third (or European colonial) World in this century and, in the decades that followed World War II, the momentous process of decolonization that resulted are responsible for this democratic change in our formal discourse. In the United States itself, the analogue of this global process was the rise and influence of the civil rights movement.

But progressive changes in the juridical status of former colonies abroad (which are now independent nations) and racial minorities at home (who now enjoy greater effective equality under the law) have not necessarily changed the way most of us really think about issues like these. Democratic changes in the way we talk about social issues have made references to racial explanations taboo. But, as we shall see in this and subsequent chapters, cultural attitudes historically allied with racial prejudice continue to undergird mainstream US academic thinking about development. And racist and ethnocentric notions about development are deeply imbedded in US popular culture as well. How valid and logical these assumptions are in explaining the historical development of the Americas is the concern of the remainder of this chapter. We will test them against evidence from the colonial history of the Americas, the period that runs from the beginnings of European conquest, about 1500, to the era of independence, roughly 1775 to 1825.

II

Climate, race, and culture are fundamental to understanding the divergent development of the societies of the Americas. But each was mediated historically by the economic roles the colonies came to play in the wider Atlantic trading system. The nature of those roles, in turn, structured the evolution of the labor systems that defined the developmental potential of each colony. Although a variety of labor systems existed in all of the American colonies, and all of them experienced free labor as well as forms of coerced labor, over time one type of labor system or the other, free or coerced, came to typify each of them. Around these systems of free or coerced labor developed characteristic patterns of social stratification, income and land distribution, political institutions, and cultural attitudes. Together, these factors structured the developmental potential of the colonies, and that of the independent states they became.

The divergent development of the American colonies is sharply framed by the paradox signaled in the title of this chapter. How did the wealthiest American colonies become the poorest nations of the hemisphere, and the poorest colonies become the core of the nation that became the richest in the world? Answering that question reveals the fallacies in explanations of United States and Latin American development that make culture, race, and climate the determining factors. The extreme examples of divergent development sketched below point instead to the centrality of colonial labor systems in the development of the United States and Latin America.

Saint Domingue/Haiti. By the end of the eighteenth century, the French colony of Saint Domingue, situated on the western third of the Caribbean island of Hispaniola, was the largest sugar producer in the world. Measured in terms of the wealth it generated, it was also the richest colony in the Americas. In 1791 its 480,000 black slaves (in a total population that included a mere 40,000 whites and some 25,000 mulattos) were producing more than 78,000 tons of sugar a year, which accounted for more than half of the value of France's colonial trade. Today independent Haiti is the poorest nation (measured in income per person) in the Western Hemisphere.

Upper Peru/Bolivia. During the sixteenth and seventeenth centuries, silver made Upper Peru the most lucrative Spanish colony in South America. Most of the silver was extracted by Indians forced by Spanish authorities to labor in the mines. In 1570, the population of Potosí, located at the richest mine, numbered some 160,000, making it the largest city in the Americas. Silver was by far the most important export of colonial Spanish America, and, along with Mexico, Upper Peru produced almost all of it. Yet today independent Bolivia has the lowest per capita income of Spain's ex-colonies in South America.

New England. In contrast, the British colonies of New England were initially the poorest of the Americas. Having neither precious metals, nor the warm climate to produce agricultural staples in demand in Europe, they met their subsistence and local needs largely through small-scale diversified farming and craft production based on family and free wage labor. By the end of the colonial period, however, these societies were among the most prosperous and dynamic in the Americas. Following independence, and the victory of the North over the South in the Civil War, their institutions shaped the nation that became the richest and most industrialized in the hemisphere.

South Carolina. Quite different was the experience of the British colonies of southern North America. The rice-exporting region of eastern South Carolina, for example, an economy based on slave labor, had the highest white per capita wealth of any part of British North America in the late eighteenth century. Yet by 1900 this region was the poorest part of the poorest census zone in the United States.

These are extreme examples, but they highlight broader patterns of colonial development in the Americas. They show how climate, natural resources (particularly precious metals), and labor supplies deeply influenced the economic possibilities of the American colonies, and the role each would play within the wider Atlantic system.

The European powers created the Atlantic system as a consequence of their chronic trade deficit with Asia. Except for precious metals, which they mined in limited quantities, Europeans produced little that they were able to exchange for the spices and luxury items they imported from the East. Mercantilism, the theory that guided the economic policies of the European states in the sixteenth and seventeenth centuries, was a direct response to these balance-of-trade problems. Acting on mercantilist principles, governments sought to maximize the nation's exports, minimize its imports, and accumulate bullion (gold or silver) in the hands of the state. Colonies outside Europe came to play a central role in mercantilist strategy. They served as sources of the bullion and raw materials European nations could not produce for themselves. Colonies also consumed exports, preferably high-value manufactures, of the metropolis. Each European power sought to acquire an empire, and, by monopolizing trade within it, pursued maximum advantage against its European rivals. War between the powers was often the result. The colonies were the spoils.

The European explorers of the fifteenth and sixteenth centuries sought new sources of gold more than anything else. Exploration also aimed at reducing the cost of Asian imports by seeking a way around the Near-Eastern middlemen who controlled the trade between Europe and Asia. Beginning in the fifteenth century, the Portuguese located supplies of gold in Africa, and by the end of that century they had discovered the way around Africa to Asia. It was the Spaniards, however, searching for a shorter, more direct western route to Asia, who discovered America and appropriated its most valuable parts.

Once in the New World, the Spaniards' quest for gold quickly led them to the great highland agrarian civilizations of Mexico and Peru. There they discovered the most numerous and most tractable labor force in the Americas. In Mexico, as was to happen all over the Americas, European contact led to rapid population decline among the native Americans. Indians died resisting European conquest and settlement. They lived shorter lives as a result of labor exploitation and reorganization of patterns of land use and settlement. Most of all they died from European diseases, from which they had no immunity. The result was a demographic disaster of a magnitude unequalled in recorded human history. In central Mexico alone an indigenous population estimated at 25 million on the eve of conquest in 1519 fell to little more than a million a century later. The Spaniards extracted tribute and labor service from this rapidly declining Indian population. Slowly they consolidated the large rural agricultural estates worked by dependent labor that came to characterize Spanish colonial society throughout the Americas.

But mining, not agriculture, was to be Spanish America's primary role in the Atlantic system during the colonial period. By the mid-sixteenth century the Spanish had discovered great silver mines in Mexico and Upper Peru, and silver became the main export of Spanish America to Europe during the next two and a half centuries. American silver had a major impact on European development, contributing to the economic decline of Spain and the rise of Spain's Western European rivals, especially Britain. Silver-driven price inflation undercut the competitiveness of Spanish manufactures and financed Spain's costly and ultimately fruitless military pretensions in Europe. Manufactures from Britain, funnelled legally through Spanish merchant monopolies, or illegally through the contraband trade, eventually supplied the bulk of the import needs of Spanish America, and those of Portuguese Brazil as well.

The Portuguese in Brazil encountered Indian peoples much smaller in numbers than those the Spaniards found in Peru and Mexico. These lowland peoples were also more egalitarian in social structure and less sedentary and dependent on agriculture than the Indian societies of the highlands. For all these reasons the Indians of Brazil—like their counterparts in the rest of lowland South America, the Caribbean, and North America north of central Mexico—proved much more resistant to European encroachment and labor demands. They fought a running battle to maintain their way of life along the advancing frontier of European settlement. Eventually, all these peoples—in Brazil and in the rest of the Americas outside the South and Central American highlands—were virtually exterminated.

The Portuguese then turned to African slaves for labor. They already controlled the West African coast and had developed a trade with Europe in African slaves. Slaves provided the labor for the large sugar estates the Portuguese established in northeast Brazil in the sixteenth century. Slaves produced all the major exports of Brazil during the next three centuries. They mined the fabulous gold and diamond reserves discovered in central Brazil in the eighteenth century. They produced the coffee, grown in the south-central region, which by the time of abolition in 1888 supplied roughly two-thirds of world demand. Brazil alone consumed almost half of the estimated ten million African slaves shipped to America.

On the Caribbean islands, many of which, like Saint Domingue, were originally claimed by Spain but fell to other Western European powers in the seventeenth and eighteenth centuries, the pattern was much the same. The indigenous people were rapidly exterminated and eventually huge numbers of African slaves (almost half those sent to America before the nineteenth century) were brought in to produce staples, primarily sugar, for export to Europe.

Table 1, drawn from Ralph Davis, *The Rise of the Atlantic Economies*, reveals the timing and magnitude of reliance on slave labor in the European colonies of the Americas. Readers should be aware that these figures are estimates. The precise numbers of slaves imported into the Americas remain in doubt.

Table 1   Imports of Slaves to America (in thousands), 1600–1781

	Before 1600	1600–1700	1700–1781	Total
British North America	–	–	256	256
Spanish America	75	293	393	761
Brazil	50	560	1,285	1,895
Caribbean				
British	–	261	961	1,222
French	–	157	990	1,147
Dutch and Danish	–	44	401	445
Total	125	1,315	4,286	5,726

While the Spanish and Portuguese were the first to rely on slave labor, by the seventeenth century and, especially, the eighteenth the other European powers, the British primary among them, were importing massive numbers of slaves into their colonies in the Americas.

Before they turned to slave labor, however, the non-Spanish European colonies of the Caribbean—as well as those of the North American mainland—depended on another form of coerced labor, indentured servitude. Under this system workers (primarily young males) contracted in Europe to come to America on the condition that they work for three to five or more years. Following their service they were to be granted land, a wage (often paid in kind as a quantity of sugar or tobacco), or tools and clothing. They could then aspire to become independent farmers or artisans, or at least free wage workers. Indentured servants, like slaves, had no political rights and were often subjected to brutal exploitation. Like slaves they could be punished for insubordination or attempted flight with whippings or even mutilation.

Reliance on the labor of indentured servants differentiated the American colonies of the other European powers, especially those of Britain, from the colonies of Spain and Portugal. During the seventeenth and eighteenth centuries population growth and the rapid commercialization of the British and Western European economies created a large pool of uprooted poor, many of whom seized the opportunity to improve their situation by binding themselves in temporary servitude in the New World. Spain and Portugal, in contrast, experienced no such fundamental internal transformation. The modest number of immigrants they sent to the New World were usually free and often of considerable means. Unable to take advantage of coerced white labor drawn from the mother country, the Spanish and Portuguese depended from the beginning on coerced Indian labor and African slaves in their American colonies.

But while the other European colonies in America initially depended heavily on the labor of white indentured servants, only some of them eventually came to rely on African slaves to meet their labor needs. Why did some of these colonies come to depend on slave labor, while others did not? The answer to this question holds the key to understanding the paradox of American development. It is revealed most clearly in the experience of the British American colonies, especially those that eventually formed the United States.

From virtually the beginnings of settlement, all of the American British colonies depended on indentured servants to meet part of their labor needs. Most of these colonies—from New England to the West Indies—developed initially as diversified agricultural economies, in which patterns of landholding and income distribution were, certainly by European standards of the day, relatively egalitarian.

Wherever there was a shift in these colonies to large-scale production of agricultural staples for export, however, African slaves, not white indentured servants, came to supply the bulk of the labor force. Scholars estimate that during the whole period up to the time of the declaration of US independence in 1776, a million and a half slaves were imported into the British colonies in America. Roughly a million and a quarter of these slaves went to the sugar colonies of the West Indies, most of the rest to the southern colonies of the North American mainland. The best estimate of the number of indentured servants who came to British America during the same period is 350,000, more than a quarter of the slaves imported.

The decision by planters in the British colonies to rely increasingly on African slave labor was a complex one, and the relative weights of the numerous considerations involved are still debated by historians. Contrary to modern myth, white servants proved capable of hard agricultural labor in the tropics. Yet Europeans never considered enslaving their own kind. Racial and cultural attitudes reserved the brutality of outright slavery for black, initially non-Christian, aliens. The temporary bondage of Europeans from the laboring classes did, however, prove an attractive alternative to African slavery, at least at the beginning. As noted above, in Britain during the seventeenth and eighteenth centuries there was an abundant supply of unemployed or poor farmers, artisans, and laborers who were willing to indenture themselves in America in the hope of eventually improving their condition. Indeed, indentured servants continued to stream into the southern as well as the northern mainland British colonies until the end of the colonial period.

Initially, at least, the cost to planters of a servant's passage to America was similar to the cost of an African slave. And unlike owners of slaves, masters of servants had special reasons for working their servants to death, which many seem to have done. During the seventeenth century most indentured servants in North America died before their service was up, eliminating any need to compensate them. Toward the end of that century, however, in places like Virginia, mortality rates declined and the option of buying a slave for life, rather than contracting with a servant for a few years, became more attractive.

The decision by planters to shift away from reliance on white indentured servants toward African slave labor seems to have been decisively affected by their judgments of the relative capacity of their laborers to resist. Unlike slaves, servants could appeal to the courts. And because they were white, and shared the culture and spoke the language of the free people in these societies, they had special reasons to insist on their rights and even to believe they might escape. Indentured servants were also armed psychologically by the fact that they had voluntarily submitted themselves to temporary bondage in order to improve their situation in life. When those expectations were frustrated they could become an explosive social force.

This dynamic has been documented most clearly in the shift toward slave labor in Virginia. The shift began in earnest in the tobacco-producing region of the colony in the 1680s, following a major revolt known as Bacon's Rebellion. That rebellion began as an assault on Indian lands by land-hungry whites. It ended in a movement that challenged royal authority and the planter elite itself. The rebels included some slaves promised freedom by the insurgents, but the majority were whites, primarily debt-ridden small farmers and indentured servants.

Plantation export agriculture dependent on slave labor eventually transformed all the British American colonies with warm enough climates to grow commodities that Western Europe wanted but could not produce efficiently itself. Beginning in the West Indies in the early seventeenth century, export agriculture enveloped the British colonies all the way to Maryland by the end of that century. Between 1700 and 1781 these colonies alone consumed well in excess of a million African slaves (see Table 1). As export agriculture transformed these colonies, African slaves replaced white indentured servants as the primary labor force, and land became highly concentrated. White small farmers were forced to sell out to big planters and migrate to areas where opportunities were greater. As sugar transformed the British Caribbean colony of Barbados in the early seventeenth century, for example, thousands of small farmers sold out and migrated to British North America. As tobacco transformed the tidewater area of Virginia a century later, smallholders were forced to migrate inland.

These trends were especially pronounced in sugar production, the most important American agricultural export to Europe during the colonial period. Sugar production for export required heavy investment in expensive milling machinery, which in turn encouraged extreme concentration of landholding and extreme reliance on slave labor. The same pattern of large-scale production, land concentration, and dependence on slave labor occurred in rice cultivation in eastern South Carolina, which involved large investments in irrigation.

Tobacco, the major export from the British mainland colonies, had more limited capital requirements and could be grown competitively for export by both large and small producers. Large-scale production developed where planters had sufficient capital to purchase prime land and a labor force that could be permanently denied access to it. Planters in tidewater Virginia, many of them European investors, provide the clearest example. In contrast, small-scale white tobacco producers using relatively few slaves were able to survive in the interiors of Virginia and the Carolinas.

Wherever this transition to export agriculture and slavery occurred within British America, the relatively egalitarian distribution of land and wealth, products in part of the indentured labor system, began to break down, and society became polarized into a small wealthy elite of white planters and a large class of impoverished black slaves. Land, wealth, education, literacy, and political power were monopolized by the few and denied to the vast majority. This polarization went furthest in the small sugar-producing islands of the Caribbean like Barbados and Jamaica. But it is readily discernible in the larger, geographically and economically more diverse colonies of the North American mainland such as tobacco-producing Virginia. On the mainland, however, it was rice-producing South Carolina that most closely resembled the Caribbean sugar colonies. There, blacks became a majority as early as 1708.

Nothing of this sort happened in the British colonies of New England and the mid-Atlantic seaboard, although slavery was present there as well. Despite important differences in the economies of these two groups of northern colonies, all of them depended throughout the colonial

period on farming and craft production oriented toward domestic consumption. Fishing provided an important supplement to the economy of
New England, and eventually shipbuilding became an important addition
to the economies of both regions.

Production in these northern British colonies was based on family
labor and an ever-growing proportion of free wage workers. Indentured
servants continued to flood into the northern colonies during the eighteenth century, the vast majority going to the mid-Atlantic colonies of
Pennsylvania, New York, New Jersey, and Delaware. The small numbers of
slaves in the northern colonies were employed mainly as urban domestic
servants and artisans. As production grew and society became more prosperous, the northern colonies experienced prodigious internal
population growth and, in relative terms, relied less and less on the
importation of labor from abroad. These population and labor trends,
which sharply differentiate the development of the northern British
colonies from those of the south, are graphically illustrated in Table 2.
(The table is also adapted from Davis, and carries the same warning
about the reliability of the absolute numbers.)

Table 2 Population of the British Colonies in America excluding
Canada (in thousands; slave population in parentheses), 1640–1775

	1640	1700		1775	
New England	20	130		676	(25)
New York, New Jersey, Pennsylvania, Delaware	–	65		623	(50)
Virginia, Maryland	8	87		759	(230)
Carolinas, Georgia	–	12		449	(140)
Barbados	–	54	(42)	86	(68)
Jamaica	–	53	(45)	210	(197)
Other British West Indies	20	43	(31)	113	(97)

Comparison of the British colonies, northern and southern, helps us
to understand the relationship between culture, climate, race, and labor
systems in the divergent development of all the European colonies of the
Americas. In the British colonies the influence of British culture was a
constant, so it is easier to assess the independent action of climate, race,
and labor. All the British colonies were products of the same colonizing
power, all were peopled initially by immigrants from British society, all
were subject, more or less, to the same imperial institutions.

It is true that significant differences existed in the manner in which
the British colonies were initially organized and settled. Some began as

collective efforts by people of some means to establish societies based on religious tenets, others were granted to a single proprietor, who proceeded to distribute land to others at a price, and others were run for profit by companies of investors. But by the start of the eighteenth century, the two distinct economic and labor systems that would decisively affect their subsequent development were firmly set in place. The southern colonies from Virginia to the Caribbean specialized in producing export crops, especially sugar and tobacco, with slave labor for the world market. The northern colonies from New England to the mid-Atlantic produced food and manufactures largely for the domestic market using family and free labor.

The southern British colonies became the great economic success stories of Britain's mercantilist American empire. The more specialized they were in export production, the more heavily dependent on slave labor, the more concentrated and undemocratic their landholding patterns, the wealthier they became. These, not their poor northern neighbors, were the colonies that contributed handsomely to the British metropolis. They provided sugar and tobacco for the rapidly growing British internal market. They furnished commodities for industrial processing and for re-export. And they generated, through these transactions, sizeable tax revenue for the state. On the eve of the independence of the colonies that became the United States, exports per person averaged £4.75 for the British West Indies, £1.82 for the Virginia-Maryland region, £1.78 for the Carolinas and Georgia, £1.03 for the mid-Atlantic colonies, and only £0.84 for New England.* Figures on average wealth per person in the thirteen colonies at the same point in time were £54.7 for the southern colonies, £41.9 for the middle colonies, and £36.6 for New England. As these figures reveal, the northern colonies were of limited use to Britain. What exports they had generally competed with British goods. And far from producing revenue for the government, their administration and defense were an absolute drain on the imperial treasury.

Comparison of the British colonies in America helps us isolate the determining role of labor systems in the divergent development of all the European colonies in America. Slavery, and other forms of coerced labor—and the concentration of land and wealth that accompanied them—had similar effects in all the colonies where they took hold, whether they were Spanish or British, Portuguese or French. Coerced labor took hold in the Americas everywhere the Europeans found viable indigenous labor supplies, or opportunities to produce precious metals

---

* Throughout this paragraph the eighteenth-century currency is expressed in decimals for convenience.

or tropical agricultural exports. To stress this point is not to deny real differences in the culture and institutions of the European colonizing powers. It is simply to point to the overwhelming similarities that coerced labor and large-scale production of export commodities created despite these initial differences.

New England and the mid-Atlantic colonies were exceptions to the pattern of coerced labor that influenced the development of all the European colonies to their south. It was not some unique cultural or racial attribute that explains their exceptionalism. It was their fortuitous location on lands lacking precious metals and with a climate unsuited to cultivation of the agricultural commodities Europe wanted. Their inability to produce primary commodities for export to Europe, their relative isolation from the main circuits of trade within the Atlantic system, allowed them to preserve and develop their unique free-labor system.

Paradoxically, however, by the eighteenth century New England and the mid-Atlantic colonies were able to assume a function within the Atlantic economy that in some ways resembled the role of European metropolis more than it did that of American colony. Unable to produce much that Britain needed, yet dependent on imports of British manufactured goods, these northern colonies began to balance their trade with Britain by provisioning the slave-based economies of the southern North American mainland and the Caribbean. This new role set the northern colonies on a path toward industrialization and political democracy that sharply distinguished their development from the other colonies of the Americas. To understand how that happened we must look more closely at the relationships between the American colonies and the workings of the Atlantic system as a whole.

III

The Atlantic system, as it operated from the sixteenth through the eighteenth centuries, can be usefully described as a great triangular trade between Europe, Africa, and the Americas. Europeans traded manufactures in Africa for slaves, then sold them in America. Slaves in America produced staples, primarily sugar and tobacco, and along with other workers, free and coerced, they mined the precious minerals that were America's other major export to Europe. European nations, especially Britain as time went on, sold America manufactures and financed the commerce of the whole triangular trade.

The role each point of the triangle played in this vast Atlantic trading network fundamentally influenced its economic and social evolution over

time. Imports of European manufactures undercut African artisan industry, while the slave trade deprived African societies of many of their most
productive members. With the infusion of slave labor the American plantation societies grew rapidly. Their economies, like those of the mining
colonies of the American interior, came to revolve around the production
of primary commodities for export. Meanwhile, imports of European
manufactures and mercantilist restrictions stunted the growth of their
manufacturing sectors. European commerce benefited from the influx of
precious metals, and imports of agricultural commodities lessened the
importance of domestic agriculture. Europe's exports to Africa and
America stimulated the development of its manufacturing industry.
Finally, because Europe controlled Atlantic commerce, it reaped profits
and tax revenues on virtually every exchange within the triangular trade.
It also furnished the ships, warehousing, and the insurance that made the
trade possible. In elemental terms, if economic development is defined as
the emergence of an expanding industrial economy, then the triangular
trade fostered economic development in Europe, economic growth but
not development in America, and economic retrogression in Africa.

This understanding of the Atlantic trading system owes much to the
work of Caribbean historian Eric Williams. Williams's scholarship, particularly his classic work *Capitalism and Slavery*, challenged the climatic,
racial, and cultural assumptions that have traditionally informed mainstream European and US understandings of the development of the
modern world. His book prefigures subsequent efforts by Latin American
scholars to explain Latin American underdevelopment and European
development in terms of the exploitative economic relationships between
them.

Williams was born the son of a postal clerk in Port-of-Spain, Trinidad,
in 1911. An outstanding student, he won a scholarship to Oxford, where
in 1938 he completed a doctoral dissertation on the abolition of the
slave trade and slavery in the British West Indies. That same year he jour-
neyed to the United States, and began to teach at Howard University in
Washington, DC. There he broadened his doctoral research to study the
association between slavery and the rise of British capitalism. The book
he published in 1944, *Capitalism and Slavery*, incorporated both his dissertation and his new research in a bold, overarching thesis. As he put it,
the book was "strictly an economic study of the role of Negro slavery and
the slave trade in providing the capital which financed the Industrial
Revolution in England and of mature industrial capitalism in destroying
the slave system" (p. vii). The book went through several editions, and
was translated into French, Japanese and Russian, although its reception
by many US and British academic historians was cool, if not hostile. In the

decades that followed Williams continued his scholarship, but he increasingly devoted himself to politics and the cause of Trinidadian independence. In 1962 he became the first prime minister of independent Trinidad and Tobago, a post he held until his death in 1981.

Williams conceptualized the abolition of the slave trade and slavery in the British West Indies (acts accomplished, respectively, in 1807 and 1823) as part of a momentous transition from mercantilist to liberal economic thought and policy-making in Britain. The great proponent of liberal economic theory was Adam Smith, whose *The Wealth of Nations* appeared the same year, 1776, the colonies that became the United States declared their independence. While mercantilists had stressed the need for government control and commercial monopolies to promote the economic power of the nation, liberals like Smith argued for *laissez faire*, the idea that the role of government in the economy should be sharply limited to allow private individuals and market forces free rein. Mercantilists sought to promote the economy of the metropolis by creating an empire of colonies that was self-sufficient and impervious to commercial penetration by rival nations. Liberals, in contrast, claimed that colonies were a wasteful burden on the national economy. For them, maximum economic advantage depended on a nation's comparative advantage in global free trade.

Williams saw the growing political appeal of liberal economic assumptions in Britain and abroad in the late eighteenth and early nineteenth centuries as a consequence of the Industrial Revolution. There was no place in liberalism for the mercantilist system of preferential access to the British market by the British Caribbean sugar colonies, or for the British commercial monopolies that provided them with slaves and manufactures. For Williams, therefore, the importance of the rise of abolitionism in Britain in the early nineteenth century lay not in its humanitarian content, but in the way it served the economic interests of the rising class of British industrial capitalists. By the early nineteenth century, he contended, Britain could buy its sugar more cheaply outside the British West Indies, and the countries that purchased its textiles and other industrial products needed free access to the British market to pay for these imports.

Williams's thesis offended the sensibilities of those who stressed the humanitarian impulses behind British abolitionism, and his work still figures prominently in the ongoing debate among historians over the origins and timing of abolitionism. But it was the other dimension of his argument that had the broadest implications and generated the greatest, and most enduring, controversy. His argument that slavery was a powerful impetus to the Industrial Revolution challenged common understandings of the development of modern civilization itself. All of us appreciate that the Industrial Revolution, which transformed the British economy between 1780 and 1850, and quickly spread abroad, marks a quantum leap in the productive capacity of human society. Williams implied that this momentous achievement was not essentially the result of British cultural values and technical ingenuity. Nor did it depend simply on internal capital resources, the availability of free labor, the existence of good internal transport, and a large domestic market. He maintained that it depended as well on an external commerce in human flesh and the brutal exploitation of African slave labor in the British sugar colonies of the Caribbean. In precise and measured prose, he argued that the triangular trade "provided one of the main streams of that accumulation of capital in England which financed the Industrial Revolution" (p. 52).

Williams advanced his argument in powerful, engaging language backed by an array of hard economic statistics and hundreds of pithy quotations culled from British archives. He traced the growth of the English slave-trading ports of Bristol and Liverpool. He analyzed the links between British commerce in slaves and sugar and the growth of the English merchant marine and the shipbuilding industries, and the connections between both and naval power. He outlined the importance of sugar-processing plants within British industry and showed the importance of the re-export trade in sugar for the British exchequer. He even found connections between Caribbean capital and the development of James Watt's steam engine, between slavery and the insurance firm Lloyd's of London, and between West Indian planter fortunes and the consolidation of Barclay's bank.

Williams effectively demonstrated the weight of British West Indies trade within overall British commerce, but he was less successful in demonstrating direct links between the trade in slaves and sugar and the development of the textile industry, whose transformation beginning in the 1780s marks the advent of the Industrial Revolution. The triangular trade, he correctly noted, gave a "triple stimulus" to British industry.

> The Negroes were purchased with British manufactures; transported to the plantations, they produced sugar, cotton, indigo, molasses and other tropical products, the processing of which created new industries in England; the maintenance of the Negroes and their owners on the plantations provided another market for British industry . . . . (p. 52)

Williams was able to document links between the trade in slaves and sugar and a variety of British industries, including the iron works that provided manacles for slave ships and American plantations. But he failed to make a convincing case for the links to the textile industry itself. In fact, his chapter on "British Industry and the Triangular Trade" barely mentions that subject.

His problem lay not in the strength of his general idea, that the triangular trade was intimately connected with the Industrial Revolution, but in the limits he placed on himself for demonstrating that connection. He confined himself exclusively to the role of the British West Indies in that process. He left aside, for example, Brazil, the largest of the American slave societies. By the late eighteenth century, although Brazil was still nominally under Portuguese political control, it was in fact already a virtual British protectorate, its economy, including its massive imports of slaves, dominated by British interests. Williams ignored the whole of Spanish America as well, which, as one can see in Figure 1, came to constitute by far the major foreign market for British textiles in the decades between 1820 and 1840.

Williams also believed that he had to prove direct economic links between, for example, the profits made by English slave traders and investments in industry. In fact, however, the decisive influence of the Atlantic economy on British industrialization was much more general and indirect than he thought. The eminent British historian Eric Hobsbawm, for example, has argued that the existence of a potential world market for textiles, accessible to the seaborne British, was the single most important prerequisite for the revolutionary breakthrough to industrial production.

The current consensus among historians about the causes of the Industrial Revolution tends to confirm Williams's emphasis on external factors, although the weight of explanation among Europeanists still rests on internal conditions. In the words of Peter Stearns, who has synthesized that scholarship, the role of Europe's colonial expansion and the influence of its dominant position in world commerce have "moved up the causation ladder" in explanations of the Industrial Revolution. But Stearns also shows that, in recent years, the question of internal causation has grown in complexity and its focus has moved backward in time. Historians have shown that reductions in family size in early modern Europe may help explain the Industrial Revolution. Other historians argue that during the sixteenth and seventeenth centuries, long before the advent of the urban Industrial Revolution of the late eighteenth century we customarily think of, its essential elements, including wage labor, were already worked out in large-scale textile production in the countryside. Yet even these early internal changes may be closely connected with the growing commercialization of domestic economies that accompanied European expansion after 1500 into the Atlantic and the world beyond.

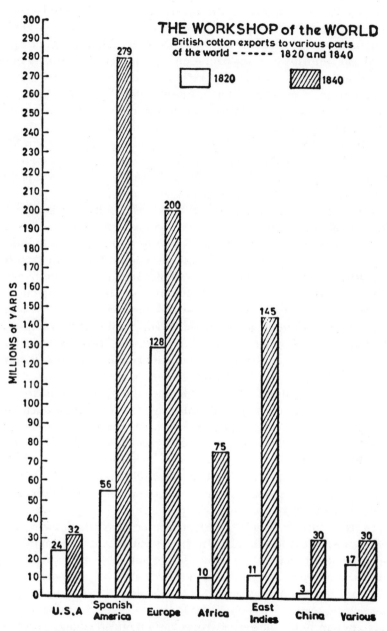

Reprinted from Eric Hobsbawm, *The Age of Revolution* (New York 1962). The graph indicates the extraordinary growth and importance of British cotton textile exports to former Spanish colonies in the Americas following their independence. Enormous profits from the textile trade fueled the development of heavy industry in Britain, which by 1850 had become the world's first mature industrial economy.

Study of industrialization in the Americas reinforces the idea that external factors defined the potential for industrial transformation. Only one region in the Americas, the northern part of the United States, experienced an industrial transformation in the century following independence from Europe. Neither the southern British colonies, including those of mainland North America, nor the former Spanish and Portuguese colonies industrialized in the nineteenth century. In fact, the newly independent Latin American republics, like the southern United States, experienced an intensification of their traditional roles within the Atlantic system during the nineteenth century. They produced a growing volume of agricultural and mineral exports for the rapidly industrializing economies of the North Atlantic.

Once again, focus on the British colonies, and, following independence, on the southern and northern regions of the United States, allows us to evaluate the role of British culture in the industrialization process. As we have seen, in important respects the northern British colonies developed in a way similar to that of Britain itself. Initially, they engaged in diversified farming and livestock production for the domestic market. Their land and labor systems were far more democratic than those of England, however. Large landed estates employing tenant farmers existed in the northern colonies. But the rule, reinforced by an expanding frontier of agricultural settlement to the north and west, was the family farm, which often employed some wage workers. As these northern British colonies grew and became more prosperous, towns and cities developed as commercial centers and sites of craft production, which was also based on family and free wage labor. Wages in these economies were high by European standards, which helps to explain the attraction they held for European immigrants, free workers and indentured servants alike. Wages were kept high, and the democratic structure of landholding patterns maintained, by the availability of land on the frontier.

High wages encouraged the growth of an internal market in the northern colonies, but at the same time they reduced the international competitiveness of domestically produced agricultural and manufactured goods. As revealed in Table 3, which is adapted from Williams's work, during the eighteenth century the northern colonies suffered a severe trade deficit with England. The deficit was a result of their inability to sell much to Britain, and their heavy dependence on British manufactures to meet their growing needs.

During the eighteenth century, the northern British colonies solved the problem of their trade deficit with England by helping to provision the slave economies of the Caribbean and, to a lesser extent, those of the

Table 3   British Trade with British America and Africa, 1714–73, and as a
Percentage of All British Foreign Trade

	British imports from	% of total British imports	British exports to	% of total British exports
West Indies	101,264,818	20.6	45,389,988	6.2
Southern North American mainland	47,191,919	9.6	27,560,778	3.8
New England and mid-Atlantic	7,160,300	1.5	37,939,422	5.2
Africa	2,407,447	–	15,235,829	2.0

southern North American mainland. Not all of this trade was with British colonies, however. A large and growing part of it was an illegal, contraband trade with the burgeoning French and Spanish Caribbean sugar colonies, particularly Saint Domingue and Cuba. The northern colonies provided these highly specialized slave monocultures with grains, fish, and forest products, cattle for meat, mules for traction in the sugar mills, and slaves imported from Africa. They also furnished them a range of manufactures, from textiles to iron implements, many of them imported from Britain and then re-exported to the Caribbean. From the West Indies, the northern colonies imported sugar and molasses, much of which they refined into rum. The bulk of these imports supplied the domestic market. But the northern colonies also sent rum and manufactures to Africa to purchase slaves, most of whom they sold in the West Indies and the southern mainland.

Trade with the Caribbean and participation in the larger triangular trade stimulated the growth of commerce and the shipbuilding industry in both New England and the mid-Atlantic colonies. The impact of this trade on the development of the different northern colonies, however, was uneven. Drawing on a maritime tradition begun in fishing, New England concentrated on shipping and the financial and commercial aspects of the trade. Its poor soils and cold climate limited the capacity of its small farmers to respond to Caribbean demand. In the mid-Atlantic colonies the rewards of the trade seem to have been spread more widely, with farmers among the primary beneficiaries. These trends help to explain differences in the concentration of wealth in these two groups of northern colonies at the end of the colonial period. Wealth was less concentrated in the mid-Atlantic colonies than in either New England or the southern mainland colonies. In New England, in contrast, wealth was even more highly concentrated than in the rich southern mainland colonies. But in New England (as in England itself), participation in the Atlantic trade tended to concentrate wealth in the hands of merchants, bankers, and manufacturers, not, as in the southern colonies, a planter class.

By the time of independence, the northern region of the British mainland colonies had assumed a role in the Atlantic system that in important respects resembled that of Great Britain itself. To be sure, its manufacturing sector lagged far behind that of its British metropolis, and the magnitude of its Atlantic trade was still small. But in the century following independence, industry developed rapidly in the North and by the turn of the nineteenth century, the United States was ready to challenge British industrial and commercial supremacy in the Americas and the world at large.

Contrary to Bemis's argument, climate does not directly explain the divergent development of the European colonies in America. That is, it did not in some mysterious way imbue the predominantly white population of the northern British colonies with "climatic energy" that somehow explains their subsequent ability to develop manufacturing industry and stable democratic political institutions. What climate explains is the *inability* of the northern British colonies to respond, as did the British, French, Spanish, and Portuguese colonies to their south, to the demand for tropical and subtropical agricultural commodities in Europe.

Nor does "culture," as we commonly use the term, explain the vast differences in the historical development of American societies. If British cultural values and institutions account for the subsequent development of the northern British colonies, why did not Virginia and South Carolina, or Barbados and Jamaica, develop in similar ways? Slavery and other forms of coerced labor had profound cultural consequences in all the American societies where those labor systems became prevalent, regardless of the European power that settled and controlled them. These labor systems created or hardened class and racial attitudes which gravely compromised the potential for industrial and democratic development. Among these cultural attitudes was widespread disdain for manual labor and the people who performed it, and the idea that people of African, Indian, or mixed descent were congenitally inferior to whites, if not subhuman.

Finally, race, in and of itself, does not account for the fact that the economy and politics of the United States evolved in such a different way from those of Latin American nations. The failure of the British colonies of the Caribbean and the southern North American mainland, like that of the Spanish and Portuguese colonies, to develop in the manner of the northern British colonies was the result of their success in using coerced labor to produce agricultural and mineral exports for Europe during the centuries of colonial rule. These societies failed to develop in the post-independence era in the way their once-poor, predominantly white, northern neighbors did not because they had too many blacks, but because they had too many slaves.

IV

During the century following independence the paradox of American development was fully, and in most places tragically, revealed. Those European colonies that were the economic success stories of the mercantile, colonial era found it extremely difficult to adjust to the liberal principles of the Atlantic world's new industrial capitalist order. Only one area found the transition to liberalism, with its promise of political democracy and industrial development, relatively easy: the once-poor, free labor northern colonies of the North American mainland.

In the United States during the eighty years following its independence from Britain in 1781, the development of the nation's northern and southern regions diverged radically. The political arrangements worked out at independence preserved and protected the expansion of the South's slave-labor system. But northern interests prevailed on the issue of tariff protection for manufacturing industry. During the first half of the nineteenth century a series of crucial compromises enabled both the North and the South to extend their characteristic labor systems to newly settled territories to the west. The South's economy grew rapidly, paced by cotton exports that provided the bulk of the raw material for Britain's voracious textile industry. The North, meanwhile, developed an industrial economy that far overshadowed that of the South. Industry provided the material basis for the North's victory over the South in the most costly and destructive war yet seen in human history, the Civil War of 1860–64. During the war, and in the decades that followed, the North used its control of the government to abolish slavery and enact legislation dealing with land settlement, banking, tariffs, and railroad construction that helped consolidate the largest industrial capitalist society in the world.

The societies of Latin America and the Caribbean, like the US South, experienced no such industrial transformation. Some grew rapidly as producers of staples much in demand in the industrializing North Atlantic. Cuba's slave-based economy, for example, became the world's premier producer of sugar during the nineteenth century. Brazil, as noted previously, depended on slave labor to become the world's largest supplier of coffee during the same period. These two societies became the largest importers of slaves during the nineteenth century. (In contrast, the slave trade to the United States was abolished in 1808 and the South depended for its growing labor needs in cotton production on the natural increase of its domestic slave population.) The spectacular economic growth of Brazil and Cuba and the strength of their planter classes enabled them to avoid the extreme political instability and civil warfare typical of the Spanish American mainland during most of the nineteenth century.

Elsewhere in Latin America and the Caribbean, however, economic stagnation was the rule. The British West Indies, victims of soil exhaustion, loss of preferred access to the British market, and British abolition of the slave trade and slavery, produced a declining portion of the world's sugar during the nineteenth century. In Saint Domingue, a massive uprising of slaves, stimulated by the ideals of the French Revolution, drove white French planters from the island, defeated a 25,000-strong army Napoleon sent to re-establish French control, and by 1804 made Haiti the first independent nation in the Americas south of the United States. The uprising destroyed the plantation economy of the largest sugar-producer in the world. Former slaves turned land they acquired to production of food for themselves. But if the revolution halted Haiti's export-oriented growth, it was a boon for US expansionism. It induced Napoleon to sell Louisiana to the United States in 1803, effectively doubling US national territory.

In Spanish America as a whole, following the costly struggles for independence between 1810 and 1825, efforts to establish independent republics and organize viable economies based on liberal principles embroiled the newly independent states in incessant civil warfare. In the context of stagnant or declining exports, free trade brought a flood of imports of foreign manufactured goods. The chronic balance-of-trade deficit that resulted led to specie drain and eventually to default on the debts contracted in Britain during the era of independence. In many areas resumption of economic growth and the return of political stability came only in the last decades of the nineteenth century. In most places renewed economic growth depended on large-scale infusions of foreign capital, which came primarily from Britain, but increasingly from the United States as well. These developments consolidated Latin America's modern role as an exporter of primary agricultural and mineral commodities to the industrialized world.

As this brief sketch of post-colonial economic and political trends makes clear, the problem of "order," emphasized by Bemis, threatened the stability and even the existence of all the former European colonies in the Americas in the nineteenth century. Making the transition from colony to independent republic required fundamental reorganization of the polity. The problem was especially acute because of the liberal democratic precepts that dominated elite political discourse and popular aspirations in Europe and the Americas by the late eighteenth century. These ideas included the notion of inalienable individual political rights and the concept that legitimate government rested on the consent of the governed. These principles justified the drive for independence and defined the formal goals of the new republics. Everywhere, however, they were corrupted and compromised in the interest of preserving the social status quo and the power of political elites.

In Latin America the struggle for political liberalism foundered on the economic and social legacy of colonialism. Although slavery was eventually abolished, the legacy of coerced labor revealed itself in the highly exploitative labor systems—forms of obligatory labor service, debt peonage, tenantry, and sharecropping—that remained typical on the great rural estates and plantations of the region. Liberal laws governing the partition of public lands, the break-up and sale of the extensive landholdings of the Catholic Church, and the division of the communal lands of Indians all sought to free up land and labor in a capitalist marketplace. They were justified as efforts to create a numerous class of small, independent farmers. Yet almost everywhere the resources and power of the great landowners, merchants, and elite professionals sabotaged these social goals. The result, in many areas, was even greater concentration of land and wealth. Given this social and economic reality, liberal political reforms, which sometimes contained quite radical provisions (such as the abolition of property and even literacy requirements for suffrage) were quickly reversed or subverted in practice. The chaotic, violent politics of nineteenth century Latin America assumed liberal forms, but remained authoritarian in practice.

Nineteenth-century Latin American politics has traditionally been explained as a cultural and institutional legacy of Spanish and Portuguese colonialism. Among US academics, these cultural arguments often slid into overt racism. As late as 1932, for example, an eminent Latin American historian at Berkeley, Charles Chapman, was explaining Latin America's violent and authoritarian nineteenth-century politics as a function of the region's black and Indian heritage. It is closer to the truth to say that liberal ideals were undermined by the insidious legacy of coerced labor, and by the extreme concentration of land and wealth that went hand in hand with it.

The legacy of successful export production in the colonial era found expression in the politics of the newly independent British colonies as well. Again, comparison of the former colonies of the North American mainland disabuses us of the cultural and racial explanations commonly used to explain Latin American politics of the era. None of the thirteen colonies that originally formed the United States was, at the outset, politically very democratic in modern terms. Suffrage was restricted to free adult males who commanded a certain amount of property or income. But because of the family and free-wage labor systems of the northern colonies, and the relatively egalitarian distribution of land and wealth they promoted, by the time of independence more than half of their free male adult population had the vote. These colonies, whose political institutions would subsequently spread to the West, and be imposed on the South, already figured among the most democratic polities on earth.

In the former colonies of the southern mainland, however, things were quite different. Slaves, of course, could not vote. Nor did they enjoy any of the basic civil liberties on which democracy depends. The skewed nature of economic and political power, a product of plantation export agriculture, left elected bodies in control of the planters. Like their counterparts in Latin America, such as the slave-owning Venezuelan cacao planter Simón Bolívar, these wealthy white men played a major role in articulating the democratic ideology that justified independence from European colonialism. But their high-sounding democratic rhetoric was contradicted by their need for a system of political representation able to preserve their social power and protect their labor system. The system devised for the new nation enabled them to do that until the Civil War. For example, representation in the most democratic institution of the new republic, the House of Representatives, was calculated to preserve the planters' power by counting each non-voting slave as three-fifths of a person.

The simplest way to understand the differences in the political evolution of the United States and Latin American nations in the century following independence is to realize that, unlike the United States, Latin America had no "North." No Latin American nation had a region where a free labor system in the colonial era had produced a relatively egalitarian, rapidly industrializing society in which liberal political ideals could flourish. Latin American liberalism enlisted a geographically diffuse but growing number of reformers drawn from elite and popular classes alike. All viewed liberal economic reform as responsible for the prodigious advance of "civilization" in the leading nations of the West. But the most powerful class committed to liberal economic reform in Latin America, the large landowners who benefitted most from the region's expanding role as a supplier of agricultural exports to the industrialized world, were necessarily also committed to preserving their position within the grossly unequal distribution of wealth and power inherited from the past. They could hardly countenance fundamental reform of the land and labor systems they depended on.

Even in the United States, where the struggle over liberalism was decisively resolved by the victory of the North over the South in the Civil War, the legacy of coerced labor continued to compromise the South's transition to a liberal social order. The denial of basic civil liberties and voting rights to blacks was typical in the region from the late nineteenth century until well after World War II, when large-scale civil rights protest succeeded in expanding them. And until recently, the industrial growth of the region was also limited. Southern industry developed in part as northern corporations fled unionization of their plants and moved south, a process that began at the turn of the nineteenth century and intensified following the organizational gains of industrial workers in the 1930s and 1940s.

In fact, as we shall see in more detail in subsequent chapters, the legacy of coerced labor in the south undermined worker organization there and in the nation as a whole, not only in the nineteenth century but throughout the twentieth. Everywhere racial prejudice among white workers undercut labor unity, and northern employers often imported black and white workers from the low-wage south to undercut unionizing efforts in northern industry. When workers won support from the national government for union organizing during the crisis of the 1930s and World War II, capitalist interests cemented an alliance with southern elites that effectively limited government support for union rights in the postwar era. In recent decades, as corporations have eluded the power of industrial unions in their plants by relocating in low-wage, union-free parts of the southern United States, the strength of the organized labor movement in the nation as a whole has been eroded.

The information in this brief account of the post-colonial history of the American nations is, of course, not new. And the US side of it is well known to US historians and the readers of their texts. What is novel and significant about the story sketched here is the way it reveals the essential *unity* of US and Latin American history during the nineteenth century and beyond. This unity revolves around the common struggle of the independent American republics for liberal reform. US readers need not know much about nineteenth-century Latin American history to appreciate the significance of the failure of liberal reform in Latin America in the nineteenth century and the implications of that failure for twentieth-century developments. They have only to imagine what the nineteenth- and twentieth-century history of the United States would have looked like had the whole of the country developed in the colonial period as the South did, or had the South, not the North, won the Civil War.

Unfortunately, most US historians fail to see the unity in this history. By customarily treating US history in isolation from that of the rest of the Americas, they convey to their students the parochial notion that the history of their nation is unique and special—that it is "exceptional." Such treatment, by default, gives free (if often implicit) rein to cultural notions (only yesterday buttressed by the climatic and racial assumptions of distinguished historians like Bemis) to explain the successful march of US history toward the liberal democratic industrial order we know today. Latin American history, treated separately as a different domain of study, can thus be apprehended by US historians (and other academics, their students, and the public at large) in these same cultural (cum racial) terms. Except here culture is used to explain the failure of the nations south of the US border to develop successfully along a liberal path—in a word, to "modernize."

These cultural understandings of US and Latin American history were buttressed by broader trends in the US academy in the decades following World War II. During this period US academics (and many in Europe as well) fashioned an elaborate theory to explain development and under-development in the modern world. "Modernization theory" explained development as a function of cultural values. It held that, over time, modern values—rationalism, secularism, the "need to achieve"—yielded the scientific and technological progress, the self-generating industrial economies, the fluid social structures, and the democratic politics of developed capitalist societies like the United States. If most of the world had failed to develop along these lines, they argued, the root cause lay in the fatalistic, superstitious value systems of their "traditional" societies. Development of traditional societies, they maintained, depended on the diffusion of modern values through capital investment, education, technical missions, and, not least, widespread understanding of mod-ernization theory itself.

Modernization theory was "modern" in that it jettisoned the climatic and racial determinisms that Western scholars like Bemis had long relied upon to explain the world around them. It thus accommodated the rise of nationalism in the European colonial world and the process of decol-onization that accompanied it. It also served to legitimize the expanding economic, political, and cultural role of the United States in the postwar world.

Modernization theorists were never very clear, however, about the his-torical origins of the modern values they championed. Once they were forced to give up climate and race as the material cause of modern civilization, they drifted in a kind of nebulous idealism. Modern cultural values seemed to "drop from the sky," or else (as in standard US college courses in Western civilization) they arrived in the modern West via a tortuous cultural journey that began in classical Greece. Either way, an implicit invocation of race restored their connection to the material world.

During these same postwar decades Latin American scholars challenged these cultural assumptions by developing a body of thought often called "dependency theory." Building on assumptions like those of Eric Williams, they found the locus of underdevelopment in the workings of the world economic system. While modernization theorists found the cause of underdevelopment in cultural values *internal* to traditional societies, dependency theorists located its origins in the *external* ties that bound colonial societies and their modern national successors to the metropolitan capitalist nations of the West. Their solution to the problem of underdevelopment called for reform of the economic and social legacy of these historical ties and advocated fundamental restructuring of contemporary relationships between developed and underdeveloped societies.

This essay has tested the logic of these two positions through comparative analysis of the history of the European colonies in the Americas. Rejecting the cultural assumptions of "modernization" theory, it has built on the assumptions of "dependency" thinkers to argue that the labor systems of the American colonies, forged in response to the economic needs of European colonialism, best account for the later success or failure of the colonies in developing into capitalist industrial democracies. To the extent that "modern" or "traditional" cultural values can be singled out and associated with these developments, they would seem to be a consequence of this process, not its cause.

To my mind, this simple interpretation best explains the historical evidence on the comparative development of American societies. Yet my sense is that, while few US historians would contest the specifics of the argument I have made, few incorporate ideas like these into their teaching and research. And based on my experience with undergraduates and with graduate students specializing in US history, the interpretation advanced in this chapter is "news."

Certainly, general US political discourse and historical understanding at the end of the twentieth century is far from appreciating the legacy of colonialism in the Americas and the meaning of the struggle for liberalism in the newly independent nations of the hemisphere. Evidence for this assessment comes from the way we in the United States use—or, better, abuse—the term "liberal."

In mainstream contemporary US political debate self-proclaimed "conservatives" of the Republican Party blame the so-called "liberals" of the Democratic Party for a variety of evils, primary among them an embrace of government regulation and social welfare programs. In fact, as we have seen in this chapter, it is liberals who have historically sought a minimum of government control and regulation of private economic interests. In this sense, leaders of the Republican Party in the United States today could more appropriately be called liberals than their counterparts in the Democratic Party.

The social welfare benefits and labor rights that are today the targets of self-styled "conservatives" in the United States were put in place by social reformers of the Democratic Party backed by organized labor during the great crisis of liberalism in the 1930s (a subject I shall review in chapter 5 of this study). Members of the Democratic Party who continue to support these reforms are more properly called social democrats, not liberals.

Political leaders in the United States and throughout the hemisphere who today seek to reduce the strength and legal protections for labor, privatize government services, and promote unrestricted free trade in the hemisphere are the heirs of the liberal tradition in the Americas. Liberalism—let no one mistake its purpose—is the preferred ideology of the industrial capitalist order.

In the next two chapters, and, in a more general sense, in the remainder of the book as a whole, we will be following the legacy of American colonialism into the twentieth century. Because the struggle for liberal reform of this legacy was unsuccessful in nineteenth-century Latin America, movements there for democratic social reform in the twentieth century became far more radical than in the United States. From nineteenth-century political struggles to create a viable liberal capitalist order, they evolved into powerful nationalist movements, supported by organized workers, and aimed at fundamental social reform. These movements went far beyond the struggle to establish basic civil, political, and trade union rights witnessed in the United States. US movements for democratic reform in this century, including the struggles of mobilized workers, were effectively contained within the boundaries of an expanding liberal capitalist order. In contrast, the twentieth-century Latin American social revolutions challenged basic elements of the liberal capitalist order itself. They thus not only confronted the opposition of capitalist interests at home, but earned as well the hostility of US investors, the US government, and, ironically, the increasingly pro-capitalist organized US labor movement itself. The most tragic consequence of the paradox of American development was thus to pit labor in the Americas against itself.

Appreciation of the paradox of American development provides a democratic foundation for understanding crucial features of the twentieth-century history of the United States and Latin America, and prepares us for interpreting the dynamics of the relationships between them. It allows us to explain the great disparities of power and wealth that divide the developed and underdeveloped parts of the hemisphere without resort to ethnocentric and racist arguments. In particular, it enables us to redefine the concept of "order," which Bemis correctly identified as the overriding issue affecting the history of US–Latin American relations. The ongoing struggle for a peaceful, progressive order in those relations has been stymied not, as Bemis would have it, by the disorderly proclivities of non-white people of tropical American climes. Rather, it has been thwarted by elite opposition to something every US citizen should readily understand and most should easily identify with—an ongoing effort to democratize Latin American societies by overcoming the legacy of colonialism. Why this simple truth proves so elusive for most US citizens, generalists and academic specialists alike, is a question that will engage us throughout the remainder of this book.

Further Reading

The publications listed below include major works that have influenced the interpretation advanced in the chapter as well as books and articles that can serve as guides to the general literature on the subjects addressed.

Amerman, David L., and Philip D. Morgan, *Books about Early America*, Williamsburg, VA, 1989.

Bailyn, Bernard, *Voyages to the West*, New York 1986.

Bemis, Samuel Flagg, *The Latin American Policy of the United States*, New York 1943.

Bergquist, Charles, *Coffee and Conflict in Colombia, 1886–1910*, Durham, NC, 1978.

Bushnell, David, and Neill Macaulay, *The Emergence of Latin America in the Nineteenth Century*, New York 1988.

Coatsworth, John H., "Notes on the Comparative Economic History of Latin America and the United States," in Wolfgang Reinhard and Peter Waldmann, eds., *Nord und Sued in Amerika*, Freiburg 1992, pp. 595–612.

Coclanis, Peter, *The Shadow of a Dream*, New York 1989.

Curtin, Philip, *The African Slave Trade*, Madison, WI, 1969.

Davis, K.G., *The North Atlantic World in the Seventeenth Century*, Minneapolis 1974.

Davis, Ralph, *The Rise of the Atlantic Economies*, London 1973.

Drake, Paul W., *The Money Doctor in the Andes*, Durham, NC, 1989.

Furtado, Celso, *The Economic Development of Latin America*, Cambridge, UK, 1970.

Green, Jack P., and J.R. Pole, eds., *Colonial British America*, Baltimore 1984.

Hobsbawm, Eric, *The Age of Revolution*, New York 1962.

James, C.L.R., *The Black Jacobins*, 2nd edn., New York 1962.

Mintz, Sidney W., *Sweetness and Power*, New York 1985.

Moore, Barington, *Social Origins of Dictatorship and Democracy*, Boston 1966.

North, Douglas C., *The Economic Growth of the United States, 1790–1860*, New York 1961.

Solow, Barbara L., and Stanley L. Engerman, eds., *British Capitalism and Caribbean Slavery*, Cambridge, UK, 1987.

Stein, Stanley J., and Barbara H. Stein, *The Colonial Heritage of Latin America*, New York 1970.

Stearns, Peter N. *Interpreting the Industrial Revolution*, Washington, DC, 1991.

Williams, Eric, *Capitalism and Slavery*, Chapel Hill, NC, 1944.

A cartoon reprinted from John J. Johnson, *Latin America in Caricature* (Austin, TX, 1980), depicting colonial dependencies acquired by the United States following the War of 1898. Entitled "Cares of a Growing Family" and drawn by J. Campbell Tory, it was published in *The New York Bee*, 25 May 1898. In it, US President William McKinley ponders how best to deal with these new territories, which include Cuba and Puerto Rico. Images like this reveal the centrality of race in understandings of modern social evolution and suggest links between racial attitudes at home and imperialistic ventures abroad.

2

The Social Origins of
US Expansionism

No feature of US–Latin American relations during the twentieth century is more important than the expansion of US economic interests in Latin America. The preconditions for the growing economic integration of the two parts of the hemisphere were set in the colonial period and the nineteenth century. Industrialization in the United States created economic and social conditions that drove political and cultural elites toward an expansionary course in Latin America. At the same time, elites in Latin America viewed expanded trade and foreign investment as a way to end political instability and modernize their economies.

Since the last decades of the nineteenth century US policy has consistently sought to increase and protect US investments in Latin America. Government officials promoted foreign expansion as a way of insuring the economic growth and political stability of the United States itself. For their part governments in Latin America have alternatively sought to attract and control US investment, always under the rationale of stimulating economic growth and the political and social development of their own societies. Despite the superficial harmony of these official goals, however, the reality of expanding US economic interests in Latin America has led to severe political conflict between the nations of the hemisphere. These issues have received a great deal of attention in the literature on US–Latin American relations and are analyzed in detail in the next chapter. Less well understood—and virtually ignored in that literature—is the role of social conflict, particularly labor struggles, in the origins of US expansion itself. It is this neglected and important subject that is the focus of this essay.

The history of US expansion beyond the North American continent falls into two distinct stages. The first began in the late nineteenth century and continued until the advent of the Great Depression of the 1930s. The second began during World War II and continues to this day. During the first period, expansion focused primarily on Latin America.

Economic and political elites sought markets for a growing quantity of agricultural and manufactured goods. Financiers extended loans to Latin American governments to finance public utilities and communication and transport systems, especially railroad construction. The bulk of direct US private investment in Latin America went into the production for export of industrial minerals and fuels, such as copper and petroleum, and agricultural commodities, especially sugar and bananas.

After World War II, the scope of US foreign trade and investments became increasingly global, and although the traditional activities of US investors in Latin America continued, their relative importance declined. The distinguishing feature of this second period is the growth of manufacturing production abroad under the aegis of United States-based multinational corporations.

Most US historians have viewed the expansion of US interests abroad before World War II as a marginal development, largely unconnected to the march of national history. The most telling example, discussed in detail in this chapter, is the way they traditionally explained the War of 1898 with Spain. The war began when the United States intervened in Cuba's struggle for independence from Spain. It ended with the United States committed to a formal policy of imperialism. Yet for generations US historians argued that the war was simply an unfortunate "accident." And although for three decades following the war, the US intervened with force in Central America, Mexico, and the Caribbean, this period of "Dollar Diplomacy" appears in standard US accounts as an "aberration" (that is Bemis's language) or as an unimportant appendage to the main story of US history. At center stage is domestic reform during the "Progressive Era," US involvement in Europe during World War I, and cultural change during the prosperity of the 1920s.

In contrast, US historians generally acknowledge that the global expansion of US interests since World War II has deeply affected the domestic history of the nation. They recognize that the decades of international rivalry with the Soviet Union influenced economic development (the "military-industrial complex"), politics (McCarthyism, and internal division during the war with Vietnam), and even culture (the plots of Hollywood movies, the "counterculture" of the 1960s). US historians debate the motives behind the expansion of US commitments abroad during this period. Most stress ideological and strategic goals, although revisionists writing in the 1960s and 1970s showed how those goals were closely related to economic interests.

Neither of these periods of expansionism, however, is interpreted by US historians as a product of social or labor struggle at home. Revisionist diplomatic historians (known in US studies as the "Wisconsin School") emphasize the centrality of expansionism in the history of the nation, but they have only a marginal interest in labor history. [Most US labor historians, on the other hand, although their specialized work has become increasingly sophisticated and revisionist in other respects, have curiously ignored the relationship between class conflict at home and expansion abroad.]

This essay links the history of US labor with the history of US expansionism. It connects the insights of revisionist diplomatic and labor historians, and reflects on the intellectual and political implications of uniting those heretofore largely separate fields of historical inquiry. The essay focuses on the first period of expansion, leaving treatment of post-World War II developments to chapter 5.

I

The best single study of the origins of US imperialism in 1898 is Walter LaFeber's *The New Empire*, a book published in 1963. A revised version of LaFeber's doctoral dissertation written at the University of Wisconsin in 1959, the book broke decisively with traditional interpretations of the War of 1898. As noted earlier, those interpretations explained the war as an unfortunate accident that could have been avoided by strong political leadership. They argued that a weak President McKinley allowed the nation to drift into war under the pressure of public opinion. The people were whipped into war fever by an irresponsible "yellow" press, which sensationalized Spanish atrocities in Cuba, in part to increase the sales of mass-circulation dailies. According to the most influential work in this tradition, Julius Pratt's 1936 book *The Expansionists of 1898*, US business interests opposed the war.

LaFeber attacked this traditional interpretation head on. He argued that the war was a logical result of a consensus built over decades and shared by influential leaders in business, government, religious, and academic circles. All agreed on the vital need to expand markets abroad to preserve unchanged a domestic economic, social, political, and cultural order they believed was gravely threatened by social forces slipping from their control.

LaFeber conceptualized the social origins of US expansionism more explicitly at the start of his dissertation than he did in his revised book-length study. He began the dissertation by emphasizing how elite fears of the "danger" and the "threat" posed by the rise of rural and urban radicalism drove policy-makers toward an expansionary course. He quoted a sweeping statement by historian H. Von Holst on the crisis facing US

democracy following the bloody government repression of the great
Pullman railway strike of 1894.

> Fearful is the responsibility that rests upon this people, not only for themselves
> and for their posterity, but for all mankind. Never before have all the condi-
> tions been so favorable for making self-government a permanent success;
> never again can they be so favorable. If we fail now, after what those who pre-
> ceded us have achieved and left us [as] a priceless heritage, we shall stand in
> history more deeply branded than any other people, for our guilt will be
> greater than that of any nation that has ever trod the face of the earth.

Von Holst feared that if labor's demands for fundamental social reform
continued to be violently repressed, the prospects for US democracy
were doomed. LaFeber shared Von Holst's assessment of the magnitude
of the challenge posed by labor in the 1890s and the critical issues it
raised for the future of US democracy. Writing with hindsight, however,
he would show how elites found the solution to democratic pressure at
home not through basic domestic reform but by taking the fateful course
of foreign expansionism.

LaFeber never makes this argument very explicit in *The New Empire*,
however. The labor history of an era marked by the rise of powerful organizations like the Farmers' Alliance, the Knights of Labor, and the
American Federation of Labor (AFL) is largely absent from the book.
The massive, bloody strikes of the era—the great railway strike of 1877,
Haymarket (1888), Homestead (1892), the tremendous, overlapping
national strikes of miners and railway workers in 1894—enter LaFeber's
account only tangentially. Readers of the book find no description of
the radical democratic visions of an alternative society articulated by
farmers and workers during the 1880s and 1890s.

But a phantasmagoric popular social threat pervades LaFeber's book
nonetheless. It appears in twisted form in the perceptions of the businessmen, statesmen, and intellectuals LaFeber continually quotes
verbatim. Through the minds of this power elite, LaFeber establishes the
link between their class fears and the chronic economic depressions and
popular mobilization that define the last quarter of the nineteenth century.

LaFeber placed his interpretation squarely in the context of the maturation of the US industrial economy. He outlined the rapid growth of
industry during the 25-year cycle of fitful depression that began with the
Great Depression of 1873–78 and ended with the crisis of 1893–97. By the
end of the century US industry was producing more than Britain and
France combined, and the value of manufactured exports accounted for
a third of all US exports. Agricultural production and exports expanded

during this period as well, despite a dramatic decline in the world prices of major commodities, especially wheat. These trends, LaFeber argued, generated a widespread perception that the US economy was producing more than it could consume or place abroad, and led to ever wider concurrence about the need for new export markets. These would have to be found, it was felt, not primarily in Europe, where competition was fierce, but in Latin America—and beyond it in Asia—where agricultural staples and manufactured goods would find millions of new consumers.

LaFeber linked this analysis of the drive for expansion with the psychological impact of the official closing of the western frontier, which was (prematurely) announced by the US Census Bureau in 1890. He was thus able, in one of his most important chapters, to incorporate into his argument the thought of the famous US historian, Frederick Jackson Turner. Speaking at the World's Fair in Chicago in 1893, Turner advanced what became the most influential interpretation of US history ever developed, the so-called "Frontier Thesis." Turner held that "American" individualism, political institutions, and national character—in a word, the country's unique democratic calling—rested on the economic power generated by expansion across free land on the frontier. Now that the frontier had disappeared, the thesis implied, what would become of these unique American institutions and values? Here was the nub of the matter, the idea that the whole "American system" was at risk and that to preserve it expansion was necessary.

But LaFeber was not content to demonstrate the expansionist implications of the "Frontier Thesis." He went on to show that as early as 1891 Turner was aware of the "amazing new cure-all" of "open-door" economic diplomacy. This kind of expansion would be the hallmark of a new empire, where economic advantage could be won without the burdens of formal colonialism. In Turner's paper "The Significance of History," LaFeber found a statement which, as he put it, "offered to historians the Ariadne thread for unraveling American foreign policy after 1890."

> [O]nce fully afloat on the sea of worldwide economic interests we shall soon develop political interests . . . . [P]erhaps most important are our present and future relations with South America, coupled with our Monroe Doctrine. It is a settled maxim of international law that the government of a foreign state whose subjects have lent money to another state may interfere to protect the rights of the bondholders, if they are endangered by the borrowing state.

"It is difficult to overemphasize the significance of this statement," LaFeber concluded, "and unnecessary to elaborate upon it" (pp. 69–70).

LaFeber took special pains to deal with the generally accepted idea among historians that businessmen opposed the War of 1898. He showed among other things that McKinley was deeply sympathetic with the expansionist goals of the newly formed National Association of Manufacturers. He demonstrated how many businessmen who initially opposed the war did so primarily out of fear that warfare could stifle the embryonic economic recovery from the severe depression of the mid-1890s, which was underway by 1898. He documented how, in the weeks immediately preceding the declaration of war, influential elements of big business swung away from that position, hoping that war would end the chronic uncertainty generated by the situation in Cuba.

The bulk of LaFeber's analysis focused, however, on the intellectuals, politicians, and diplomats who put elite fears into systematic form and provided the blueprint for US expansionism. He analyzed the writings of the naval strategist Alfred Mahan, the intellectual and cultural concerns of Brooks Adams, the missionary zeal of Josiah Strong. He probed the diplomatic records of a string of powerful secretaries of state, including James G. Blaine, Walter Q. Gresham, and Richard Olney, to show that market advantage became the single overriding goal of US foreign policy in the late nineteenth century.

LaFeber established these broad economic, intellectual, and strategic trends in the first part of his book. He devoted most of the rest of it to case studies, drawn from his dissertation, of US policy in Latin America during the 1890s. He reviewed policy toward the Chilean Revolution of 1891, the Brazilian Revolution of 1894, the Venezuelan Boundary Crisis of 1895–96, and finally, the Cuban crisis that led the United States into war with Spain in 1898. This diplomatic history is not very attractive to Latin American historians because it neglects entirely Latin American sources and fails to analyze adequately the internal Latin American dimensions of these events. But for LaFeber's own purposes these case studies worked admirably, if a little monotonously, to hammer home his thesis that US policy-makers consciously, consistently, and ruthlessly sought markets, markets, markets.

For LaFeber, then, the advent of a formal policy of imperialism in 1898 was no accident. It was the conscious, logical result of a process that brought US business, policy, and academic leaders to a consensus about how best to preserve the social status quo.

II

The New Empire was so impressive as a piece of historical research and writing that the American Historical Association awarded it the prestigious Beveridge Prize and funded its publication in 1963. Yet for all its apparent prestige among US historians, *The New Empire*'s interpretation of the origins of US imperialism has not become the dominant one in US history textbooks today. These textbooks often list *The New Empire* in their suggestions for further reading and most include the search for markets as part of their explanation of the origins of US expansionism. In a critical sense, however, they fail to come to terms fully with LaFeber's argument, which, as outlined above, places US expansionism explicitly within the context of economic developments, and implicitly, by treating the class fears of elites, in the context of popular mobilization.

The history textbooks, of course, do not ignore the issues of industrialization and economic depression in the late nineteenth century. And most contain considerable detail and useful analysis of labor and agrarian unrest. But they treat these subjects in chapters separate from the ones devoted to the advent of imperialism. Conceptually, they delink domestic economic and social developments from the story of expansionism. Urban labor's story is recounted in chapters dealing with the rise of industry. Separated from labor's story, and usually treated in chapters dealing with the debate over the currency and the tariff, is the history of agrarian unrest and the rise of the Populist Party. Finally, these texts do not deal with the link established by LaFeber between expansion and intellectual trends, particularly his searching analysis of the most famous interpretation of US history, Turner's Frontier Thesis.

That the authors of mainstream textbooks do not come to terms fully with LaFeber's contribution is not surprising. To incorporate his thesis would undermine the liberal ideological and political message of these texts, and subvert the way they organize the story of American history to sustain that message. The history textbooks share a common liberal faith in the democratic progress of the nation. They organize the history of the late nineteenth and early twentieth centuries as a progression of periods defined by domestic political developments—the Civil War, Reconstruction, the "Gilded Age,"* and Progressivism. They treat the advent of imperialism as a sidelight to this story, rather than, as LaFeber would have it, its defining characteristic.

In contrast, for LaFeber (and for the "Wisconsin School" in general) 1898 marks the great watershed of post-Civil War US history. Preceding it are decades of large-scale industrialization and escalating class conflict

---

* This curious term, in standard use by US historians today, derives from the title of a novel by Mark Twain and Charles Dudley Warner. It focuses attention on the new wealth and political corruption of the last decades of the nineteenth century rather than on industrial transformation and the violent class conflict that accompanied it.

that drive the US elite into imperialist adventure. Following it (just as Von Holst predicted) is a century in which the demands of empire resolutely undermine the democratic promise of the nation. In the trenchant words of William Appleman Williams, LaFeber's most famous mentor at Wisconsin, the twentieth century revealed the "tragedy of American diplomacy," the bitter, undemocratic fruit of "empire as a way of life."

One would think that US labor historians might have seized upon LaFeber's analysis to link their study of domestic working-class life and labor struggles to the expansionist thrust of foreign policy. In recent decades labor scholars have worked in an intellectual environment that is more open to dissent and innovation than was the repressive Cold War climate that prevailed in the 1950s and 1960s when a brave young LaFeber researched and wrote *The New Empire*. Authors of some of the best recent works on US labor build on Marxist or radical precepts that reject the liberal assumptions of mainstream studies and textbooks on US history. They qualify, for example, the liberal notion that US society became more democratic over the course of the late nineteenth and twentieth centuries. They emphasize the centrality of class struggle and the extent of the repression faced by workers' organizations at the end of the nineteenth century. Their studies have increased our appreciation of the breadth and depth of popular democratic struggle in the United States during the last decades of that century. They reinforce, in other words, LaFeber's thesis that domestic social mobilization impelled the power elite into foreign expansion. Yet the authors of these studies ignore LaFeber's contribution and write as though they are unaware of the imperialist corollary of their own revisionist arguments.

Illustrative of these trends are three especially important books by US labor scholars. Each deals with a major facet of labor struggle in the United States at the close of the nineteenth century. And each is especially relevant to the question of the social origins of US expansionism. Two of these studies, Lawrence Goodwyn's *Democratic Promise: The Populist Moment in America* (1976) and David Montgomery's *Workers' Control in America* (1979), are widely acknowledged as major contributions to US social history. The third, *Segmented Work, Divided Workers*, a collaborative effort by Marxist economists David Gordon, Richard Eduards, and Michael Reich, published in 1979, helps place late nineteenth-century US labor history into the broad sweep of modern capitalist development.

Although these works ignore the issue of imperialism, they nevertheless enable us to specify with greater clarity than LaFeber did the links between social struggle at home and expansion abroad. Moreover, each of these works advances a way of viewing labor history that transcends its specific nineteenth-century US subject matter. (I will return to these

insights in chapter 5 when I discuss the problem of constructing a democratic labor politics in the world today.)

Goodwyn's book is a major reinterpretation of the largest popular
movement in US history. It demonstrates the movement's cooperative
ethos, its radical reform program, its democratic potential. Reading his
book one can well appreciate how LaFeber's elites must have shuddered
at the prospect of growing Populist power. Goodwyn shows how the movement united millions of rural workers across racial, regional, political,
and—not least important—class or property divisions. The Farmers'
Alliances brought together rural smallholders, sharecroppers, and day
laborers and attracted railroad and even urban workers to their fold.
They linked whites with blacks, Southerners with Westerners, and one-
time Democrats with former Republicans. Building on these coalitions
they mounted a radical civil crusade against the power of bankers, merchants, railroad tycoons, and established political elites.

Goodwyn's book argues that the Populists' well-known emphasis on
monetary issues, particularly their advocacy of the free coinage of silver,
was a superficial aspect of their program for radical economic reform.
That program rested on the development of producer and consumer
cooperatives and on the Sub-Treasury Plan, which would have radically
democratized access to credit. It was the issue of free silver, however, that
dominated the pivotal presidential election of 1896. Populists merged
with Democrats and met defeat at the hands of William McKinley, who
championed high tariffs and the gold standard, and had major support
from business interests. The election inaugurated a period of Republican
control of the White House that, except for the years of Woodrow Wilson,
lasted until the Great Depression of the 1930s.

Goodwyn empathizes profoundly with the Populists, and sees in their
movement important lessons for those who would construct a democratic politics in the nation today. But he does not address the links between
the radical agrarian movement he celebrates and the resolution of the
national crisis it created through imperialism. Veteran Populist Tom
Watson, who helped lead the powerful bi-racial agrarian movement in the
South and served as the Populists' vice-presidential candidate in 1896,
grasped this link very clearly. "The Spanish War finished us," he would
later say. "The blare of the bugle drowned the voice of the Reformer"
(quoted in George Brown Tindall, *America: A Narrative History*, 2nd edn.,
New York 1988, p. 897).

David Montgomery's book eloquently demonstrates the transcen-
dence of the struggle by workers to exert control over the labor process
in US industry. That struggle underlies the violent labor conflicts of the
1880s and 1890s. Although by the end of the nineteenth century many

US workers labored in large factories, skilled workers, not management, still largely controlled the way work was done and set the pace of production. In their efforts to cut labor costs and increase efficiency, capitalists sought to break the power of skilled workers, many of whom were organized into powerful craft unions. The name widely associated with this capitalist offensive is that of Frederick Winslow Taylor, who propagated the principles of what he called "scientific management." That doctrine called for division of the productive process into its simplest components, and increases in the speed and efficiency with which workers executed them. Using these techniques, management sought to appropriate the knowledge of skilled workers, reduce their numbers, and extract the greatest effort at the lowest cost from the semi-skilled factory machine operatives who replaced them.

Montgomery also documents the ethos of mutuality that pervaded the US labor movement at the end of the nineteenth century. That sentiment proved explosive when translated into the sympathy strikes that became the hallmark of the massive labor struggles of the 1890s. Labor protest met with severe private and public repression, and with effective counter-strategies by capitalists and the state. Especially telling was the use of court injunctions against sympathy strikes. Faced with this repressive reality, many skilled workers turned toward a more moderate and restricted unionism, embodied in the American Federation of Labor, whose star began to rise in the 1890s. Montgomery demonstrates that the struggle of US workers over control issues continued well into this century. But after 1900 conservative craft unionists maintained control of the AFL, the largest and most powerful labor federation. Like Goodwyn, Montgomery mentions no link between foreign expansion and the conservative institutional outcome of the radical labor struggles he analyzes.

Gordon, Eduards, and Reich's book links stages in the evolution of the US economy, from the beginnings of industrialization to the present, with parallel developments in labor markets and the labor process. Of particular interest to the authors is the connection between "long waves" of capitalist development in the world economy, roughly fifty-year periods of growth and stagnation, and what they call "social structures of accumulation" within these waves. By the latter term they mean the conditions, broadly conceived, under which capitalists are induced to invest and thus expand production during long periods of time. Structures of accumulation include banking and currency laws and government trade policies. They encompass the organization of work and production, forms of worker resistance, and the legal regime used to channel and repress labor organization.

A major section of the book treats the 25-year period of downturn in the long wave that coincides with the maturation of the US industrial economy and the massive worker protest and organizational drives of the 1870s, 1880s, and 1890s. This is the period of chronic depressions and price deflation between 1873 and 1898 that forms the conceptual foundation of LaFeber's argument, helps explain the agrarian mobilization described by Goodwyn, and fosters the explosive labor protest analyzed by Montgomery.

Gordon, Eduards, and Reich define this period as one of economic crisis and uncertainty, in which workers and capitalists alike struggled to create new institutional and organizational forms favorable to their class interests. Best known among the initiatives by capitalists is the growth in the size of corporations and their concentration into huge oligopolies known in the United States as trusts. This process, identified and documented by Lenin, occurred throughout the industrialized world. According to Lenin's famous theory of imperialism, the concentration of industry and the growing power of banks led to a massive export of capital to less-developed world regions, to a scramble for colonies, and ultimately to war between blocs of capitalist nations over spheres of influence and territory worldwide. Gordon *et al.* describe this process of economic concentration but downplay its imperialist outcome. They focus their analysis, as does Montgomery, on the efforts by capitalists to lower labor costs and increase production by breaking the control of skilled workers over the labor process.

The struggle by workers and capitalists for control of the labor process helps to explain some of the major questions in US labor history of the late nineteenth century. It illuminates, for example, the meteoric rise and rapid decline of the Knights of Labor, which organized millions of skilled and unskilled workers in a common vision of a democratic society of producers in the 1880s. It helps explain the unity of landed and landless agricultural workers who flocked to the Populist movement. It furthers understanding of the causes of the violent resistance by workers to efforts by management to restructure production in basic industries like steel. It places in context the emergence of such innovative labor tactics as the sympathy strike, and the changes in the law and the uses of state repression to curb labor mobilization in the 1890s.

Control issues also illuminate the growing success of the moderate craft unionism championed in the 1890s by the AFL. Management and government tolerance of that organization, which would dominate the labor movement until the 1930s, represented a kind of compromise with skilled workers outside the large-scale firms that formed the core of US industry by the turn of the century. That compromise, however, left aside most unskilled and semi-skilled workers in large-scale manufacturing production, the most important and dynamic sector of the economy.

The other aspect of Gordon *et al.*'s framework, their emphasis on long waves and structures of accumulation, helps illuminate the genesis of US expansionism, particularly the role of the War of 1898 in that process. Viewed from this perspective, the war appears as the decisive event that bolstered investor confidence in the long-term prospects for economic growth and profit. The national euphoria that accompanied victory in what John Hay, Secretary of State between 1898 and 1905, called a "splendid little war" cemented into place all the separate pieces of a new structure of accumulation. These disparate pieces, fashioned by capitalists in the struggle with labor in preceding decades, included, as we have seen, large-scale, more concentrated units of production and the key capitalist advance in the structuring of the labor process known as Taylorism. They included as well changes in the law and the use of the courts to effectively repress worker dissent, a process which in turn fostered new, more conservative, forms of worker organization. In monetary and fiscal terms, the new structure for investment rested on the gold standard and a high protective tariff. In political terms, it found expression in the consolidation of Republican political hegemony in the election of 1896, and in the denaturing and defeat, through fusion with the Democratic party, of the Populist party. In military terms the new structure for investment revolved around the building of a battleship navy and acquisition of imperial beachheads to protect overseas commerce. Victory in the War of 1898 yielded the strategic territory, Cuba and the Philippines, that would protect a Central American canal designed to open up the Latin American market, help unify the national market, and open the way to the markets of Asia.

Strange as it may seem, however, the issue of foreign expansion does not enter into Gordon *et al.*'s discussion of the forging of a new structure of accumulation during the late nineteenth century. The word "imperialism" does not figure in the index; LaFeber is absent from the bibliography. Yet the imperialist thrust of 1898 coincided with the end of a quarter-century of economic uncertainty and the beginning of the long wave of capitalist expansion that lasted until the 1920s. In the Americas this period witnessed a great burst of US investment in Latin America, US intervention to assure the separation of Panama from Colombia, the building of the Panama Canal, and the consolidation of informal US control over the whole Caribbean Basin. It coincided, in a word, with the advent of LaFeber's *new* empire, one controlled through informal economic and political mechanisms, not (for the most part) through the formal acquisition of colonies.

The intellectual and political implications of the failure of seminal works like these to relate labor's struggle to the process of expansion are tellingly revealed in the treatment of the late nineteenth century in an otherwise admirable US history textbook published in 1992. Inspired by the celebrated US social historian Herbert Gutman, the American Social History Project's *Who Built America?* (references below are to Volume 2) seeks to emphasize the central role of working people in the history of the nation. The book attempts to synthesize the "dramatic discoveries" about working people contained in the "new" social history of the last three decades. These discoveries, the authors announce in their introduction, allow them "to think and write differently about familiar topics, including the rise of industrial capitalism, US *overseas expansion* [my emphasis], successive waves of internal migration and foreign immigration to the nation's cities, depression and war, the rise of industrial unionism, and the widening struggle for civil rights" (pp. ix–x).

The book's treatment of the late nineteenth century, however, gives the impression that labor protest of the 1880s and 1890s (during the so-called "Gilded Age") led only to domestic reform (the "Progressive Era"). Imperialism is left out of the equation. Yet the authors recognize that the end of the 1890s marks a watershed in US and labor history. Summarizing their chapter 4, on the "class wars" of the 1880s and 1890s, they declare that the United States "would never again witness such a broad or fundamental challenge by working people to the claims of capital" (p. 157). But they link expansionism neither to worker protest of the late nineteenth century nor to labor's more moderate twentieth-century course. Rather, expansion comes into their study in the following chapter, which covers the period 1900 to the start of World War I. There it is treated in the conventional manner of the mainstream liberal textbooks discussed above. Expansionism is "[d]riven, in many ways, by economic needs," that is, by the search for markets, and by the "example" of European powers. The labor struggles of the 1890s enter their analysis only indirectly, as a spur to a "strident nationalism," voiced by "politicians and religious leaders" (pp. 161–62). LaFeber's *The New Empire* does not figure in the extensive bibliographies for these two chapters. A final indicator of their disregard for the importance of US imperialism and expansion is the index to the volume itself, where neither term appears.

The interpretive and political implications of the authors' failure to link the domestic and international dimensions of the struggle of US workers during the 1890s are starkly illustrated in their treatment of Attorney General Richard Olney during the dramatic labor conflicts of 1894. After describing the sorry fate of Jacob Coxey's march on Washington at the head of an "industrial army" of the unemployed in

May of that year, and noting the existence of larger, more radical armies in the west, which sometimes commandeered trains for their purposes, they turn to Olney, a former railroad corporation lawyer, who "played a particularly important role in shaping administration policy." "Olney obtained federal court injunctions, deployed large numbers of US marshals, and finally brought in US troops to end the train seizures." These measures led to considerable conflict, but in the end they stopped the train hijackings and, "more important, halted the eastward march of the industrial armies" (p. 140). In mid-summer, however, with tens of thousands of coal miners already on strike, Eugene V. Debs's powerful new American Railway Union launched a nationwide boycott in support of striking workers at the Pullman car works that brought most of the nation's railway traffic to a halt.

Olney now enters their narrative a second time.

[B]uilding on the tactics he used earlier against Coxey's Army, [Olney] obtained a sweeping injunction in early July from the federal courts, effectively outlawing the boycott . . . .

Federal troops and state militia were quickly dispatched in six states. The arrival of the U.S. Army in Chicago on the Fourth of July precipitated a violent confrontation that left thirteen dead, more than fifty wounded, and hundreds of thousands of dollars of railroad property destroyed. Working-class resistance to the troops spread rapidly across the country over the course of the next week, encompassing twenty-six states in all from Maine to California . . . . By July 11, an estimated thirty-four people were killed; Debs and other ARU leaders were arrested. (p. 142)

The authors go on to analyze the weak support given the American Railway Union by the leadership of the American Federation of Labor, and the bitter aftermath of the strike, which led to prison terms for Debs and other leaders and to the blacklisting of many of the strikers.

Now, although the authors of *Who Built America?* do not give us this information, this is the same Richard Olney who just one year later, as Secretary of State, issued a famous pronouncement that put the world on notice of US intentions to play a forceful new role in the hemisphere and the world of power politics. "Today," he declared in blustering legal diction, "the United States is practically sovereign on this continent, and its fiat is law upon the subjects to which it confines its interposition" (quoted in Bemis, p. 120). The immediate intent of Olney's declaration was to thwart British designs on territory claimed by Venezuela. But the broader legacy of his pronouncement, widely recognized by students of US diplomatic history, was the way it transformed the Monroe Doctrine into a "positive" instrument. After 1895 policy-makers increasingly used the

Doctrine to justify the right of the United States to intervene in the affairs of Latin American nations whenever they felt US interests were threatened.]

In contrast to the authors of *Who Built America?*, LaFeber stresses the relationship of Olney's "epochal" foreign policy pronouncement both to domestic economic and social issues and to the subsequent history of US foreign expansionism. He begins his coverage of Olney, like the authors of *Who Built America?*, by noting that before he accepted the post of Attorney General in 1892 Olney was one of the "best-paid" railroad lawyers in New England. But then LaFeber enters more complex terrain. In order to understand US actions in the Venezuelan boundary dispute in 1895, he contends, two aspects of Olney's thought must be understood. First, Olney

> had changed his views concerning the cause of the depression during the course of 1893 and 1894. In 1893 he attributed the depression to a normal downturn of the business cycle. By June, 1894, however, his understanding of the economic picture had matured to the point where he interpreted the depression as a great "labor revolution" resulting from the introduction of machine technology into the economy. (p. 256)

LaFeber says that Olney hoped this "revolution" could be channeled in peaceful ways, but he reminds us that as Attorney General he did not hesitate to use force in the Pullman strike and that he regarded Eugene Debs with contempt.

The second crucial aspect of Olney's thought, according to LaFeber, was his understanding of the course of US history. He believed by 1895 that the United States had emerged from the period of internal development and was "by necessity expanding outward" (p. 256). The significance of the Venezuelan boundary issue thus begins to become clear in LaFeber's analysis. In challenging Great Britain's ambition to control, at Venezuela's expense, the mouth of the Orinoco River, which many in the US government believed was the gateway to the commerce of northeastern South America, Olney was escalating the policy of commercial expansion that culminated in the War of 1898. In enunciating the "Olney extension" of the Monroe Doctrine in 1895, the US government was saying, as LaFeber bluntly puts it, "that the Western Hemisphere was to be under American [US] commercial and political control, not European" (p. 242).

In ignoring Olney the diplomat, the authors of *Who Built America?* artificially split the man, and the history they write, in two. The pair of ideas outlined by LaFeber coexisted and complemented each other in Olney's mind. They informed his innovative, aggressive interpretations of both domestic and international law. They linked his ruthless repression of the Pullman strike in 1894 and his forceful diplomacy of 1895. Perhaps the thought and actions of no other single historical figure testify so powerfully to the social origins of US imperialism.

III

How is one to explain the reluctance of US scholars to recognize the social origins of US imperialism? And what are the implications of taking what would seem to be such a simple, logical step? One might argue that to do so is to distort the historical record, that the democratic social threat to the system was not so great or radical, or that it had crested or had been resolved by the mid-1890s. This would probably be the line adopted by the authors of the liberal textbooks I have described. But this argument misses the point. However one weighs the scope, intensity, and timing of popular mobilization by rural and urban workers—qualities that recent scholarship by historians like Goodwyn and Montgomery clearly tends to weigh more heavily on the side of real threat than much work done earlier—the issue under consideration is the *perceptions* of that threat by privileged social sectors. LaFeber persuasively documents those perceptions. To discount his work, and evidence from recent scholarship on worker mobilization that can buttress and extend his argument, historians must refute his analysis of such perceptions, and explain away, somehow, the links he establishes between elite class fears and imperialist action.

As for that recent labor scholarship itself, which, as I have noted, builds on radical or Marxist, not liberal, assumptions, it might be argued that the subject for historians like Goodwyn and Montgomery is social struggle, not imperialist expansion. The problem here is that the issue of imperialism is intertwined with their story, including, as I hope to show in this section, its outcome.

In ignoring the relationship between US imperialism and the trajectory of the labor movement, the studies I have reviewed by Goodwyn, Montgomery, and Gordon, Eduards, and Reich are not exceptional. Mainstream US historians, including most labor historians, have systematically obscured the connections between foreign expansion and the history of the labor movement at home. A recent state-of-the art survey by Leon Fink of work on labor history published over the last two decades confirms this generalization. Part of a volume (*The New American History*, edited by Eric Foner) commissioned and published by the American Historical Association in 1990, Fink's analysis of studies dealing with the late nineteenth and early twentieth centuries mentions neither expansion nor imperialism, nor any other link between international and domestic affairs (pp. 240–43).

In contrast, the architects of US imperialism seem to have had the purpose of expansion and its intended effects on US workers clear in their minds. Secretary of State Henry Cabot Lodge defended the acquisition of the Philippines before the Senate in 1900 on the grounds that the islands held tremendous potential as markets for US goods and sites for capital investment. He also stressed their strategic location for access to the markets of Asia. He emphasized above all that acquisition was in the best interest of the people,

> most particularly for the advantage of our farmers and our workmen, upon whose wellbeing, and upon whose full employment at the highest wages, our entire fabric of society and government rests.

The so-called anti-imperialists who opposed acquisition of the Philippines fully endorsed these commercial and social goals. They believed, however, that these ends could be achieved without the costs of formal colonialism. Incorporation of territory densely populated by darker, primitive races—"Malays, Tagals, Filipinos, Chinese, Japanese, Negritos and various more or less barbarous tribes," in the words of the leading anti-imperialist spokesperson, the naturalized German immigrant Carl Schurz—threatened democratic institutions at home. Were such overseas lands to become US territories they would eventually become states of the Union and their congressional representatives would have a say in legislation affecting the vital interests of the white majority at home. (Speeches by Lodge and Schurz are reproduced in Theodore P. Green, *American Imperialism in 1898* (1955); the quotations are from pp. 72–3 and 79.)

Most of the published evidence we have on the impact of imperialism on US labor comes from the work of Philip Foner. He was a prolific historian whose orthodox Marxist-Leninist interpretations are customarily ignored or discounted by mainstream US historians. Viewed dispassionately, however, his work serves as a partial corrective to mainstream US scholarship on the subject. Foner made a major (and much-neglected) contribution to the study of the origins of the War of 1898, *The Spanish-Cuban-American War and the Birth of American Imperialism*, a two-volume work published in 1972. The book documents the racial and class fears of US policy-makers as they monitored the increasingly radical nature of the Cuban independence movement. By the late 1890s leadership of the movement had passed from the white elite to black and mulatto revolutionaries who threatened existing property relations and the social and racial hierarchy. Foner's book thus nicely complements LaFeber's. It demonstrates the international class and racial dimensions of LaFeber's exclusively national argument.

Foner also edited, with Richard C. Winchester, *The Anti-Imperialist Reader*, a study published in 1984. The first volume covers the period from the Mexican War to 1900 and includes a large sample of domestic responses to imperialism by leaders of the organized labor movement, socialists, and African-Americans. Before his death in 1995 Foner also completed the first volume of a study entitled *US Labor Movement and Latin America* (1988), which covers the period up to World War I. [These two works show that the initial opposition to imperialism by most sectors of the US labor movement was shallow, and that it soon evolved toward accommodation with expansionism.] The response of Samuel Gompers, the leader of the AFL, was typical. Gompers originally opposed imperialism, fearing that political incorporation of backward, low-wage societies would take away domestic jobs and undercut the earnings of organized workers. Once he understood that US policy was aimed primarily at commercial expansion abroad, not the political incorporation of foreign territory, he came to endorse that policy.

Nevertheless, although Foner's work reveals an awareness of LaFeber's book, and of its place in an evolving literature on the origins of imperial expansion, he interprets its thesis in the same limited way the liberal textbooks do. He focuses entirely on the quest for markets. He ignores [LaFeber's implicit argument that the democratic struggle of rural and urban workers in the 1890s impelled the national elite into their imperialist adventure.]

Moreover, in emphasizing the accommodation with imperialism by the leadership of much of the organized labor movement, Foner's conclusions mirror Lenin's indictment of the opportunism of the "labor aristocracy" of advanced capitalist nations. For Lenin, this labor elite, suborned by a small slice of the profits of imperial expansion, could never be expected to fulfill the historical mission of the industrial proletariat envisioned by Marx. Leadership of the socialist revolution that would overthrow capitalism would come instead from a vanguard party of Communists who understood what was in the best interest of the working class even if workers themselves did not.

The anti-democratic implications of Foner's Leninist assumptions are obvious to us today. The socialist experiments of this century, inspired by Lenin's precepts, doomed the development of democracy in the polity and in the workplace. In the long run, they also destroyed the potential for economic development. (These issues are discussed more fully in chapter 5.) But the implications of Leninist thinking should not blind us to the importance of the accommodation, documented by Foner, of mainstream labor to imperial expansion. [This is true most broadly because, as the dominant leadership of the organized labor movement abandoned its opposition to imperialism in the early twentieth century, it moved at the same time to accommodate itself to the burgeoning capitalist order at home.]

Documenting these links between imperial expansion and the trajectory of the labor movement is difficult because most US historians, labor historians in particular, do not frame the issues they study this way. They, like the studies and textbooks they write, disconnect social from diplomatic history, fragmenting the history of the nation they study into separate, largely unconnected spheres. For an outsider looking in, especially one who specializes in Latin American history, theirs is a curious and distorted perspective on historical reality. For US historians, in contrast, it is a natural and perfectly normal way of viewing the past.

Because US historians do not "see" the question of links between expansion and labor history as a problem, they don't study it. As a result, even if there are such links, there is little evidence in their work that a non-specialist can point to to develop the argument I am suggesting here.

I can illustrate these perceptual issues and the "Catch-22" situation in which they place the non-specialist by reproducing a particularly illuminating critique of the argument I have made up to this point. The critique comes from David Brody, the leading US labor historian specializing on the twentieth century. Brody is responding to an earlier version of this essay, which circulated as a working paper in 1993.

April 15, 1993

Dear Chuck:

Thanks for sending me your Working Paper No. 2, which I read with much interest. It's a stimulating treatment of LaFeber et al., which is true of everything you do that tears us out of our national parochialism and makes us see what we (and the U.S.) do from the other end of the stick so to speak. I did think, however, that your criticism of Montgomery, Goodwyn etc. has a rather obvious answer. It seems to me well accepted by those of us who find LaFeber persuasive that the labor and agrarian upheavals of the 1890s did trigger the anxious expansionism that led to the 1898 war with Spain. Maybe LaFeber doesn't emphasize this enough, but he most certainly says so and, as in the empirical basis for the book generally, gives us quotations enough to satisfy us of the strength of his claim. For the text I and others recently published, I reread LaFeber and accordingly made this argument in my imperialism chapter, but like all the others you cite, I don't say anything about imperialism in my labor chapter. The problem for US labor historians of virtually all political persuasions except unreconstructed Marxist-Leninists is that the process seems to go in only one direction; class struggle may lead to imperialism, but we don't see how imperialism leads back to the class struggle, so the social origins of US imperialism becomes a kind of footnote for us. At the receiving end in your neck of the woods, of course, the impact of US imperialism is devastatingly clear and no footnote to Latin American history. Now this omission may be false consciousness on our part (although I would not concede that until it could be demonstrated just in what degree and in what ways US imperialism did matter for US labor history in this era). And this in turn goes back to one of the central problems with which LaFeber wrestles. The fact that expansionists thought that access to overseas markets was crucial to social stability in the US does not mean this was objectively the case; and LaFeber concedes as much; he acknowledges that foreign trade was not a big deal for the US economy as it was ca. 1900. His is a study of perceptions, and their consequences, and he says so. The haziness of the underlying realities I would submit is what at least in large part accounts for the silence of labor historians on imperialism. If we don't see its impact, how can we write about it? I don't think it's enough to belabor us for ignoring imperialism, or more precisely, for segregating it from labor history proper. You have to show us why that's the wrong thing to do. Anyway, you can see that your working paper set my juices flowing.

. . . .

All the best, David

In this pithy and illuminating critique Brody accepts the thrust of the argument I have made to this point about the social origins of US expansionism. In fact, he makes it his own. Yet he admits that in the history textbook he has just co-authored (James Henretta, Elliot Browlee, David Brody, Susan Ware, and Marilynn Johnson, *America's History*, 3rd edn., forthcoming) the chapter he wrote on labor makes no mention of imperialism. His reasons are most revealing. First he argues that he, like other US labor historians (except "unreconstructed" Marxist-Leninists like Philip Foner), finds the relationship of labor to foreign expansion as going in only one direction. Labor mobilization may contribute to imperialism, but US historians can't see that imperialism affects labor. Second, he emphasizes, correctly, that LaFeber's thesis (like my own argument in this essay) concerns the *perception* by elites that foreign expansion was crucial to social stability and that this "does not mean this was objectively the case." He concludes that it is the "haziness of these underlying realities" that "in large part accounts for the silence of labor historians on imperialism."

My response to Brody's defense of US labor historians emphasizes two points. First, even if imperialism had no effect on the subsequent history of labor, it still seems to me important to convey the idea (which Brody says he accepts) that labor's democratic struggle at home motivated elites to pursue expansionism. Second, as each of the essays in this book tries to demonstrate, *perception* is all we have to work with—there is no other "objective" reality. Brody addresses directly the problem of perception that undergirds my critique of US labor historians and frames my own dilemma as a non-specialist writing about US history. "If we don't see [imperialism's] impact," he says, "how can we write about it?" He then urges me to do what he and his colleagues who are specialists in the field cannot: show, as he puts it a few lines earlier, "just in what degree and in what ways US imperialism did matter for US labor history in this era."

To accept Brody's challenge fully would entail becoming a US history specialist and embarking on a major primary research project. For disciplinary and professional reasons I discuss in chapter 5, that is a course a Latin American historian like myself is unlikely or unwilling to undertake. What I can do, writing as a non-specialist in US history, is more modest. I can try to suggest, on the basis of reading in the published work of US labor historians, how expansionism helps to explain what these historians identify as the most important analytical problem in twentieth-century US labor studies.

That problem usually takes the form of a question. Why and how did the increasingly organized and powerful US labor movement of the first two decades of the twentieth century fall apart—materially, ideologically, and tactically—in the 1920s? That question is implied in the title of another major study by David Montgomery, *The Fall of the House of Labor* (1987), which examines the six decades of labor history that culminated in the collapse of the 1920s. Montgomery promises (p. 71) to deal with the subject of imperialism in the later chapters of his book. Except for minor references (pp. 348 and 406) made in passing, however, he does not. Yet many of the themes he and other US historians develop to explain the crisis of labor in the 1920s are in one way or another connected to expansionism. Before we turn to this interpretive question, we must first briefly review this US labor history, then see how US labor historians explain it.

After 1898 the economy of the United States entered a phase of rapid growth that, with short interruptions, continued through World War I. During the same period the relatively tight labor markets fostered by economic expansion and, later, wartime mobilization, favored the struggles of US workers. Union membership expanded four times, from half a million to over two million, between 1898 and 1903 alone. It doubled again between 1915 and 1920, rising from more than two and a half million to more than five million. That meant that almost 20 percent of the non-agricultural labor force was unionized in the latter year. Strike activity during the same period reached heights that dwarfed anything seen previously. In 1919 alone some four million workers went out on strike, roughly a fifth of the nation's workforce.

Much of this labor mobilization was led by socialists, in and outside the American Federation of Labor, and by the militants of a radical new organization of workers formed in 1909, the Industrial Workers of the World (IWW). Socialists advocated a wide spectrum of democratic reforms, and their proposals included plans to nationalize the railroads and the coal industry. "Wobblies," as IWW members were called, went much further. They denounced the "wage slavery" of capitalism and the inherently repressive nature of the state itself. They advocated the unity of all workers, skilled and unskilled, and celebrated workers' dignity and the ideal of worker control. The IWW and many militant socialists opposed US involvement in World War I and during the war they organized powerful industrial strikes. Some of these strikes, like those in the Northwest timber industry (which produced light-weight spruce lumber for aircraft production), and those in East Coast munitions plants, affected the war effort directly.

Through this whole period, however, the moderate leadership of the AFL, and of the craft unions that formed its core, withstood these radical challenges from within and without the federation. Under Gomper's leadership, the AFL defined the goals of working people in increasingly narrow economic ("bread and butter") terms, and sought increased benefits and influence for labor through accommodation with capitalists and the government. The AFL was spared the severe government repression directed at the IWW and radical labor in general during World War I and the postwar period. During the 1920s its craft-based union philosophy continued to inhibit the organization of workers in the large-scale industries that formed the core of the economy. Despite heroic organizational efforts and some temporary successes during the war, workers in industries like steel, meatpacking, and textiles, and the great new firms engaged in automobile and electrical goods manufacture, and chemical and petroleum production, remained unorganized. In these new industries especially, management took the lead during the 1920s in developing personnel practices and extending benefits to workers aimed at eliminating the appeal of independent unions.

Following the severe postwar depression of 1920–22, economic growth resumed, but at a slower rate than before the war. High unemployment during the postwar depression sharply undermined previous union gains. By 1923 union membership had fallen to about three and a half million. Thereafter, although levels of manufacturing production continued to rise, employment in manufacturing stagnated. Despite new immigration laws that sharply limited the influx of foreign workers, significant levels of structural unemployment persisted throughout the decade.

Meanwhile, management implemented what came to be called the "American Plan," a set of initiatives that boosters called a unique solution to the problem of industrial conflict. Businessmen launched an effective "open shop" drive that successfully eliminated independent unions from many industries, and fostered plans to win worker loyalty by extending to them pension, savings, and health plans, often through company-controlled unions. Average real wages rose some 25 percent in the course of the decade and many workers were able to purchase homes, automobiles, and domestic appliances, often using the new method of installment buying. Corporate profits, however, rose at a much higher rate than wages during the same period, roughly 40 percent, a trend that fostered growing inequality of income distribution. During the 1920s the income share of the richest 5 percent of the population rose from about one-fourth to a third of total income while the richest 1 percent saw their income share rise from about 12 to 19 percent. These trends contributed to what many analysts have called the "crisis of consumption" that overcame the economy in the late 1920s and plunged the nation into the Great Depression.

US labor historians extract from this history a number of important themes to explain the trajectory of labor, particularly its decline in the 1920s. They emphasize racial and ethnic divisions in the labor movement, which were magnified by patterns of domestic and international migration. They show how the narrow craft unionism of the AFL proved incapable of addressing the organizational needs of semi-skilled operatives in large-scale industry. They point to the failure of the labor movement to break out of the political embrace of the Republican and Democratic parties and found a viable labor party of its own. They note the effectiveness of management initiatives in large-scale industry in stifling independent unionism by extending benefits to workers and forming company unions to diffuse worker grievances. They probe the negative implications for worker activism of new patterns of consumption, living arrangements, and forms of popular entertainment. And they stress the extent of the repression unleashed against radical labor by an increasingly powerful state.

Although the labor historians do not stress the fact, all of these developments were closely related to the extraordinary growth of the US economy after 1898. Between 1898 and 1929, despite the disruptions of World War I and a slowdown in growth during the 1920s—a result in part of increasing investment of US capital outside the domestic economy—the economy grew at an average rate of 3.7 percent per year (in the eleven years immediately following the War of 1898, the average annual growth rate was a whopping 5.2 per cent). During the same period, 1898–1929, US foreign trade expanded almost fivefold, with Latin America providing more than one-fourth of total US imports and taking almost one-fifth of US exports by the latter year. US foreign investment grew rapidly during the same period, facilitating the expansion of US foreign trade. By World War I direct foreign investment represented a bit more than 7 per cent of the value of all the goods and services produced in the US, the same level reached in the 1980s. Half of this investment was in Latin America, as Table 4, based on Department of Commerce statistics, indicates.

Table 4   US Direct Foreign Investments, 1919 and 1929*

(book value in millions of US dollars)

	1919	1929
Europe	694	1,340
Canada and Newfoundland	814	1,657
Mexico	644	709
Cuba and other West Indies	567	1,026
Central America	112	251
South America	665	1,720
Other (Asia, Africa, Oceania)	259	725
Total	3,765	7,428
Total Latin America	1,988	3,706
Share Latin America	52.8%	49.9%

Source: Adapted from Mira Wilkins, *The Maturing of Multinational Enterprise* (Cambridge, MA, 1974), Table III.1, p. 55.
*Excludes direct investment in banking, which was listed, probably erroneously, as $125 million in both 1919 and 1929.

Total US foreign investment was much higher than these figures on direct investments suggest. It is estimated that more than half of US foreign investment at the start of World War I was indirect. That is, it was not directly invested in things like mines, plantations, transport and communications systems, commercial establishments, and banks, but rather took the form of stocks, bonds, and securities. Initially, most indirect foreign investment was in Europe, but during the 1920s it expanded rapidly in Latin America as well. By 1929 indirect foreign investment in Latin America totalled some $1.6 billion, a little less than half of the value of direct US investments in the region. As these figures make clear, foreign expansion was an integral part of the tremendous economic boom of the decades after 1898.

[The impact of sustained economic growth on the strength of the US labor movement was pervasive and in some ways contradictory.] On the one hand, the relatively tight labor markets fostered by economic expansion favored the bargaining power of labor and contributed to its growing organizational success. On the other hand, the phenomenal economic growth of the era bolstered the perception among elites, and among many in the middle and working classes as well, that the economic and social system of the nation, for all its flaws and problems, worked remarkably well. This basic perception, more than anything else, explains the ideological weakness and political vulnerability of radicals in the labor movement during the first three decades of the 20th century. It helps explain the ascendancy of AFL moderates over their radical contenders, the failure of advocates of a labor party to break the allegiance of most workers to the two traditional parties, the growing acceptance of the AFL as a legitimate interlocutor among capitalists and state officials, and public acquiescence in the use of repression against radical unionists and the left in general.

Labor activists know that it is difficult to win a strike unless it has the support or at least the sympathy of the public at large. Without that sympathy, workers' struggle to improve their lot—which by definition challenges the economic and social status quo—is subject to the repressive might of the capitalist state. No one who reads the labor history of the late-nineteenth- and early-twentieth-century United States can fail to appreciate the magnitude of government repression, largely unchecked by public opinion, of militant labor. Repressive actions included an arsenal of legal constraints aggressively interpreted by conservative judges and the courts. They ranged from denial of the use of the mails to left-wing journals to the application of naked force by local police, state militias, and federal troops against striking workers. What changed for labor during the Great Depression of the 1930s was the widespread and growing perception among citizens in all walks of life that the nation's economic system was not working very well at all. The dramatic organizational success of labor during that decade (discussed in chapter 5) depended on this changed political climate and on government policies that sought to channel and moderate labor's demands through concessions, not simply repress them.

It is within this broad interpretive framework that specific links between foreign expansionism and domestic labor developments should be understood. Although in general US labor historians do not see these links, some recent works provide highly suggestive clues to their nature and importance.[This is especially true of work on what many see as the central problem faced historically by the US working class, its division along racial and ethnic lines.]

US labor historians have shown again and again how racial and cultural attitudes, especially the prejudice of white (often skilled) workers against domestic blacks and foreign immigrants (who were generally forced into unskilled jobs), undermined the solidarity of working people and weakened their organizational efforts. Racial attitudes, inherited from Europe, and reinforced by the legacy of slavery, also reflected a massive structural problem that bedeviled the working class during the late nineteenth and early twentieth centuries. Large-scale migration to US industrial centers during this period seriously undercut the organizational efforts of labor. Part of this migration was internal, as rural black and white workers sought employment in industrial cities. In addition, millions of foreign immigrants from Asia, Mexico, and especially southern and eastern Europe flooded into the US labor market. During the Depression-ridden 1890s on average almost half a million immigrants entered the country each year. Their numbers topped a million annually during the expansionary years before World War I. Most were willing to accept wages and working conditions far below the levels established workers were struggling to achieve. Capitalists used immigrant labor to break strikes and manipulated ethnic solidarities to undermine worker solidarity in the workplace and in the community. Racial and ethnic divisions within the working class were reinforced by notions of Anglo-Saxon superiority championed by the elite and members of the middle class and propagated in the schools, the press, and the churches.

[Labor historians have yet to investigate the connection between racism and imperialism, however, although doing so would seem to be a logical step.]The most provocative recent study of the role of race in the making of the US working class, David Roediger's *The Wages of Whiteness* (1991), suggests (by omission) how such analysis might proceed. Roediger argues that as the US working class came into being in the middle of the nineteenth century it defined itself as white. Workers expressed their fear of dependence on wage labor and resisted industrial discipline by creating a black "other" they both longed to be like and hated—a pre-industrial rural black slave, who was primitive, carefree, sensual, and lazy. These dubious psychological benefits, Roediger contends, were an essential part of the "wages of whiteness." They were complemented by the public benefits of white citizenry, especially political rights, which were made more meaningful by being denied to blacks.

Roediger shows, however, that this racial working-class exclusiveness, formed in the decades before the Civil War, began to break down following abolition and especially during the era of reconstruction following the war. Unfortunately, he ends his study in the 1870s, precisely at the point when the period of working-class mobilization that characterized the last decades of the nineteenth century began. This period, like the first two decades of the twentieth century, furnishes impressive evidence of the capacity, against tremendous odds, of US workers to transcend divisions based on race and ethnicity. Such solidarity has been amply documented by US labor historians. It seems to have occurred primarily during periods of intense labor mobilization and strike activity. It is true, however, that many of these instances of working-class unity ended tragically, a consequence that often accompanied worker defeats. And in the end, as Roediger is at pains to emphasize, racism became institutionalized within the labor movement, especially within the craft unions of the AFL.

[Roediger somewhat lamely explains this outcome as the resurfacing of dominant attitudes forged in the pre-Civil War era. In more immediate terms, however, they seem to have been bolstered by racial and cultural identities fostered by the course of expansionism.]

Persuasive evidence for the link between an intensification of domestic racism and foreign expansionism comes from a seminal study of US political cartoons by US Latin Americanist John Johnson, *Latin America in Caricature* (1980). Johnson's work demonstrates that images of Latin American "others" with qualities not unlike those of the stereotypes of blacks Roediger analyzes for the 1840s and 1850s become pervasive in the United States in the decades following 1898. (Representative examples of these cartoons, drawn from Johnson's selection, appear on pages 44 and 80.) His evidence shows, moreover, how racial and cultural stereotypes were consistently enlisted in the service of US foreign policy objectives. When Latin American countries or revolutionary forces within them challenged US political and economic interests, the cartoons often portrayed them as unruly, shabbily dressed, razor-wielding, watermelon-loving, black children speaking caricatured Southern US black dialect. Alternatively, they were depicted as obstreperous, sombreroed, gun-toting, unshaven, pint-sized *mestizos*. These characters were likely to feel the forceful, civilizing hand of white Uncle Sam. He might settle for giving them a good bath or a haircut or resort to a good caning or a paddling in the woodshed. In contrast, when Latin American states accommodated US security and economic interests, they appear as white, attractive, pliable Latin women or as well-groomed, light-skinned, attentive schoolboys properly dressed in Western fashion. These last subjects appear eager to accept the blandishments and paternalistic guidance of Uncle Sam. The few examples Johnson found of Latin Americans depicted as grown-up Caucasian males occur when Latin American government officials provide extraordinary service to the economic and security goals of US policy. The most notable case is Porfirio Díaz, the Mexican dictator whose support for foreign investment in the decades preceding the Mexican Revolution of 1910 made him the darling of the US foreign policy establishment.

This line of analysis is partially confirmed in the work of one of the few US historians who have addressed the connections between imperialism and domestic issues of racial, ethnic, and national identity at the turn of the twentieth century. In a dissertation done at Brown University in 1992, Matthew Jacobson shows how leaders of the Irish-, Polish-, and Yiddish-American communities he studied initially opposed imperialism, seeing it as an undemocratic, corrupting force that could transform US society into the image of the repressive European polities they had left. But as the post-1898 debate developed over annexation of colonies populated by "darker races," many of these same people began to identify with the nationalist and racialist assumptions that rationalized expansionism.

How economic expansionism and concomitant military and strategic concerns played themselves out in a key industry is suggested in a rare study of US labor by an author sensitive to the links between domestic class struggle and imperial design. Paul Krause's *The Battle for Homestead, 1880–1892* (1992) shows that Andrew Carnegie had already secured lucrative naval contracts for battleship armor before he decided to break the control over production exercised by organized workers at his largest and technologically most sophisticated mill. With the timely support of 8,500 state militiamen, who replaced the 300 Pinkerton detectives the workers had routed, Carnegie's managers crushed worker resistance and reopened the mill on a non-union basis. Workers in the Homestead mill, it turns out, made the armor plate for the battleship *Maine*, whose mysterious sinking in Havana harbor precipitated the War of 1898. And the corporation lawyer who masterminded the repression of radical unionists at Homestead, Philander Knox, in 1909 (after serving for a time as Attorney General for McKinley) became Howard Taft's Secretary of State, in which capacity he served as principal architect of the policy of "Dollar Diplomacy."

Meanwhile, Andrew Carnegie, who had sold his interest in the first billion-dollar US corporation, United States Steel, devoted himself to philanthropy and to the cause of international peace. He donated money to the Central American Court of Justice, created with the support of the US government in 1907 to promote the stability of the region. When the court condemned as contrary to international law Knox's decision to send 2,700 marines into Nicaragua in 1912 to prop up a government friendly to US interests, the United States simply ignored the decision. Knox, who in the employ of Carnegie had demonstrated his ability to manipulate domestic law to condemn the Homestead strikers as traitors to the nation, thus exhibited his willingness to flout international law when it stood in the way of US interests. [Like Olney before him, Knox steadfastly pursued the interests of capitalists at home and abroad throughout his career.] Carnegie described him, in a letter recommending his services as Attorney General to McKinley in 1896, as "the best lawyer I have ever had for our interests" (quoted in Krause, p. 272).

[US labor historians have not addressed the links between foreign expansion and the growth and militarization of the state,] although Montgomery raises the issue in *The Fall of the House of Labor* (p. 71). Clearly, the decisions to build a battleship navy, to go to war with Spain, to engage, under the policy of "Dollar Diplomacy," in a series of armed interventions in Central America and the Caribbean to protect isthmian canal routes, and ultimately, to enter into World War I all reflected the drive for foreign expansion. And all these decisions, especially the last, had grave implications for US labor. The relationship between labor and the state that developed during the course of World War I included far more than the ruthless repression of the IWW and other radical labor militants. Government efforts to insure labor cooperation in the war effort led to institutional arrangements that temporarily favored labor. These arrangements, as labor historian Melvyn Dubofsky has shown in *The State and Labor in Modern America* (1994), prefigured those worked out on a more enduring basis during the 1930s and World War II.

A final example of the link between foreign expansion and the course of US labor history comes from the work of David Brody himself. In his essay "The Rise and Decline of Welfare Capitalism," which appears as the second chapter of his celebrated study *Workers in Industrial America* (2nd. edn. 1993), Brody examines the fate of what is commonly called the "American Plan" of industrial relations. This combination of modern personnel management, worker benefits, and company-controlled employee representation schemes was promoted in the 1920s by leading industrialists and corporate managers as the definitive solution to industrial conflict. Brody takes those claims seriously, argues that these company plans appealed to many workers, and concludes that the "paternalistic course of American industrial relations might well have continued but for the Great Depression" (p. 78).

Brody shows that the new approaches to labor relations had their most ardent managerial supporters and took hold most fully in very large manufacturing corporations, such as General Electric and Standard Oil of New Jersey. What he does not emphasize is that [many of these huge firms, which were often oligopolies, had large foreign operations. The system of industrial relations at the core of the "American Plan" took shape in John D. Rockefeller's Standard Oil of New Jersey following the massacre of workers and their families by state militiamen at a Rockefeller-owned operation in Ludlow, Colorado, in 1913 and another bloody confrontation with striking workers at Standard Oil's Bayonne, New Jersey, refinery in 1915. The man Rockefeller subsequently hired to develop his employee relations scheme, Clarence J. Hicks, was later credited by company officials with having done for modern industrial relations what Frederick Taylor had done for the organization of capitalist production. Jersey Standard's "generation of industrial peace" (the phrase comes from the title of a company publication issued in 1947) was underwritten, at least in part, by the massive profits of the corporation's extensive foreign operations. By the 1920s, for example, Jersey Standard's Venezuelan subsidiary, Creole, was already producing the lion's share of the oil that made Venezuela the premier oil-exporting nation in the world.

The story is similar for General Electric, the giant of the burgeoning US electrical industry. Brody emphasizes the role of Gerard Swope, who became president of General Electric in 1922, in "spread[ing] the new gospel" of the "American Plan" during the 1920s (p. 52). He does not mention that Swope ascended to that position after serving as head of GE's newly formed and wholly owned subsidiary for international operations. General Electric's largest market in Latin America was Brazil, where the company's rapidly expanding volume of light-bulb sales (the most profitable segment of the electrical industry during the 1920s) led it to open its first wholly owned manufacturing subsidiary in Latin America in 1922.

These examples, though limited, illustrate the interpretive potential of linking the traditional domestic subject matter and concerns of US labor historians to the issue of expansionism after 1898. Foreign expansionism began as an elite response to the democratic struggles of US workers. The psychological, strategic, and economic consequences of the "splendid little war" with Spain inspired the confidence of capitalists, whose investment decisions underwrote the three decades of economic expansion that followed. The sustained economic growth of the first three decades of the twentieth century affected the labor movement in manifold ways. It influenced the volume of international and internal migration, which in turn had serious implications for domestic working-class solidarity. It structured the relative tightness of the labor market, and thus the bargaining power of workers on the job. It informed people's perceptions of the efficacy of the economic system, the justice of social relations, and the

legitimacy of the political system. US penetration of less-developed societies, particularly in Latin America, worked to strengthen the racial and
cultural myths that explained US economic success and growing military
might as God-given attributes of white, Protestant, Anglo-Saxons. These
attitudes, in turn, complicated the struggle for domestic worker unity,
undermined the labor movement's search for political allies, and helped
rationalize state repression of radical labor reformers.

IV

LaFeber's book merits the continuing attention of all American historians, US labor historians primary among them. Beyond its specific
interpretation of the origins and nature of US expansionism, it contains
within it the rudiments of a democratic history of US imperialism. It
diverges in fundamental ways from Lenin's classic treatment of the subject, most significantly in the way it views the role of popular struggle in
the industrial core of the capitalist world economy. Lenin's vision of the
origins of imperialism is economistic. It privileges impersonal economic
forces (the "logic" of capitalism) and thus has the ironic ideological
effect of empowering capitalists as a class. It denigrates the democratic
struggles of working people in the industrial capitalist nations, confusing
the results of labor's defeats and the conservative outcomes of compromises between capital and labor at one stage of struggle with the nature
and power of labor's democratic vocation itself. Out of that confusion
came the rationale for a revolutionary vanguard, with its sorry sequel of
authoritarianism in the workplace and the polity in the socialist regimes
of this century.

The traditional liberal explanations of the origins of US imperialism
with which LaFeber had to contend were also fundamentally undemocratic. They blamed the people of the United States for the imperialist
War of 1898. LaFeber was determined to place the blame where he
thought it really lay, in the hands of the power elite. But in accomplishing that goal so single-mindedly, he neglected two other essential and
related tasks. By neglecting the story of worker mobilization itself in his
study, he missed a chance to emphasize labor's democratic role in bringing the elite to consciousness of the need for expansion. And by failing
to stress the democratic dimensions of popular support for the war, he
lost an opportunity to reinterpret the very evidence on which the traditional explanations rested their case. Did not most people who devoured
the stories of Spanish atrocities in the "yellow press" and favored US
intervention in Cuba in 1898 sympathize with the Cuban revolutionaries

and want to aid in their struggle to liberate themselves from colonial oppression? Had LaFeber emphasized the democratic elements in popular support for the war, he could have subsumed the rival liberal interpretation and enlisted it in his argument. Had he fully incorporated the history of late-nineteenth-century labor mobilization into his argument, he could have challenged the democratic credentials of orthodox Marxist interpretations of the origins of US imperialism.

US labor historians have developed the empirical knowledge and interpretive sophistication to bolster and extend LaFeber's seminal work. By neglecting LaFeber and ignoring the origins in popular struggle of US imperialism, they not only miss an opportunity to contribute to a more [democratic understanding of the origins of imperialism,] but also underestimate and distort the very social forces that they all hope can lead toward a more democratic future. Finally, they fail to come to terms with the institution, imperialism, that (as we shall see more fully in subsequent chapters) has worked most of the time in this century to strengthen labor's class antagonists and weaken labor's own democratic vocation, including its solidarity with democratic forces abroad. Contrary to the vision of most US historians, foreign expansion after 1898 is intimately connected with the course of domestic history, including the trajectory of the labor movement in the first decades of the twentieth century.

The era surveyed in this chapter is similar in many respects to the period of crisis and intense class conflict that led to the wave of US expansion in our own time. Out of the era of the Great Depression of this century and the remarkable labor mobilization of the decade after 1935 came institutional arrangements initially much more favorable to labor in this country than the one cemented into place after 1898. The hallmark of the response by elites to labor mobilization at the end of the nineteenth century was a "new" imperialism, which sought markets and promoted investments in utilities, transportation, and production of raw materials abroad. In the period since World War II, those activities have continued, but the primary vehicle through which US capitalists have subverted compromise with a powerful labor movement at home has been the multinational manufacturing corporation. I will survey the negative consequences of that strategy for the labor movement, for the economy, and for US democracy itself in chapter 5. Recognizing that the movement of capital in the world economy owes much of its impetus to the national democratic struggles of working people—not only in the era discussed in this essay but in the contemporary period as well—helps us appreciate the futility of solutions to labor's problems conceived within the confines of single nation-states. It helps us envision the international coalitions that will be necessary to control, democratize, or transform capitalism in our own time.

Further Reading

American Social History Project, *Who Built America?*, 2 vols., New York 1992.

Andrews, Greg, *Shoulder to Shoulder?*, Berkeley, CA, 1991.

Brody, David, *Workers in Industrial America*, 2nd edn., New York 1993.

Drake, Paul W., *Money Doctors, Foreign Debts, and Economic Reforms in Latin America from the 1890s to the Present*, Wilmington, DE, 1994.

Dubofsky, Melvyn, *The State and Labor in Modern America*, Chapel Hill, NC, 1994.

Foner, Eric, ed., *The New American History*, Philadelphia 1990.

Foner, Philip, *The Spanish-Cuban-American War and the Birth of American Imperialism*, 2 vols., New York 1972.

—— *US Labor Movement and Latin America*. South Hadley, MA, 1988.

Foner, Philip, and Richard C. Winchester, eds., *The Anti-Imperialist Reader*. 2 vols., New York 1984.

Goodwyn, Lawrence, *Democratic Promise*, New York 1976.

Gordon, David, Richard Eduards and Michael Reich, *Segmented Work, Divided Workers*, Cambridge, UK, 1979.

Green, Theodore P., *American Imperialism in 1898*, Boston 1955.

Jacobson, Matthew F., "Special Sorrows: Irish-, Polish-, and Yiddish-American Nationalism and the Diasporic Imagination," unpublished PhD dissertation, Brown University 1992.

Johnson, John J., *Latin America in Caricature*, Austin, TX, 1980.

Krause, Paul, *The Battle for Homestead, 1880–1892*, Pittsburgh 1992.

LaFeber, Walter, "The Latin American Policy of the Second Cleveland Administration," unpublished PhD dissertation, University of Wisconsin 1959.

—— *The New Empire*, Ithaca, NY, 1963.

—— *The American Search for Opportunity, 1865–1913*, New York 1993.

Lenin, V.I, *Imperialism*, New York 1939.

May, Ernest, *Imperial Democracy*, New York 1961.

Montgomery, David, *The Fall of the House of Labor*, Cambridge, UK, 1987.

—— *Workers' Control in America*, Cambridge, UK, 1979.

Pike, Fredrick B., *The United States and Latin America*, Austin, TX, 1992.

Pratt, Julius, *The Expansionists of 1898*, Baltimore 1936.

Radosh, Ronald, *American Labor and United States Foreign Policy*, New York 1969.
Roediger, David, *The Wages of Whiteness*, London 1991.
Williams, William Appleman, *The Tragedy of American Diplomacy*, New York 1959.
—— *Empire As a Way of Life*, New York 1980.

CARTOON COMMENTS ON CURRENT EVENTS

A view, by US political cartoonist John T. McCutcheon, of the Mexican Revolution, reprinted from John J. Johnson, *Latin America in Caricature* (Austin, TX, 1980). Uncle Sam administers a "pacification pill" to a pint-sized Mexican *mestizo* revolutionary in 1916 while a clean, light-skinned, docile group of Central American students in Western dress look favorably on. During the political crisis of World War I and the economic crisis of the 1930s, US hostility toward the Mexican regime abated and the revolution achieved its most important economic and social reforms. The cartoon originally appeared in the *Chicago Tribune* in 1916 and is reproduced here with the permission of the publisher.

3

Latin American Revolution,
US Response

US expansionism after 1898 had ironic, unforeseen effects. Viewed by members of the US elite as a solution to economic instability and social unrest at home, it stimulated democratic social struggle abroad. If imperialism worked to subvert workers' efforts to democratize US society, it had the effect of strengthening democratic reform forces, including organized labor, in Latin America. Among the primary targets of the Latin American reformers were the interests of US capitalists themselves.

Throughout this century Latin American reformers have sought to promote national development by dismantling the legacy of colonialism. They have tried to democratize the highly unequal distribution of wealth and power that was the heritage of the coercive labor systems of colonial rule. Latin American struggles for reform have involved people from all classes, but their fates have depended in large part on the actions of workers, especially those engaged in production for export. While reform efforts have been pervasive, and domestic and foreign resistance to them has made the politics of the whole region highly unstable and often violent, only rarely have they reached revolutionary dimensions. Revolutionary coalitions often developed in precisely those areas where US penetration after 1898 was greatest.

The twentieth-century Latin American social revolutions are the most dramatic expressions of democratic struggle in the history of the Americas. Precisely for that reason, study of US responses to them reveals more clearly than any other aspect of US–Latin American relations the nature and limits of democracy in the US itself. The US government has consistently opposed the democratic reforms championed by Latin American revolutionaries and has gone to great lengths to subvert their radical implications. It has justified these actions, however, by claiming it was acting to preserve democracy, not subvert it.

US government officials and mainstream academics consistently have contended that US policy obeys not economic interests but security concerns, particularly the threat allegedly posed by international Communism in the post-World War II era. This chapter challenges these interpretations, arguing that behind the official rationale for US policy, and the justifications of it by many US scholars, lies a sobering historical reality. Policy toward Latin America has sought, fundamentally, not to make the region safe for democracy, but to make it safe for the interests of US capitalists.

The thesis of this chapter is not new. Revisionist US historians, particularly those of the "new left" writing during the era of the Vietnam War (Carl Oglesby's polemical essays, cited in the readings for this chapter, are good examples), and the archival-based diplomatic histories of contemporary exponents of the "Wisconsin School" (see, in particular, Thomas McCormick's *America's Half-Century*, 1989) have produced a progression of studies that demonstrate the capitalist rationale behind US foreign policy in this century. Many Latin American specialists, especially those working within Marxist traditions, have done the same, particularly in studies of the individual Latin American social revolutions and US policy toward them. For the most part, however, all this work continues to be dismissed or ignored by US policy-makers, mainstream academics, and the public at large.

What is new in this chapter is the way it challenges the logic and common sense of these mainstream understandings. In it, I look comparatively at the four "classic" cases of revolutionary reform in Latin America—Mexico, Cuba, Bolivia, and Guatemala—and engage the most systematic analysis of US policy toward them, Cole Blasier's *The Hovering Giant* (1976). This exercise in comparative logic demonstrates the democratic aspirations of Latin American reformers and revolutionaries and the undemocratic lengths to which the US government has gone to stymie their reforms. Understanding the logic behind US policy, I argue, allows us to transcend the simple notions of "economic" versus "security" concerns in the history of US–Latin American relations. It enables us to comprehend the consistency of US policy from the beginning of the century (before Communist states existed) to its end (when the Cold War is over). In the post-Cold War world we live in, such an understanding has democratic implications for all Americans. It provides a sobering, realistic appraisal of the obstacles to democratic reform in both parts of the hemisphere today.

I

The expansion of US capital into Latin America in the last decades of the nineteenth century and the first decades of the twentieth was part of a larger process, a massive transfer of capital, technology, and even people from the industrialized North Atlantic to the underdeveloped world. Led by Great Britain, whose investments in and trade with Latin America far overshadowed those of the United States until World War I, this process brought an end to the economic stagnation and political instability that had enveloped Latin America since independence. One by one the Latin American nations developed the capacity to produce one or more agricultural or mineral commodities for export to meet the expanding demands of the industrialized world. Argentina, for example, came to export cereals and meat; Chile, nitrates and copper; Bolivia, tin; Brazil and Colombia, coffee; Venezuela, oil; Central America, coffee and bananas; Cuba, sugar; and Mexico, a variety of mineral and agricultural commodities, including oil. Success in developing these export economies allowed Latin American nations to pay for expanded imports of capital, machinery, and manufactures from Western Europe and the United States. Taxes on imports furnished revenue that greatly strengthened the power of the governments of Latin America. Initially, at least, economic growth worked to stabilize Latin American politics.

Over time, however, export-led economic growth generated powerful social and political tensions within the nations of Latin America. On the one hand, it strengthened the political power of the large landowners who generally monopolized agricultural production for export, the merchant class involved in the burgeoning export-import trade, and the foreign capitalists who invested in export production, as well as in commerce, transport, communications, and utilities, and who lent Latin Americans and their governments money. On the other hand, export-led growth fostered the development of two other social groups who would work—sometimes in tandem—to reform and democratize Latin American societies in this century. One group included professionals, students, small business people, and military officers, whose numbers expanded to fill service positions in these modernizing economies. The other group was composed of workers, urban and rural, who saw their position in society strengthened as the economic growth of the region proceeded. Of the two groups, workers, especially those engaged in export production, processing, and transport, proved to be the most powerful and consistent force for democratic change.

Two general patterns stand out within the overarching story of the struggle for reform in Latin America during this century. Where production for export demanded large investments and sophisticated technology, as was the case in mining and petroleum, and some forms of export agriculture, such as sugar and bananas, foreign capitalists usually acquired control. In these societies the struggle for reform typically acquired a leftist (anti-imperialist, anti-capitalist) dimension, and the potential for social revolution was great. Examples include Mexico, Bolivia, Guatemala, Cuba, and Chile, countries whose attempts at social revolution are surveyed in this chapter. Where, in contrast, export production depended primarily on control of land resources and labor, and demands for capital were limited, Latin American capitalists retained control. In these societies—Argentina, Brazil, and Colombia are good examples among the larger Latin American nations—reform movements were more muted and moderate than in the first set of countries, and the appeal of socialist alternatives proved limited.

US policy toward Latin America in this century has not been unduly concerned with those nations in which movement toward democratic reform has been moderate and its results modest. It has endeavored to protect and expand US influence in these societies, using its preeminent position in their foreign commerce, the lure of investment capital, and the manipulation of economic and military aid to achieve this goal. On occasion it has even used its influence to promote limited democratic reform. This last strategy became particularly important in the 1960s following the consolidation of the Cuban Revolution. At that time the United States pledged major assistance, through a program called the Alliance for Progress, to Latin American nations planning to engage in moderate reform, a goal US policy-makers saw as necessary to head off the prospect of general social revolution in the region.

It is with the societies undergoing revolutionary change that US policy toward individual Latin American nations has been most intensely concerned. Toward these nations the US government has used literally every means at its disposal, including armed intervention, to protect what it has defined as its interests in the region. Analysis of US policy toward the Latin American social revolutions of this century reveals most fully the guiding principles behind policy toward the region as a whole.

II

Until 1970, four countries in Latin America had experienced social revolutions—fundamental, democratic transformations of their economic and social structures and dramatic change in the goals of their political regimes. Latin American specialists customarily date these revolutionary transformations as occurring between 1910 and 1940 in Mexico, between 1946 and 1954 in Guatemala, between 1952 and 1964 in Bolivia, and between 1959 and the present in Cuba. Since 1970 two additional social revolutions have occurred in Latin America, in Chile between 1970 and

1973, and in Nicaragua between 1979 and 1990. This chapter focuses on comparative analysis of US policy toward the first four. But its conclusions about the nature of policy toward Latin American social revolutions apply as well to the more contemporary examples of Chile and Nicaragua.

In three of the four countries that experienced social revolutions before 1970, US economic penetration before the revolution was great, and played an important role in the social process that led to revolutionary reform. In Mexico, during the dictatorship of Porfirio Díaz (1876–1910), US investments, most of them in mining, agriculture, and railroads, expanded rapidly to the level of about $1 billion. Control by US capital of the bulk of Mexican oil production proved especially important in the revolutionary process, particularly the relationship between the revolutionary regime and the United States. By the early 1920s Mexico had become (temporarily) the largest oil exporter in the world and taxes on petroleum provided more than a fifth of Mexican government revenue. In Cuba, US capitalists invested heavily after 1898, and, by the time of the first major effort at social reform in 1933, controlled more than half of Cuban sugar production, by far the most important sector of the Cuban economy. US investments in Cuba were also important in mining and public utilities. United Fruit was the biggest US investor in Guatemala, producing the bulk of the banana exports that accounted for roughly a fifth of the nation's foreign exchange. The company also held a controlling interest in the nation's most important railroad and in the utility company that provided much of the nation's electrical power.

Only in Bolivia were US investments limited. The tin industry, which produced most of the country's foreign exchange, was dominated by three companies run by Bolivian nationals. Nevertheless, European and US capitalists held important investments in these firms, and they controlled the processing of tin ore in refineries located in the United States and Europe. At the time of the revolution of 1952, US investors owned an estimated 15 to 20 percent of the largest tin-mining operation. In other sectors of the economy US investment was small, although Standard Oil of New Jersey had a long-standing interest in Bolivia's potential oil reserves.

In all four countries the United States dominated foreign trade, taking the bulk of each country's exports and providing the largest share of its imports at the time of the social revolutions we are considering. The United States' preeminent position in the foreign trade of these countries allowed its government to exercise great influence in their internal affairs. In Bolivia, for example, US decisions over the purchase of tin determined the vitality of the national economy and even the health of the Bolivian people, since tin exports were used to purchase much of the food supply. Since the 1940s such decisions have decisively influenced the fate of Bolivian governments. In Cuba, US manipulation of the sugar quota helped destroy the reformist government of 1933. In the early 1960s, the revolutionary Cuban government preserved itself in the face of a cut-off in US sugar purchases when it found in the Soviet Union a new client for its major export.

The social revolutions of all four countries were spearheaded by multiclass coalitions whose support depended in large part on elements of the middle and working classes. Labor mobilization helped destabilize the old order in all four countries, and labor organizations were among the primary beneficiaries and supporters of the revolutionary regimes. The struggles of Mexican oil workers and Bolivian tin miners precipitated the most dramatic and important seizures of property during the Mexican and Bolivian revolutions. The mobilization of Cuban sugar workers in 1933 and Guatemalan banana workers in the 1940s began the process that eventually led to the expropriation of land owned by the US firms that had long dominated those economic sectors.

Despite commonalities like these, the history of these Latin American social revolutions has been written in national not comparative terms. To be sure, the history of each of these revolutions is unique and particular. Separated in time, they took place in countries of different size and geography, whose social and economic structures, ethnic composition, and historical experience varied widely. Some of the finest work (examples are listed among the selection for further reading) in the field of Latin American history has focused on these individual social revolutions. In general, however, historians have failed to emphasize their similarities. In the broadest sense, as we have seen, these similarities are democratic consequences of a common experience of European colonialism and US expansionism. But it turns out that the similarities are more specific and exact than this, and it is here that the comparative method of a social scientist like Blasier proves so enlightening.

Through comparison Blasier was able to identify significant commonalities in the nature and evolution of all these revolutions and in US policy toward them. His primary purpose, however, was to explain not these commonalities, but a major difference within policy toward these revolutionary regimes. He wanted to know why the United States ultimately accommodated revolutionary reform in some of these societies, and backed armed intervention to overthrow the revolutionary regimes of others. He contended that US security concerns, especially the fear of Soviet communism in the post-World War II era, explained both the instances of accommodation and the attempts at suppression.

Although I will argue that Blasier's assumptions are flawed, and that his conclusions are confused and misleading, his book is fundamental to understanding US policies toward revolutionary change in Latin America. No other book helps clarify with such precision the terms of the debate over the relative importance of security and economic concerns in determining the Latin American policy of the United States. And although Blasier's account of policy toward individual Latin American revolutionary regimes, written almost two decades ago, has been superseded in some respects (noted below) by subsequent research, his emphasis on security concerns remains typical of mainstream academic scholarship on US foreign policy in the United States. In recent years, even some representatives of the Latin American left have bought into the argument that security concerns explain the historical hostility of the US government to Latin American social reform. The most prominent example is Mexican political scientist Jorge Castañeda, whose 1994 book *Utopia Disarmed* received a great deal of attention in US circles. Focus on security concerns leads liberal US academics like Blasier to emphasize the potential for peaceful democratic reform in Latin America. It leads Latin American leftists like Castañeda to emphasize potential US support for social democratic reform in the region now that the Cold War is over.

For all these reasons, coming to terms with Blasier's analysis is central to the task of understanding US–Latin American relations. It helps us weigh the importance of security and economic concerns in determining the Latin American policy of the United States in the past. And it enables us to gauge the probability of US support or hostility toward fundamental democratic reform in Latin America in the future.

Blasier brought to the study of US policy toward Latin American revolutions, and especially the question of the role of Communist influence in them, a very special set of credentials. "My professional life has been divided down the middle, half concerned with Eastern Europe and half with Latin America," Blasier wrote in the preface to a sequel to *The Hovering Giant*, a book entitled *The Giant's Rival* (1983), which assessed the history of Latin American–USSR relations. "I have lived and traveled about as much in one region as the other and know their languages equally badly" (p. xiii).

Blasier began his professional research in 1947 in Chile, where he undertook study of that country's Communist Party. He did his graduate work in international relations at the Russian Institute of Columbia University, and spent most of the 1950s as an officer in the US Foreign Service, including a stint in Moscow. He returned to study of Latin America in the 1960s, teaching at the University of Pittsburgh and helping to build that university's interdisciplinary program in Latin American studies. After publication of *The Hovering Giant* in 1976 he visited Eastern

Europe on several occasions, and in 1979 became the first US scholar to undertake resident research at the Institute for Latin America in Moscow. Blasier's reputation among Latin Americanists won him election to the presidency of the US-based Latin American Studies Association in 1987. Between 1989 and 1994 he served as director of the Hispanic Foundation of the Library of Congress in Washington.

Blasier's treatment of his subject is quintessentially liberal, a stance implicit in his efforts at the beginning of *The Hovering Giant* to establish his ideological independence and define his goals. "My approach was not facilitated or burdened by explicit doctrinaire predispositions." "Conservative, liberal, and radical writers all have made arguments of one sort or another which I consider persuasive, but I do not identify totally with any single school . . . ." Blasier hoped his work would convey a better understanding of the past in order to "help US leaders and Latin American revolutionaries conduct themselves more effectively in their mutual relations." He stated that his analysis was not based on a "perception of the policy-making process as rational, orderly, or consistently manageable." But, he believed, knowledge of the past could help make it more so. "Men of power often are ignorant of, conceal, or defy facts; my commitment to this study is based on my continuing faith that they cannot be or do so forever" (p. xvi).

Implicit in these statements are the assumptions that his interpretation flows directly from the "facts," that conflict within the hemisphere can be made more manageable through judicious compromise, and that education can mitigate the irrational and violent dimensions of human behavior. These are core ideas in contemporary liberal scholarship and politics, and they support the idea that Blasier's book is important both for what it says as about US–Latin American relations and for what it reveals about mainstream US scholarship on that subject in the postwar period.

Throughout *The Hovering Giant* Blasier insists on a formal stance that identifies with neither US officials nor Latin American revolutionaries. He consistently refrains from passing judgment on their conflicting policy goals. He claims only to be a political realist, who recognizes that great powers pursue their national interests as they see them, not according to some high moral standard based on equitable or ethical treatment of lesser powers. He endorses both the reality of capitalist organization of the societies of the hemisphere and the inevitability of Latin American efforts to reform them. He believes that peaceful compromise with Latin American revolutionaries best serves US interests, especially fundamental US security interests. Given the magnitude of US economic and political power, he contends, the United States can achieve its fundamental goals

without resort to armed force. US efforts based on force to resolve its conflicts with Latin American revolutionary regimes, he argues, even if
temporarily successful, are inherently unstable. In the case of Cuba, he
demonstrates how the failed attempt to suppress the revolution brought
the United States to the brink of nuclear war with the Soviet Union. The
possibility of nuclear holocaust during the Cuban Missile Crisis of 1962
created the greatest security threat ever faced by the United States,
indeed, by the world as a whole.

Blasier's analysis thus justifies a middle-of-the-road reformist path
between the goals of Latin American revolutionaries and conservative
US policy-makers. If both learn to understand each other better and to
compromise with one another more effectively, he argues, Latin
American social reform and US security can both be achieved. Blasier's
formal disavowal of ideological commitment notwithstanding, this liberal vision of peaceful progress in the hemisphere infuses every aspect of
his interpretation.

III

The pattern Blasier finds in the four Latin American social revolutions
and US responses to them is quite simple. The revolutionary process
begins when a coalition of democratic reformers comes to power. The
reformers favor political democratization, such as an end to dictatorial
rule, free elections, and expanded suffrage. They extend labor rights
and promote unionization. They envision land reform and greater control over foreign investment. In most cases, US policy is initially receptive
to working with these reformist governments. But as the reform process
threatens the property rights of foreign investors, US policy quickly turns
against them. Typically, US hostility contributes to the overthrow of the
reformist regime. That outcome radicalizes the reformers, and when
with time they return to power they implement radical reform measures.
The most fundamental of these transform landholding patterns, fostering much wider distribution of ownership, sometimes along cooperative
or collective lines. The reforms also restrict the prerogatives of capitalists,
especially foreign capitalists involved in export production. Typically,
these policies result in the nationalization of large firms in the export sector. US policy forcefully opposes these measures, and insists on what it
defines as "just" compensation for expropriated property.

At this point, in two of the cases analyzed by Blasier, Guatemala and
Cuba, the United States decided to remove the revolutionary regime
through armed intervention. In the other two, however, Mexico and

Bolivia, the United States resisted that course and pursued a policy of compromise with the revolution. US accommodation to these revolutions, Blasier shows, succeeded in moderating the radical course of revolutionary change, particularly policies toward US investors. US support of armed intervention to reverse the revolutionary process, on the other hand, had mixed results. In Guatemala, it resulted in the overthrow of the regime and a complete reversal of its reforms, including the expropriations of US property. In Cuba, in contrast, armed intervention failed to destroy the regime, and the revolutionaries proceeded to nationalize the bulk of the economy along state socialist lines and to ally themselves with the Soviet Union.

In his historical analysis of the revolutionary process Blasier emphasizes the fact that the initial measures proposed by reformist governments were extremely moderate. All sought modest changes within a framework of democratic capitalism. Blasier identifies this moderate reformist stage as occurring between 1911 and 1913 in Mexico, between 1943 and 1946 in Bolivia, and between 1945 and 1951 in Guatemala. (For reasons having to do with certain political variables that need not concern us here, Blasier does not include analysis of the Cuban reformist government of 1933, although he acknowledges its similarity to the other reformist regimes and notes its importance as a prelude to the revolution of 1959; for his reasoning, see pp. 33–4). Table 5, adapted from Blasier (p. 35), conveys at a glance the similarity of the modest liberal measures taken by these three reform governments.

These early reformist governments, Blasier affirms, "did not represent political extremes of the right or left, but were, broadly speaking, centrist" (p. 65). "Why," he asks, "was the United States unable to come to terms with governments which came closer to approximating expressed American ideals than most Latin American governments of the past?" (p. 64). His answer is that US government hostility reflected the interests of private investors. US and domestic capitalists were alarmed over the threat posed to their property by economic and social reform. They were also concerned over rising levels of popular mobilization and the political instability that accompanied the reform process. As Blasier puts it, "U.S. and Latin American private interests probably did not control U.S. officials in a strict sense, but both tended to think alike" (p. 68).

What Blasier terms the "aggressively hostile" nature of US actions against these regimes (p. 65) included threats of armed intervention, the withholding of diplomatic recognition, and severe economic and political pressures. These actions contributed to the fall of the reform governments in Mexico and Bolivia and to the assassination by domestic

Table 5 Reform Governments: Social and Economic Measures

	Mexico, 1911–13	Bolivia, 1943–46	Guatemala, 1945–51
Agricultural reform	Survey and recovery of illegally alienated lands; agricultural experiment stations established	—	Agricultural development program; attempt to promote cooperatives
Industry/commerce	Official study of oil exploration; plan for electrification of central plateau	Increased taxes on tin; foreign exchange controls on tin	Increased governmental control over petroleum resources; national bank established
Labor measures	Department of Labor established; studies on reduction of hours, strikes, minimum wages; National Labor office settles seventy strikes	Labor's role strengthened by growth of miner and rural unions; workmen's compensation and other labor laws	Expansion of membership of industrial/agricultural unions; new labor code, courts, and social security law
Indigenous affairs	Official investigation of Indian education	Feudal service abolished; first national Indian congress	First Indian congress
Education	New rural schools; large budgetary increases; National Congress on Education	New rural schools; education code; literacy campaign	Expansion of rural education; literacy campaign

political opponents of their leaders. In all cases, Blasier argues, US opposition to moderate reform served to radicalize the reform process, and
eventually led to governments that pursued much more fundamental
social reforms. These are summarized, again following Blasier (pp. 72–3),
in Table 6. As Blasier points out, even these radical reforms (except in the
case of Cuba) were carried out by governments clearly committed to the
principles of democratic capitalism.

The seizures of US property that resulted from these reforms—which,
it is important to point out, affected Latin American capitalists far more
than foreign investors—became a central issue in subsequent US relations with these regimes. The US officially recognized their right to
expropriate property, but insisted on "just" compensation. All four of
the revolutionary governments recognized the principle of compensation
for property they had nationalized. But they were in no position to compensate foreign owners immediately in cash, and, in any case, they
questioned the values unilaterally assigned expropriated properties by
their previous owners. As a result, discussions over compensation between
the United States and these Latin American governments, when they
occurred, involved hard and protracted bargaining over the size and
mode of payment.

Despite all the evidence and analysis reviewed to this point, however,
Blasier believes that security concerns, not economic interests, ultimately
explain US policy toward these four social revolutions. He contends that
fear of German influence in Mexico, both before and during World War
I and in the late 1930s and early 1940s led the US government to override
the special interests of certain US capitalists, especially the oil companies.
Through compromises with the Mexican government achieved in 1923,
the US had blunted the threat of expropriation of land, mines, and petroleum concessions contained in the revolutionary Mexican Constitution of
1917. Understandings reached between the two governments between
1940 and 1942 settled US claims against Mexico, including the most
volatile issue that stood between them, the 1938 expropriation of the
major oil companies operating in Mexico. This second set of agreements
was achieved in conjunction with a pledge by the United States to provide
the Mexicans with large-scale economic assistance. In Bolivia, Blasier
finds that fears that the Soviets might gain influence over the revolution
of 1952 led the United States to encourage the Bolivians to work out
acceptable terms of compensation with the previous owners of the tin
mines. These agreements were consummated in 1953 and presaged large-
scale US economic and military assistance to the Bolivian regime.

Blasier argues that US security fears over the influence of Soviet
Communism, not economic interests, were also the primary motivation

Table 6 Revolutionary Governments: Social and Economic Measures

	Mexico, 1915–40	Bolivia, 1952–64	Guatemala, 1952–54	Cuba, 1959–
Land	Haciendas broken up; lands redistributed, 25.6 million hectares to 1.6 million owners (1940). 49% of cultivated land held communally in *ejidos*	Haciendas broken up; lands redistributed to 145,000 owners	Restrictions on hacienda size; distribution of 1 million hectares to 100,000 owners	Large holdings, commercial farms, sugar lands and mills nationalized. By 1963, approximately 70% of farm land in state farms.
Extractive industries	Major foreign oil companies nationalized (1938)	Three largest tin companies nationalized; oil exploration by public corporation and foreign companies encouraged	Refused to grant foreign oil concessions	Oil refineries and nickel mines nationalized (1960)
Electric power	Federal Electricity Commission to regulate and gradually take over private plants (1939)	—	Temporary government control of US-owned plant; construction of public plants	Nationalized (1960)
Railways	Expropriation of privately owned shares in national railways, public management	—	Main rail line (United Fruit controlled) seized	Nationalized (1960)
Labor unions	Mass mobilization, linked to party and government bureaucracy	Mobilization, especially in mines; later challenged by revolutionary government	Incipient mass mobilization of industrial and rural workers	Mass mobilization, subordination to regime

behind US efforts to bring down the revolutionary governments of
Guatemala and Cuba. In Guatemala, where top US officials had close ties
to United Fruit, Blasier takes special pains to discount the possibility of
any conflict of interest between their private economic involvement and
their public actions. Guatemalan government officials claimed at the
time that the US Secretary of State, John Foster Dulles, and his brother
Allen, then head of the CIA, had close ties with the law firm that handled
United Fruit business. They claimed that John Foster Dulles himself had
drafted the United Fruit contracts with the government of the
Guatemalan dictator Jorge Ubico in 1930 and 1936. They pointed out
that Assistant Secretary of State John Moors Cabot and his family were
stockholders in United Fruit, and that the US ambassador to the United
Nations, Henry Cabot Lodge (a descendant of the pro-imperialist
Secretary of State whose views we examined in chapter 2) also had a
financial interest in the company. Most US scholars now acknowledge the
validity of these claims, and Blasier himself cites privileged information
and engages in informed speculation to lend additional support to some
of them (p. 165). Nevertheless, he insists that in the cases of the Secretary
and Assistant Secretary of State he "found nothing on the public record
or in their reputations reflecting on their financial integrity." "No doubt,
too," he concludes, "they were wiser than to risk their reputations and the
verdict of history on behalf of United Fruit profits" (p. 166).

Similarly, Blasier claims security fears over the spread of Communism,
not economic interests, explain the US decision to intervene with armed
force to overthrow the Cuban revolutionary regime. Reviewing President
Eisenhower's formal decision to authorize the paramilitary operation
against Cuba in March 1960, Blasier asserts that, given the size of US
trade and investments in Cuba

> it is tempting to rely on economic explanations to explain US responses to
> Castro. But . . . Eisenhower sincerely believed and feared that Cuba would
> become a Communist state, and concern about the potential of hostile Soviet
> influence in Cuba was paramount in his mind. Most of what is known about
> the circumstances and Eisenhower's own background supports the thesis that
> he put the nation's military security, as he saw it, ahead of private profit.
> (p. 221)

What is curious about Blasier's argument is that he believes that in all
cases (except that of Mexico) US security fears were illfounded. The
most revealing part of his argument comes in chapter 6, where he carefully weighs the evidence on the influence of national Communist parties
and the Soviet Union in the revolutionary governments of Guatemala
and of Cuba, the two cases in which the United States backed armed

intervention to topple revolutionary governments. He finds that US claims of Communist influence over the Guatemalan regime were grossly exaggerated, a conclusion he would now probably soften somewhat in light of recent research (see, in particular, the work by Piero Gleijeses cited under further reading). He shows that in Cuba the influence of the Cuban Communist Party and the Soviet Union over the regime was minimal during 1959, the first year of the revolution. It was only as US opposition to the reform measures of the regime intensified that the Cuban leadership successfully wooed Soviet support and relied more heavily on Cuban Communist cadres.

But if, as Blasier contends, US security concerns over Soviet influence in Bolivia, Guatemala, and Cuba were both similar and similarly unfounded, what then explains the differences in policy toward these regimes? Why did the United States accommodate and ultimately support the Bolivian revolution and engage in armed intervention to overthrow the Guatemalan and Cuban regimes?

Blasier's explanation emphasizes the personal dispositions of the US and Latin American officials involved in policy decisions and the degree of meaningful communication between them. He stresses, for example, that the Bolivian ambassador to Washington, Victor Andrade, played golf with President Eisenhower and later said that his most effective argument with the president was to tell him that aid to Bolivia would show the world that he "was not a reactionary inflexible Republican and could support a revolution" (p. 136).

Blasier does not emphasize the obvious structural explanation for the cordial personal relations that developed between Bolivian and US officials, and the notoriously frosty ones between the officials of the Guatemalan and Cuban revolutionary regimes and their US counterparts. Yet these very different diplomatic climates mirrored the extent of US economic interests affected by the revolutions in these two countries. Bolivia, where US economic interests were minimal, was clearly an exceptional case among the four countries Blasier is analyzing.

Mexico, the other case of US accommodation, is likewise an exception to Blasier's general argument. Here, unlike in the other three cases, Blasier finds that US security concerns were justified. One need not fully accept Blasier's contention that German influence over the Mexican government posed a major threat to US security during the world wars (in fact, some specialists do not) to accept the fact that broad geopolitical and domestic concerns moderated US policy toward the Mexican Revolution during those years. It is no accident that the high points of the revolution, the labor and economic reforms promised in the Constitution of 1917 and the large-scale land reform and oil expropriations of the middle and late 1930s, occurred at times when the United States was at war with capitalist rivals or enmeshed in the world economic and domestic social crisis of the Great Depression. Mexican reformers seized these opportunities to press forward with democratic reforms that threatened the prerogatives of private investors. The US government was forced to constrain its response, either out of fear of magnifying the scope of its external problems on the eve of war, or because it was preoccupied with resolving severe social and economic crisis at home, or both. Once freed of these constraints, US pressure to contain the radical promise of the Mexican Revolution resumed, a fact that helps to explain the hiatus in the reform process in Mexico during the 1920s, and its demise in the 1940s.

Whatever the precise weight of rival great power influence over these revolutionary regimes—questions on which Blasier and other students of these revolutions may disagree—Blasier's conceptualization of US security concerns is itself problematic. His definition of those concerns—US fear of rival great power intrusions into the hemisphere—accepts as a given an exclusive US sphere of influence in the Americas. Even on its own terms, however, that definition simplifies the relationship between the "economic" interests of private investors and the "security" or strategic concerns of US policy-makers.

What, after all, were the strategic goals of those policy-makers? According to Blasier's own analysis, they were to curtail economic and political inroads by rival, potentially hostile, capitalist powers into the hemisphere, and to contain the expansion of the Soviet Union and of Communism generally, especially in the post-World War II era. These goals were cast as a struggle to defend liberal democracy against fascist and Communist totalitarianism—which indeed they were. But success in this struggle also protected capitalist organization of the economies of the hemisphere under the aegis of the United States and its allies, and promoted the interests of the United States and friendly Western capitalists who operated within them.

When the interests of these private investors were threatened, as was the case in each of the Latin American social revolutions analyzed in this chapter, US policy-makers preferred to stress their commitment to liberal democracy in explaining their opposition to them. They chose not to emphasize their more fundamental goal of preserving the prerogatives of private investors within a US-dominated hemispheric system as a whole. They did so in part because they found it convenient to explain their goals in high moral terms rather than in base material ones. But they had pragmatic reasons as well. Given the democratic aspirations of the majority of their constituents at home, to trumpet their protection of capitalist profits was not very politic. It was not, as Blasier puts it, the best way to assure their place in history. In order to accomplish their policy goals, then, they often had to rationalize them by manufacturing or magnifying the threat of Communism to the security of democracy in the hemisphere.

Blasier convincingly demonstrates the unreality of the Communist threat at the start of the revolutionary process in each of his case studies. But he attributes the erroneous "perceptions" of US politicians to irrational hysteria, ignorance, or incompetence, not to design. He is "surprised," for example, at the fact that during the debate over the character and intentions of the Guatemalan reform government there was "virtually no expression of the Guatemalan side of the story in the Congress" (p. 62). He finds it "puzzling and disturbing" that there is "little or no evidence" that leaders in the Department of State or Congress were aware that the aggressive actions they were taking against Cuba "would lead precisely to the circumstances they claimed they were trying to avoid" (p. 208).

If, however, unlike Blasier, we were to assume that the fundamental motivation behind US policy was the protection of private investors and the "free enterprise system," then policy toward the Latin American revolutions reveals itself as consistent from beginning to end and across time and space. It was hostile in all cases to moderate Latin American reformers once US private investors were hurt by their reforms. Faced, precisely because of this initial opposition, with more radical, revolutionary reforms, US policy-makers then were left with the option of either accommodating the revolutions or attempting to overthrow them. They accommodated them when (as in Bolivia) US investors were virtually absent from the picture or were unscathed by the reforms, or when (as in Mexico) US dominance of the capitalist hemispheric system as a whole seemed threatened, that is, during the world wars and the Great Depression. Otherwise (as in Guatemala and Cuba), US policy was implacably aggressive toward these revolutionary regimes.

Blasier does not seem able to see this simple, rational pattern. Nevertheless, it is consistent with all his evidence and his entire analysis up to its final interpretive twist, when he insists that irrational "security" fears explain US policy-makers' actions. Given Blasier's liberal faith, the US government *by definition* cannot consistently act in the class interests of a small minority of capitalists. The problem is that his evidence shows that it does.

Viewed this way, the Cuban case does not reveal most dramatically, as Blasier would have it, the irrational and counterproductive nature of US efforts to crush the revolution. Rather, it illustrates the extreme risks US policy-makers were willing to run to preserve the hemisphere as an exclusive theater for private enterprise unrestrained by democratic reform. Nor was the result of US policy in Cuba completely negative, at least when viewed from the perspective of its fundamental goal. If the victory of the Cuban regime shattered US economic control over the island, the course of the revolution served to reaffirm the anti-Communist rationale that officially justified US intervention. By forcing the Cuban revolutionaries into ever-growing reliance on Soviet Communist power, US policy-makers were able to argue more effectively that what motivated US policy was the defence of democracy in the hemisphere. That argument was badly in need of confirmation since, as we shall see below, the United States has often supported authoritarian, undemocratic, dictatorial regimes in the region—as long as they defended the prerogatives of private US capitalists.

Many analysts, as Blasier's comments on Eisenhower's Cuban policy quoted above suggest, assume that the weight of US economic interests in a given country should determine the salience of economic motivation in US responses to revolutionary change in it. There is a dimension of truth in that argument, as indicated in the interpretation of US accommodation to the Bolivian Revolution outlined above.

Overall, however, what explains the consistency of US opposition to fundamental reform everywhere in Latin America in this century is the need of US policy to insure the prerogatives of private capital throughout the region, and, as time went on, throughout the world as a whole. The most fundamental of these prerogatives is the sanctity of private property. Preservation of that principle explains why the United States has insisted, even in the cases of accommodation with Latin American revolutions, on the principle of compensation. (In these cases, US readers will note, it was the US taxpayer not Latin American revolutionary regimes who ultimately paid most of the bill for upholding the principle of compensation to the capitalist interests involved.)

Preservation of the principle of private property also explains the "mystery" of US support for Latin American dictatorships that consistently violate democratic norms but just as consistently protect the interests of US investors. Ideally, of course, the United States has preferred to support liberal democratic regimes in the hemisphere, as long as they do not threaten, or allow to be threatened, the fundamental interests of capitalist investors, especially those of the United States itself. A good example is the current wave of US support for democratic regimes in Latin America, a fact that reflects the political weakness and ideological confusion of the socialist-inspired left in the region in the post-Cold War era and the current appeal of liberal solutions to economic problems. (These issues are discussed more fully in chapter 5.) But whenever fundamental social reform has become a reality in such democratic regimes, as the country case studies reviewed in this chapter demonstrate, US policy has quickly turned hostile toward them and resorted to a range of illegal and undemocratic means (both at home and abroad) to destroy them.

Review of US policy toward these four Latin American social revolutions thus reveals a staggering fact to US citizens willing to contemplate it. That policy has single-mindedly opposed fundamental democratic reform in Latin America in the interests of private capitalists. This policy has been presented to the US public as a struggle against totalitarianism, especially Soviet Communism. In fact, however, as Blasier himself would show in more general terms in his study of Soviet–Latin American relations, *The Giant's Rival,* Communist influence in Latin America throughout this century has been minimal. It became a threat to US security only where, as in Cuba, US opposition to reform fostered growing Communist influence.

That most US citizens are unaware of these simple historical truths is neither "puzzling," nor simply "disturbing," as Blasier would have it. Certainly, as many studies (including Blasier's) have shown, the US public's ignorance of the anti-democratic thrust of their country's foreign policy is testimony to the capacity of the government and private interests to manipulate information. Both distort the historical record by casting the Latin American struggle for reform as a Communist threat to the hemisphere. But, as argued in chapter 1, the vulnerability of the US public to such manipulation is, at root, a consequence of an imperfect understanding of the legacy of American colonialism itself. The cultural (cum racial) explanations of Latin American underdevelopment that pervade US academic discourse and popular understanding hardly prepare US citizens for understanding the Latin American social revolutions as indigenous struggles for democratic reform. Instead they appear in the public mind as potentially dangerous, immature, and ineffectual products of an innate Latin American propensity for volatility and disorder.

Unfortunately, liberal scholars, even those of democratic sentiments of the kind exemplified by Blasier, must share responsibility for this unhappy state of affairs. Far from unmasking the consistently anti-democratic thrust of US policy toward fundamental reform in Latin America, work like Blasier's ultimately serves to reinforce it.

As a liberal democrat and a Latin Americanist, Blasier empathizes with the struggle for reform in Latin America. And he recognizes that the consistency of US opposition to basic reform in Latin America lies in the influence of private US economic interests over the thought and activities of US policy-makers. But in the end he abandons this line of analysis to invoke US security concerns. He does so even though he recognizes, as a Sovietologist, that the alleged threat posed by the USSR to US security in the hemisphere was bogus.

In the end, in order to conserve his faith in liberal democracy, Blasier must distort his own evidence, and transform the rational consistency in US policy (the defense of capitalist interests) into irrationality (an unfounded fear of Communism). The costs of this intellectual maneuver are great. Blasier asks us to believe that US policy-makers—intelligent, rational defenders of US private economic interests threatened by demo-cratic reform in Latin America—become, in the end, irrational anti-Communists who fool themselves about the threat of Communist influence in the hemisphere. He asks us, in short, to believe that US pol-icy-makers are dumb. I do not believe they are.

IV

Like Blasier, most US historians have explained US opposition to funda-mental reform in Latin America—and the history of US Latin American policy generally—in terms of US security interests. In doing so they are simply updating Bemis, who, as we saw in chapter 1, developed the secu-rity argument up to the era of World War II. These interpretations artificially separate so-called "security" interests from "economic" inter-ests. Even on its own terms, however, as Blasier's work reveals, "security" includes protection of US capitalists and the system in which they oper-ate. For their part, many Latin Americanists who are critical of US policy fall into the opposite conceptual trap. They discount the security argu-ment completely and analyze US policy goals in simplistic, economistic terms.

Review of US policy toward the whole of Latin America over the course of the twentieth century reveals a far more complex reality than either of these doctrinaire positions suggests. How the artificial categories of "security" interests and "economic" interests are in fact inextricably inter-twined should already be evident from the analysis of LaFeber's work in chapter 2. LaFeber showed that the strategic and security dimensions of US foreign policy by the end of the nineteenth century reflected the economic and social concerns of the US elite. Foreign commercial expansion, the elite believed, would solve domestic economic problems and preserve the social order from the radical reforms championed by organized working people at home. The acquisition of territory to build and protect an isthmian canal was the centerpiece of this expansionist commercial strategy.

Once the interconnections between the "economic" and "security" aspects of LaFeber's analysis are understood, the conventional periods of twentieth-century US–Latin American diplomatic history come into sharp interpretive focus. Students of this history customarily divide their accounts into three main periods, defined in terms of changes in the US policy of armed intervention in the affairs of the Latin American nations. During the first period, the era of "Dollar Diplomacy" (roughly, 1900–1930), the United States frequently intervened with armed force in Central America and the Caribbean. During the second period, customarily called the era of the "Good Neighbor" (1930–45), the United States formally renounced the right of armed intervention in the affairs of the Latin American nations. During the third period, the era of the Cold War and the emerging post-Cold War order (1945 to the present), the United States de facto reaffirmed its right to intervene with force in the region.

Like Blasier, these historians celebrate US policies of compromise and accommodation with Latin American governments. For them, the high point of US policy toward the region was the era of the "Good Neighbor." They deplore the interventionist periods that preceded and succeeded it. Like Blasier, they show how accommodation had positive effects which furthered US economic and security goals, and argue that armed US interventionism often subverted both goals. Finally, like Blasier, they attribute the differences in US policy that define these periods primarily to the character of US policy-makers. The "Good Neighbor" policy, according to its most thorough student, Bryce Wood, was the product of a rational process in which US policy-makers learned from past mistakes and realized they could accomplish their fundamental goals without resort to force. In Wood's account, however, these lessons were unfortunately (and somewhat mysteriously) quickly forgotten in the post-World War II era.

As with Blasier, these interpretations, which emphasize the changing attitudes of the policy elite, downplay deeper structural economic and political trends which conditioned the shifts in US policy. The period of "Dollar Diplomacy" coincided with the long wave of economic expansion following 1898 that lasted until the end of the 1920s. During this period, the United States sought to exclude German influence from the region, and gradually displaced British interests. The era of the "Good Neighbor" coincided with the crisis of the world economy and the efforts of the United States and its allies to defeat the fascist powers. The post-World War II period witnessed a long period of expansion in the global economy under US leadership and the polarization of world conflict along lines of struggle between the rival systems of capitalism and Communism. This last period was split in two by the Cuban Revolution, which brought Cold War security issues into the heart of the hemisphere. Each of these periods featured a different mix of US economic and security concerns. But all reflect the fundamental goal of US–Latin American policy throughout this century, that of safeguarding the basic interests of US capitalists.

During the period of "Dollar Diplomacy" US security concerns revolved primarily around acquisition and protection of isthmian canal routes to facilitate the expansion of US commerce. The United States intervened frequently with armed force in the Caribbean Basin to accomplish this end, beginning in Colombia in 1903 when the United States insured the separation of the province of Panama. Unlike their counterparts in Bogotá, Panamanian elites were eager to accept US terms for building the canal. The following three decades witnessed armed US intervention and prolonged occupations in Haiti (1915–34), the Dominican Republic (1916–24) and Nicaragua (1912–25; 1927–33). These interventions were often justified by a 1905 emendation to the Monroe Doctrine, called the Roosevelt Corollary, which declared the right of the United States to intervene in the affairs of American republics threatened by European powers seeking payment of debts owed their nationals.

The use of the term "Dollar Diplomacy" to characterize US policy during this period is appropriate but often misinterpreted. That policy was not primarily aimed at expanding direct US foreign investment in the small, impoverished Caribbean and Central American countries that became its targets. US investments, especially loans made to such governments by US banks, did expand during this period, and repayment of the loans was often guaranteed by US claims on customs receipts, which were sometimes collected directly by US officials. But the primary goal of all these activities was to promote the stability of the strategic territory around the Panama Canal, and to prevent inroads by rival, and potentially hostile, capitalist powers, especially Germany. US investors, including direct investors, gained from such policies. And during World War I US nationals acquired German assets in many of these countries. The fundamental goal of these policies, however, was strategic and revolved around protection of the canal, as Bemis and a host of other US diplomatic historians have demonstrated in detail. What these historians fail to acknowledge sufficiently are the economic and social origins of strategic concern with the canal. They also fail to emphasize the way the canal contributed to expanding US foreign commerce and investment, especially along the west coast of South America, during the first decades of this century. Finally, they neglect the link between the canal and the growing US naval power it facilitated, which served to protect growing US economic interests beyond the hemisphere.

The era of the so-called "Good Neighbor" Policy that followed pro-vides another variant of the complementarity of strategic (security) and economic goals in US policy toward Latin America. Faced with an inter-nal economic and social crisis of unprecedented proportions, a massive decline in foreign trade, and, as the decade of world depression advanced, growing trade rivalry in Latin America with Germany, the United States officially repudiated its right to intervene with armed force in the affairs of Latin American nations. It linked this policy to efforts to expand its commerce in the region.

The renunciation of armed intervention reflected a variety of consid-erations, not least of which was the financial cost of maintaining troops abroad in a time of fiscal crisis at home. More important, however, was the tenacity of resistance to the occupations. In Haiti resistance led to brutal guerrilla warfare in rural areas and later to urban rebellion. In Nicaragua it developed under the leadership of Augusto Sandino into a major military insurgency in the late 1920s.

There was also a growing recognition in Washington that the policy of armed intervention had failed to achieve its primary aim. Far from pro-moting the stability, development, and goodwill of the countries strategically located in the region of the canal, military intervention pro-duced the opposite effects. By 1930, moreover, the extent of US economic penetration of the region often gave it sufficient power to achieve its ends without resort to force. This power was dramatically demonstrated in Cuba in 1933, when the United States' refusal to re-negotiate the Cuban sugar quota helped bring down a reformist government perceived by Washington as threatening to US interests. Probably most important of all, however, was growing resentment of US intervention in Latin America as a whole, a sentiment reflected in the insistent demand, voiced especially by representatives of the larger nations, that the United States renounce the right of intervention in the region.

The United States finally, if reluctantly, acceded to these anti-inter-ventionist demands at the meeting of the Organization of American States at Montevideo in 1933. Soon afterwards it withdrew its troops from Nicaragua and Haiti, although it left behind a US-trained national guard that subsequently supported some of the most brutal, corrupt, and enduring pro-US dictatorships in the region.

Meanwhile, the vehicle the United States devised to achieve the eco-nomic goal of expanded trade with the region was reciprocity treaties, which guaranteed preferred US access to the markets of Latin American countries in exchange for tariff concessions on Latin American exports to the United States. These treaties, in reality quasi-mercantilist agreements that violated the liberal principle of free trade, sought to reactivate the domestic US economy and insure the country's preeminent position in Latin American trade. The treaties countered the aggressive trade policy of Germany during the 1930s, which attempted to circumvent the liberal capitalist powers' control of Latin American trade by negotiating what were essentially barter agreements with Latin American nations. Together, the United States' policies of non-intervention and reciprocity advanced its goal of strengthening its political and economic control over the region "just in time," as Bemis phrased it, to insure hemispheric political and economic cooperation in the US war effort against the Axis powers.

After World War II, US strategic concerns shifted to the containment of Communist power in Europe and Asia, while its economic interests became global in scope. Latin America, where US economic and political influence seemed secure, was neglected. Despite the pleas of Latin American officials for US developmental aid, there was no Marshall Plan for the region. Yugoslavia alone received more US economic aid between 1948 and 1960 than all the Latin American countries combined. Substituted for increased aid were the rhetoric of anti-Communism and admonitions about the developmental virtues of creating a "favorable climate" for private foreign investment. During this period, in the words of Bryce Wood, the "Good Neighbor" policy was rapidly "dismantled," a fact revealed for all to see in Guatemala in 1954. Guatemalan history also illustrates the broader policy of US support for Latin American dictatorships—as long as they looked favorably on US economic interests and toed an anti-Communist line—during the entire postwar era.

That anti-Communism was not sufficient grounds for US support, however, is revealed through US policy toward the labor-supported government of Juan Domingo Perón in Argentina (1946–55). Perón was a vigorous and very effective anti-Communist, but he pursued a strategy of nationalist capitalist development, including labor reform, that threatened US economic interests. Although these policies became, over time, more rhetorical than real, they nonetheless earned him the hostility of the US government, which rejoiced when he fell from power in 1955 and was replaced by a military government more faithful to orthodox liberal capitalist principles.

Only with the advent of the Cuban Revolution and its consolidation along Communist lines, did the United States modify its postwar strategy for achieving its economic and security goals in Latin America. The Alliance for Progress, begun in 1961, was supposed to channel $1 billion in public US aid annually into Latin America over the next decade. These funds, it was hoped, would stimulate private US and Latin American investment in the region in an amount in excess of $90 billion over the same period. US public aid was made contingent on Latin American plans to promote social reform, including modest land reform. Economic growth and social progress, achieved under democratic political regimes, US policy-makers reasoned, would counter the appeal of Cuban's reforms and its Communist model of development. These goals would be assured through expanded US military aid to the countries of the region.

Within a few short years, however, even Washington admitted that the Alliance for Progress had failed. Fear that the Cuban example would prove contagious, the spread in the region of armed insurgencies inspired by the Cuban revolutionaries' success, and even the threat of the moderate social reforms now championed by official US policy made private Latin American and US investors chary. Capital flight from Latin America, not expanded private investment in it, characterized the 1960s. The expanded role and power of the Latin American military, fortified by the counterinsurgency prong of US policy in the wake of the Cuban Revolution, led to military takeovers of many previously democratic civilian regimes in the region. Meanwhile, US attention and resources were focused increasingly outside the region as the war in Vietnam escalated.

With the collapse of the Alliance, Latin American governments, many of them authoritarian military regimes, depended increasingly on private investment by multinational corporations and on foreign bank loans for external financing. By the 1980s their external debts, the bulk of them owed to US private banks, had reached mammoth proportions, and US policy became increasingly concerned with ways to avoid a general financial crisis triggered by Latin American debt default.

US policy toward Latin America during the whole post-World War II era has been officially defended and legitimated as a struggle to preserve freedom against Communist encroachments in the hemisphere. That is a correct description of reality as long as freedom is understood as the freedom of private capitalists to operate without restraint in the region. Otherwise, there is no accounting for US support of authoritarian and dictatorial regimes that have brutally constrained the freedom of ordinary citizens while protecting the prerogatives of US and Latin American private investors.

US support of such regimes has always been somewhat of an embarrassment for liberals in the United States, within both the policy-making establishment and academia. These liberals are unwilling to acknowledge that the cornerstone of US policy lies in the defense of capitalism not of democracy. So-called conservatives, on the other hand, have had less compunction about such policies. And as their grip on national politics tightened in the 1980s, they found in the work of a heretofore obscure academic, political scientist Jeane Kirkpatrick, a brash theoretical justification for US support of Latin American dictatorships.

In an influential essay, published in book form as *Dictatorships and Double Standards* in 1982 with the support of the American Enterprise Institute, Kirkpatrick addressed the question of Communist influence in reformist governments of the kind we have surveyed in this chapter. She held that when Communist cadres formed part of a revolutionary coalition in backward countries like those of Latin America they should be effectively opposed by the United States. If they were not, she argued, they would consolidate power in their own hands and establish a totalitarian Communist regime of the Soviet type.

Such Communist regimes, Kirkpatrick contended, were different from the dictatorial governments common in traditional societies like those of Latin America. Unlike these traditional dictatorships, which admittedly "tolerated" extreme social inequality, routinely violated democratic norms, and even "allegedly" engaged in torture, totalitarian Communist regimes did all that and more. They "created" social inequality and "refugees by the millions" because they destroyed the "habitual rhythms" of daily life. These "rhythms" allowed "ordinary people" to learn to cope with "the misery of traditional life," just as "children born to untouchables in India acquire the skills and attitudes necessary for survival in the miserable roles they are destined to fill" (p. 50).

History proved, Kirkpatrick concluded, that Communist regimes, once established, never relinquished absolute power. They eclipsed all hope of future transition to democratic politics. In contrast, traditional authoritarian regimes and personalistic dictatorships of the kind common in Latin America could give way to just such democratic openings. Consequently, the United States should have no qualms about supporting dictatorial regimes friendly to the United States when they were threatened by revolutionary coalitions that included Communists. Dictators served as an effective shield against Communist control, and they left open the door to democracy.

Kirkpatrick's essay, with its appeal to history to substantiate its claim that Communist regimes were impervious to democratic transition, has now obviously been overcome by the tide of history itself. But while the collapse of the Soviet Communist bloc destroyed her most fundamental assumption, the essay continues to be worthy of attention. Although Kirkpatrick made a sharp distinction between liberal (Democratic Party) and conservative (Republican Party) approaches to US foreign policy, her book in fact developed in coherent, logical form the basic assumptions that have guided the Latin American policy of all US administrations since World War II. True, Democratic administrations in the United

States like those of John Kennedy and Jimmy Carter have emphasized more consistently than those of Republicans like Richard Nixon and Ronald Reagan a respect for democratic regimes and human rights in Latin America. And it is also true that Democratic-controlled Congresses have tried to limit the illegal and clandestine operations the US government has frequently engaged in in pursuit of its Latin American policy objectives. But all these administrations, generally with widespread congressional support, have endorsed (with greater or less enthusiasm or reluctance) the main lines of the policy outlined in Kirkpatrick's book.

Kirkpatrick is not entirely off the mark in her indictment of the authoritarian tendencies of Marxist-Leninist regimes, but in other respects her argument is not supported by the evidence on the trajectory of the revolutionary Latin American regimes and US policy toward them analyzed in this chapter. Contrary to her assertions, the evidence points to the marginal influence of Communists in such regimes up to the point when the United States did what Kirkpatrick recommends and became aggressively hostile toward their social reforms. And the enduring ability of the Cuban regime to maintain itself in power in the face of US economic and political pressure owes not a little to the popular legitimacy it derived from its democratic social and economic reforms. To acknowledge that fact is not to deny the personalistic and repressive political institutions of Castro's Cuba, which are themselves a response in part to counterrevolutionary pressures the United States has placed on that regime.

The most important aspect of Kirkpatrick's argument lies not in what it says, however, but in what it leaves unsaid. Kirkpatrick leaves unarticulated the "economic" corollary to her "security" argument. Communist regimes have sought to eliminate capitalist organization and capitalist prerogatives in their societies. Traditional dictatorial and authoritarian regimes of the Latin American type customarily have extended and guaranteed capitalist privileges, including those of foreign investors. US opposition to reformist regimes that could be labeled Communist, or prone to Communist influence, thus had the primary effect, if successful in ousting them from power, of preserving undiminished the theater of operations for US capitalists. Successful opposition to such regimes also served as an example to reformers bent on curtailing the prerogatives of capitalists elsewhere. Finally, even if ultimately unsuccessful, US opposition to such regimes often had the effect of strengthening hardline pro-Communist elements within them. The Marxist ideology of these hardliners predicted the implacable opposition of capitalist powers to reforms that infringed on the prerogatives of private investors. And that same ideology offered a socialist alternative, including potential geopolitical support, to achieve fundamental social reform. In Latin America this process had the effect of strengthening the political power, prestige, and legitimacy of Marxists and Communists within reformist regimes under attack by the United States. It thus also had the effect of making the dire anti-Communist predictions of hardline US policy-makers and academics like Kirkpatrick seem to come true.

Kirkpatrick's assumptions thus provided a convenient rationale for support of the authoritarian regimes which, by repressing dissent and the forces for democratic reform, maintained a "favorable climate" for US investment. And they served to legitimate virtually any means to sustain governments seen as friendly to US interests, and to overthrow governments judged hostile to them. In Latin America US support for "friendly" authoritarian regimes has included large-scale military aid and training in sophisticated counterinsurgency and interrogation (including torture?) techniques. Efforts to topple unfriendly regimes have ranged from the suborning of journalists and union leaders to clandestine plots to assassinate public officials. In Fidel Castro's case, CIA plans included plots to poison him, blow him up with an exploding cigar, and slip him a potion that would cause his beard to drop out. These measures would be funny were they not deadly serious. Moreover, some of these plots seem to have been directly inspired by the theories of academics. The beard plot, for example, was hatched on the assumption that Fidel's great initial popularity—his "charisma," to use the concept originally developed by Max Weber—was based more on his looks than on his social reforms. Kirkpatrick's essay justified in academic garb the netherworld of clandestine and illegal activity that underlay the public US government rhetoric about upholding democracy, freedom, and the rule of law. President Ronald Reagan rewarded her by appointing her US ambassador to the United Nations.

V

We are now in a position to place the more contemporary (and for most readers, more familiar) instances of US opposition to revolutionary reform in Latin America in historical context. US policy toward the revolutionary governments of Chile (1970–73) and Nicaragua (1979–90) follows the same pattern identified by Blasier for the "classic" Latin American revolutions we have analyzed. The basic democratic reforms of both of these governments expanded the incomes of working people, fostered unionization of urban and rural workers, raised literacy rates and increased educational opportunities, improved health care, advanced land reform, and sought to promote national development through expanded involvement by the state in economic production. These reforms limited the prerogatives of large capitalists, domestic and foreign. Primarily for that reason the reformers earned the hostility of the US government, which joined with domestic conservatives to drive them from power. The primary means chosen by US policy-makers to destabilize and destroy these regimes reflected the different ways the revolutionary regimes rose to power. The revolutionary government of Chile came to power through free democratic elections. In Nicaragua the revolutionaries won power after protracted military struggle against a brutal US-backed dictatorship.

In Chile, the United States first sought to head off the electoral victory in 1970 of a coalition of reformers under the leadership of socialist Salvador Allende through large-scale economic and military support for the moderate Christian Democrat government that preceded it. When the Christian Democrats lost the election of 1970, the United States backed Chilean conservatives in a failed attempt to use the Chilean congress to block Allende's ascension to the presidency.

Once installed in power, the Allende government proceeded to raise real wages, promote unionization, speed up land reform, and nationalize the US-owned copper mines, banks, and many large-scale industries. US opposition to the government included a virtual cut-off of economic aid and a corresponding increase in military aid, thus fortifying US ties to the military officers who eventually overthrew Allende. The United States also sought to induce its European allies to join it in boycotting Chilean copper exports, the main source of Chile's foreign exchange. The United States involved itself in the assassination of the senior military officer most committed to maintaining democratic procedures and allowing Allende to serve out his six-year term of office. It provided clandestine financial support for conservative newspapers, and bankrolled transport workers willing to strike against the government. In the midst of growing economic and political chaos fostered in part by measures like these, in September 1973 the military, under the leadership of General Augusto Pinochet, moved against Allende, who died defending his office. The Pinochet dictatorship that followed, which eventually, if only partially, returned power to civilian hands in 1992, proceeded in short order to reverse most of the reforms of the Allende period. Thousands of Chilean reformers suffered death, torture, or exile in the months and years that followed.

In Nicaragua, US support for the military-backed Somoza dictatorship (a direct descendant of the government set up following US occupation of the country between 1927 and 1933) lasted until victory of the Sandinista revolutionary forces (named for the nationalist Augusto

Sandino, who had contested that occupation) in 1979. There followed a pattern of growing US opposition to the sweeping social reforms of the revolutionary government similar to that of the other cases we have surveyed. Unlike the situation in Chile, however, the army of the Somoza dictatorship had been defeated by the Sandinista insurgency and the United States adopted the strategy of arming and supplying a large counterrevolutionary force. The "contra" was composed in part of former members of Somoza's National Guard; its civilian arm was led by Adolfo Calera, a former head of the Coca-Cola bottling plant in Managua. In pursuit of this counterrevolutionary strategy, the executive branch of the US government evaded congressional restrictions through bizarre and illegal financial transactions, which included dealings with the declared enemy regime of Iran and with gangs of Latin American narcotics dealers. After years of fighting and destruction, and, as in Chile, in the context of economic collapse, a majority of Nicaraguans voted against Sandinista leadership in 1990. The newly elected government proceeded, with large-scale US economic assistance, to roll back many of the revolutionary reforms.

In both Chile and Nicaragua, US opposition to the reformist regimes was justified, publicly, under the banner of anti-Communism. In neither case, however, was the reality of Soviet Communist influence great. This was true in part because both reformist regimes sought to avoid the fate of Cuba, which by then was struggling under the dual constraints of a US boycott of trade and its client-like dependency on the Soviet Union. It was also true because of the Soviet Union's increasingly limited capacity and willingness to support and defend these regimes. And while Cuba's own support of the Nicaraguan regime was real, and grew for a time in the face of escalating US opposition to the regime, it too was limited by declining Cuban resources.

The real locus of US opposition to both of these governments, as in the four cases analyzed in detail by Blasier, lay in the threat they posed to capitalist prerogatives in general and, especially in Chile, to US investors in particular. That threat, as noted above, was both real and symbolic. President Richard Nixon and his Secretary of State, Henry Kissinger, feared that Chile's peaceful, electoral road to socialism would encourage radical social reform in other parts of Latin America and even foster the advance of electoral socialism (Eurocommunism) in faraway Western Europe. Their successors in power, especially Ronald Reagan, feared that the development of socialist-inspired reform in Nicaragua might start a "domino" effect in the Americas. US economic interests (both existing and potential) in small, resource-poor Nicaragua were hardly very important. And by the late twentieth century

Nicaragua's once great strategic importance as a potential canal site was very much diminished. But if the Nicaraguans were allowed to build a more democratic society in which organized urban and rural workers had a real voice, if they were allowed to develop a mixed economy that included a large cooperative sector, might not the Brazilians or the Mexicans (where US economic interests, real and potential, are great) be emboldened to try a similar strategy?

As in the four "classic" cases of revolutionary reform in Latin America analyzed by Blasier, the Chilean and Nicaraguan revolutions represented an inadmissable threat not to the security of the United States and its people, but to the interests of US capitalists. In its rush to defend those strategic economic interests, the US government not only violated the democratic rights and institutions of the Chilean and Nicaraguan people, but illegally subverted the constitutionally protected democratic institutions of the United States itself.

VI

The costs to democracy in the Americas of US opposition to reform in Latin America during this century have been great. These costs have been of different orders in Latin America and the United States, however, and in Latin America they have not been confined to the societies whose experience with social revolution we have surveyed in this chapter.

As we have seen, US alliances with the most conservative factions of the revolutionary coalitions in Mexico and Bolivia limited the promise of their social revolutions, and eventually helped turn the political regimes of both nations into an authoritarian mold that brought the reform process to an end. US opposition to the Cuban Revolution and its continuing support of counterrevolutionaries drove the Cuban government into alliance with the Soviet Union, led to the militarization of Cuban society, and facilitated the adoption of authoritarian economic and political institutions based on Soviet models that have to date smothered the potential for political democratization. In Guatemala, the success of the US-backed counterrevolution totally reversed the regime's economic, social, and political reforms and led to massive repression of labor and social activists. It left in power a military regime that, over the decades, has brutally repressed dissent and engaged in wholesale extermination of indigenous peoples and political opponents thought to provide support for armed guerrilla groups fighting the government. US hostility toward the revolutionary governments of Chile and Nicaragua wreaked economic havoc, destroyed the promise of democratic socialist reform, and resulted in the death, maiming, or exile of thousands of social reformers.

But the anti-democratic results of US opposition to fundamental reform in Latin America have not been confined to these revolutionary situations, where social reformers actually consolidated power. In other countries, US policy, in alliance with domestic conservative forces, has helped to cut off the prospects for social reform before it fully got underway. The most important of these instances occurred in Brazil, the largest and most populous Latin American nation, in 1964. There a constellation of nationalist reform forces including organized labor coalesced around President João Goulart in the early 1960s. In the context of severe economic crisis, caused in part by sharp reductions in US aid and loans and by large-scale capital flight, the Brazilian military, backed by domestic conservatives and the US government, deposed Goulart in April 1964. The coup, justified in the name of anti-Communism, put an end to the period of political democracy and growing popular and labor mobilization that had begun following World War II. The military regime that held power for the next twenty years engaged in massive repression of labor activists, leftist political parties, and eventually, political dissenters of any kind. Meanwhile, it provided a safe and lucrative haven for investments by multinational corporations and banks. The rapid economic growth that resulted in the late 1960s and 1970s did not transform Brazilian social inequality; income distribution remained among the most regressive in the world. It also left Brazil with a staggering foreign debt, which the current generation of Brazilian working people is being forced to pay. Nevertheless, massive foreign investment after 1964 helped make the Brazilian manufacturing sector the most advanced in Latin America. And that development nurtured a new and powerful labor movement, which in the 1980s played a central role in challenging the military regime and returning the nation to democratic rule.

The other major result of US opposition to Latin American revolutionary regimes was to convince many Latin American reformers that the only viable avenue for achieving social reform lay in armed struggle. Beginning in the 1960s, many Latin American middle-class reformers, particularly students and intellectuals, embraced the Cuban model as the solution to national problems. They founded Leninist-inspired vanguard parties to lead popular insurrections of urban and rural workers that would transform the capitalist order of their societies into a socialist one. All of these vanguard parties failed to win general working- and middle-class support, and most were effectively eliminated by national security forces that were armed, supplied, and trained in part with US support. In most countries, however, the existence of these vanguard parties and guerrilla groups had entirely negative consequences for the labor movement and the democratic left. Latin American governments, military and civilian alike, and the right-wing paramilitary groups they tolerated or supported, used the existence of these small revolutionary groups to engage in general repression of unions and political dissent, rationalizing their actions as necessary to eliminate Communist subversion.

In contrast to this bloody, tragic history of US-backed counterrevolution in Latin America, the consequences for US society of these Latin American policies may appear to be small and insignificant. They are not. US policy toward Latin America served to reinforce the national preoccupation with Communist subversion in the postwar era, and that preoccupation, in turn, had pervasive negative effects on democratic institutions at home. Especially affected was the US labor movement, which, as will be discussed in chapter 5, first limited its vision of democratic reform at home and then joined with US corporate and government officials in subverting the reformist social goals of labor organizations in Latin America. US opposition to social transformation in Latin America, justified as a war on Communism, helped rationalize massive military expenditures to "contain" the Soviet Union. Military spending sapped the national budget, distorted the national economy, and limited social expenditures. The war on Communism also helped strengthen the power and expand the purview of secret police and intelligence operations such as the FBI and the CIA, and helped intensify intolerance of dissent in US society generally. Most importantly, the war on Communism reinforced the legitimacy of liberal capitalist ideology. It polarized debate and politics—one was either for freedom and capitalist democracy US-style or taken for an authoritarian Communist aiding the cause of Soviet totalitarianism and world dominion. As a result, meaningful discussion of democratic social alternatives to the systems of both of the superpowers was effectively eliminated. As a consequence of all these developments, general progress toward more effective political and social democracy was retarded or reversed in the United States (as well as, of course, in the Soviet Union and other parts of the world, including Latin America). The democratic progress that did occur in the United States in these Cold War decades happened in the liberal domain of individual rights for racial minorities and women.

Just as US policy was not the only, or in most cases the most important, force behind counterrevolution in Latin America, so US Latin American policy was by no means the only force behind these domestic US developments. But given the proximity of Latin America to the United States, the formative and symbolic role it played in the development of US foreign policy, and the relative ease with which the United States could accomplish its diplomatic goals in the hemisphere, US policy toward the region played a considerable role in all of them. By casting the struggle for social reform in Latin America as a Communist conspiracy bent on destroying the freedom of all Americans, the US government not only presented the US public with a grossly distorted and highly undemocratic version of Latin American reality, but also successfully undermined the potential for democratic reform and social justice at home.

Since the time of the Mexican Revolution, however, a minority of US citizens have seen through the false claims of their government officials. They have understood that the struggle for democracy in Latin America was simply that, not part of a world-wide Bolshevik Communist conspiracy. Many of these people, including sectors of the labor movement, provided effective support to revolutionary reform movements in Latin America. Over time, the scope and effectiveness of this hemispheric solidarity has grown. By the 1980s large numbers of progressive religious, union, and grassroots organizations had begun to exert significant pressure on Washington policy-makers to moderate opposition to Latin American revolutionary movements, particularly in Central America. As they informed themselves and others about the true nature of the struggle for democratic reform in Latin America, they also learned to question the effectiveness of democratic institutions at home.

With the end of the Cold War it will be harder for US policy-makers to conceal their opposition to fundamental reform in Latin America behind the rhetoric of US security concerns. Today, as has been true throughout this century, the security, material wellbeing, and democratic aspirations of all Americans are best served by a Latin America able to pursue its long-standing struggle for reform free of US opposition.

Renewal of effective democratic struggle in Latin America and the United States, however, will depend on more than understanding the capitalist logic behind US foreign policy in this century. It will depend as well on critical reassessment by Americans of the merits of liberal and Marxist theory and capitalist and socialist practice. Chapter 4 begins discussion of these crucial issues on what may initially appear as unlikely, even frivolous, terrain, the Donald Duck comic book. Chapter 5 pursues these same issues through analysis of contemporary labor history.

Further Reading

Aguilar, Luis A., *Cuba 1933*, Ithaca, NY, 1972.

Baily, Samuel L., *The United States and the Development of South America, 1945–1975*, New York 1976.

Bergquist, Charles, *Labor in Latin America*, Stanford, CA, 1986.

Blasier, Cole, *The Hovering Giant*, Pittsburgh 1976.

—— *The Giant's Rival*, Pittsburgh 1983.

Castañeda, Jorge, *Utopia Disarmed*, New York 1994.

Drake, Paul W., and Ivan Jaksic, *The Struggle for Democracy in Chile, 1982–1990*, Lincoln, NB, 1990.

Dunkerley, James, *Power in the Isthmus*, London 1988.

Gardner, Lloyd, *Economic Aspects of New Deal Diplomacy*, Madison, WI, 1964.

Gleijeses, Piero, *Shattered Hope*, Princeton, NJ, 1991.

Gould, Jeffrey, *To Lead As Equals*, Chapel Hill, NC, 1990.

Green, David, *The Containment of Latin America*, Chicago 1971.

Handy, Jim, *Revolution in the Countryside*, Chapel Hill, NC, 1994.

Hartlyn, Jonathan, Lars Schoultz, and Augusto Varas, eds., *The United States and Latin America in the 1990s*, Chapel Hill, NC, 1993.

James, Daniel, *Resistance and Integration*, Cambridge, UK, 1998.

Kirkpatrick, Jeane J., *Dictatorships and Double Standards*, New York 1982.

Knight, Alan, *US–Mexican Relations 1910-1940*, La Jolla, CA, 1987.

Levenson-Estrada, Deborah, *Trade Unionists Against Terror*, Chapel Hill, NC, 1994.

Lowenthal, Abraham, ed., *Exporting Democracy*, 2 vols., Baltimore 1991.

LaFeber, Walter, *Inevitable Revolutions*, 2nd. edn., New York 1993.

Nash, June, *We Eat the Mines and the Mines Eat Us*, New York 1979,

Oglesby, Carl, and Richard Shaull, *Containment and Change*, New York 1967.

McCormick, Thomas J., *America's Half-Century*, Baltimore 1989.

Perez, Louis A., Jr., *Essays on Cuban History*, Gainesville, FL, 1995.

Schoultz, Lars, *National Security and United States Policy Toward Latin America*, Princeton, NJ, 1987.

Schmidt, Hans, *The United States Occupation of Haiti, 1915–1934*, New Brunswick, NJ, 1971.

Winn, Peter, *Weavers of Revolution*, New York 1986.

Womack, John, *Zapata*, New York 1968.

Wood, Bryce, *The Making of the Good Neighbor Policy*, New York 1961.

—— *The Dismantling of the Good Neighbor Policy*, Austin, TX, 1985.

Wright, Thomas C., *Latin America in the Era of the Cuban Revolution*, New York 1991.

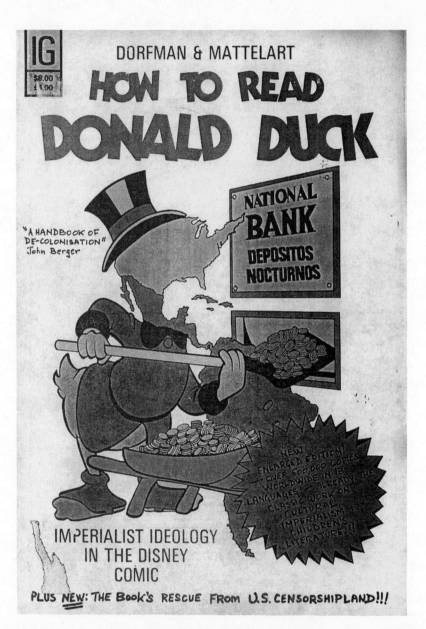

Cover of the second English-language edition of Ariel Dorfman and Armand Mattelart's *How to Read Donald Duck* (New York 1984). The book was printed in Great Britain by International General Editions. Imports into the United States were banned for several years by the US government in response to legal action taken by the Disney Corporation. The depiction of Scrooge (and thus Disney) as a hidden (nocturnal) capitalist exploiter of Latin America conveys Dorfman and Mattelart's interpretation. They hold that general readers of the duck comics, however, learn to internalize pro-capitalist, pro-imperialist values.

4

Popular Culture and
Democratic Values

How do we learn to make sense of our history? Specifically, how do Americans, North and South, come to understand how things got to be the way they are in the hemisphere today? In a sense, we have been grappling with this question in each of the previous chapters. Are Haitians poor today because they are black, or because their rich colonial society was built on slavery? Did the northeastern British American colonies become industrialized because their people were white carriers of British cultural traits, or because, being poor in the colonial era, they were able to develop on the basis of free wage labor? Does the struggle by workers for democratic reform in the United States result in foreign expansionism that erodes democratic institutions at home? Do US policy-makers use all means available to limit Latin American efforts at social reform because they fear Communist threats to US security, or because they strive to protect capitalist investment abroad, or are these simply two different ways of saying the same thing?

How we learn to judge these issues is a process that includes formal education. But it rests on deep cultural assumptions that we acquire through far more basic, often seemingly innocuous, ways—through lullabies and fairy tales, through movies and television cartoons, through jokes and sports events. The range of the social experiences that shape our values and perceptions is very wide. It includes everything from the child-rearing customs of our society to our life on the job and the history lessons we learn in school.

One particularly revealing illustration of the ways material conditions influence our cultural attitudes, and of the ways these attitudes in turn structure our history and our interpretations of it, comes from the work of the celebrated (and very conservative) US historian David Potter. At Yale in the 1950s, and later as a distinguished professor at Stanford University, Potter sought to update Turner's "Frontier Thesis," which I discussed in chapter 2. In his influential book *People of Plenty* (1954), he argued that contemporary US values were conditioned, among other things, by the twentieth-century child-rearing patterns of most US families. Thanks to central heating, for example, infants were not tightly swaddled in layers of warm clothing and were early able to move about freely. Such children were not accustomed to sleeping with siblings or parents. They got used to enjoying an individual domain in separate bedrooms of their own. Potter developed ideas like these to argue that a new frontier of industrial and technological advance could sustain the individualist values and unique democratic institutions of US society first analyzed by Turner. He emphasized neither the imperial implications of Turner's thought nor those of his own.

This chapter examines aspects of how cultural assumptions inform our understanding of the history of the Americas and of our place in contemporary society from a vantage point quite different from that of the formal academic scholarship we have considered in previous chapters. It looks at these issues from the perspective of what is commonly called "mass" culture. The concept of "mass," or, as I will term it, "popular"* culture, refers especially to forms of entertainment consumed by millions of people in our society, familiar things like "pop" music, movies, television soap operas, and comic books.

Popular culture is a subject as vast as it is complex. Questions about its influence in structuring our understanding of the world around us are much neglected, often hotly debated, and generally not very well understood. To make our inquiry manageable, we will have to delimit it sharply, and focus on a particularly illuminating example to illustrate a broader argument.

The chapter unfolds as a critique of an influential—and extremely provocative—analysis of American popular culture, Ariel Dorfman's and Armand Mattelart's *How to Read Donald Duck: Imperialist Ideology in the Disney Comic* (Valparaíso, Chile, 1971; references here are to the English-language edition of 1975). Some readers may smile at the notion that analysis of the antics of comic-book characters as seemingly frivolous and "fun" as Mickey Mouse and Donald Duck can illuminate the weighty question of how we learn to understand the world and our place within it. But the cultural values imbedded in the Disney comic, a form of popular amusement that captured the imagination of millions of children (of all ages) around the world in the middle of the twentieth century, turn

---

*These terms are loaded, as will become apparent in the course of this chapter. Here it is enough to note that "mass" culture implies manipulation of passive consumers by a powerful cultural elite, while "popular" implies an active interpretive role and choice by such consumers.

out to be no laughing matter. Dorfman and Mattelart argue that through these comics children acquire racist and ethnocentric values that reinforce and perpetuate an exploitative capitalist world order. They see the Disney comic as part of a conscious and particularly insidious conspiracy to delude us about the reality of our lives and keep the young from challenging the social status quo.

One need not accept the whole of Dorfman and Mattelart's often brilliant analysis to appreciate the intellectual and political importance of understanding what makes the Disney comic tick. Indeed, I believe that, their pioneering insights notwithstanding, Dorfman and Mattelart fundamentally misread the Disney comic. Their analysis is misleading because it neglects the comic's popular appeal. Like all art, forms of popular culture embody diverse, ambiguous, and often contradictory meanings. The Disney comic, I will argue, both reinforces our received, commonsensical understandings of the way things are, *and*, at the same time, challenges and subverts those understandings. It is the subversive (or democratic) side of the "world of Disney," I contend, that best explains its popularity.

It may not be fun for us to see our childhood heroes and friends in this critical cultural light. But, as I hope the ensuing discussion will show, to dismiss the contested meanings of popular culture is to ignore some of the most important intellectual and political issues of our time.

I

Ariel Dorfman and Armand Mattelart published *How to Read Donald Duck* in September 1971, on the first anniversary of the accession of the Allende government in Chile. Dorfman, born in Argentina in 1942, spent much of his boyhood in New York. He subsequently adopted Chilean citizenship and in 1971 was employed as a professor of Spanish American literature at the University of Chile. A member of Allende's Socialist Party, he was also on the staff of the Chilean state publishing house, Quimantú (meaning "Sunshine of Knowledge" in the language of the Mapuche Indians in Chile), where he worked in the Juvenile and Educational Publications Division. Mattelart, born in Belgium in 1936, had lived in Chile since 1962. A sociologist by training, and a Marxist, he also was a professor at the University of Chile and in 1971 was serving as head of Quimantú's Investigation and Evaluation of the Mass Media Section.

Both men saw their work as an integral and vital part of the process of socialist transformation in Chile. As they put it, in their 1975 preface to the English-language edition of the book, their effort was part of the "popular Chilean cultural offensive" that accompanied the sweeping economic and social reforms of the Allende government. Those reforms, as we saw in chapter 3, met with concerted US opposition, including an "invisible blockade" designed to destabilize the Chilean economy and topple the government. Dorfman and Mattelart emphasized the selective nature of these US-inspired sanctions in their preface. "[C]redits were denied, spare parts purchased for industrial machinery were not sent, and later, the Chilean State bank accounts in the US were blocked, and an embargo preventing the sale of Chilean copper throughout the world was organized." Two kinds of imports, however, were not blocked: "planes, tanks, ships and technical assistance for the Chilean armed forces; and magazines, TV serials, advertising, and public opinion polls for the Chilean mass media" (p. 9). Through control of the mass media, the authors contended, a small and privileged Chilean elite and their US allies prepared the ground for the "bourgeois insurrection" that materialized on September 11, 1973 and destroyed the Allende government. *How to Read Donald Duck* was conceived by its authors as a revolutionary cultural effort to immunize Chileans against this bloody, reactionary outcome. It "simply answered a practical need," the authors affirmed from exile in 1975, "it was *not* an academic exercise" (p. 10).

But if the book was not a typical academic exercise, its authors were far from abandoning what they termed "scientific rationalism" (p. 25) as the basis for their study. They located a hundred Disney comic books published in Chile, most of which contained two to four stories. Most of these comics concerned the Disney ducks—Donald, his nephews Huey, Dewey, and Louie, and Donald's uncle, Scrooge. The majority of the comics in their sample came from the 1960s; a few of them were published in the 1940s and 1950s. Although the authors admitted that their sample was "inevitably somewhat random" (p. 27), they did not speculate on its possible bias. (As we shall see below, the fact that their analysis did not center on material from the 1940s and 1950s, the heyday of the Disney comic in the United States, has important implications for their argument.) Dorfman and Mattelart studied their sample cartoons closely and documented their argument carefully, citing specific comics to buttress their analysis, and quoting dialogue from the cartoons at length. They used considerable restraint in reproducing panels from the Disney cartoons to illustrate their argument, but that did not prevent their being ensnared in legal battles with a Disney Corporation notorious for its aggressive defense of what it claimed were its copyright privileges.

Although committed to "scientific rationalism," the authors sought a language for the book "intended to break with the false solemnity which generally cloaks scientific investigation" (p. 25). "Mr. Disney," they announce in the preface, "we are returning your Duck. Feathers plucked and well-roasted" (p. 10). They did not, however, "aspire to some clumsy popularization" (p. 25). The result is a text that frequently sparkles with creative, even whimsical prose, yet also contains weighty passages that reveal the authors' debt to academic literary criticism and communications theory, and their fidelity to orthodox Marxist analysis and discourse.

It is tempting to attribute the hybrid language of the text to the different talents and disciplinary commitments of the authors, although, for political and intellectual reasons, they themselves are at pains to warn readers and critics against such an approach. "This work," they affirm, "is to be . . . considered a joint effort of conception and writing" (p. 25). It is revealing, however, that following his exile from Chile in 1973 Dorfman went on to become a major creative writer. His literary production over the last two decades has included poetry, novels, and plays (the most celebrated of which, *Death and the Maiden*, won Britain's Laurence Olivier award for drama in 1992 and was subsequently made into a major film directed by Roman Polanski). Much of this work deals with the issues raised by Chile's democratic socialist experiment and the brutal repression that followed, although Dorfman treats these themes in universal political and philosophical terms. When Dorfman returned, a decade after the publication of *How to Read Donald Duck*, to reconsider the meaning of popular culture in a lively book of essays, *The Empire's Old Clothes* (1983), he did so as a humanist who had abandoned the formal discourse (but not the assumptions) of orthodox Marxist cultural criticism. Mattelart, in contrast, reverted in subsequent works to the ponderous abstract academic language typical of social scientists in the field of Marxist-inspired communication studies. A good example is his study of Brazilian television fiction, done with Michelle Mattelart, which was published in English, in 1990, as *The Carnival of Images*.

The language of *How to Read Donald Duck* alerts us to far more important issues than the question of who is responsible for what in the book. It signals the unique and problematic contributions of the content of the study. Dorfman and Mattelart's fidelity to orthodox Marxist theory enables them to develop a powerful, highly original, and carefully documented interpretation of the Disney comic. But these same theoretical assumptions, I will argue, take their analysis in directions that are intellectually misleading, politically suspect, and fundamentally undemocratic.

They begin their analysis (chapter 1, "Uncle, Buy Me a Contraceptive . . .") by exploring a very curious feature of the world of Donald Duck. There are no fathers and no mothers in these comics, just uncles and nephews, uncles of uncles, and some cousins. And with few exceptions (such as Donald's girlfriend, Daisy, and her nieces) all these characters are male.

Dorfman and Mattelart's explanation of this strange set of family relations prefigures their entire argument. They dismiss the "hasty rationalizations" of these features by "the advocates of Disney." They rack their brains "trying to figure out the educational value of so many uncles and cousins" and are forced to "the paradoxical conclusion that in order to conceal normal sexuality from children, it is necessary to construct an aberrant world" (p. 34). In Disney, they argue, characters function only through suppression of "their personal history, their birth and death, and their whole development in between, as they grow and change." If their past is eliminated, characters are denied the "opportunity of self-examination" in the present. The absence of the father in these comics does not mean the absence of paternal authority, which is far more severe and arbitrary than in any real-life biological family. "Within this family perimeter, no one loves anyone else, there is never an expression of affection or loyalty towards another human being . . . ." Children are deprived of their "true" qualities—trustfulness, spontaneity, the capacity for unconditional love, and unbounded imagination. Children learn "fear and hatred" through Disney, for lurking just beneath the superficial attractiveness of the little Disney creatures lies "the law of the jungle: envy, ruthlessness, cruelty, terror, blackmail, exploitation of the weak" (pp. 34–5).

The authors then introduce a key feature of what has now become (for them, at least) the frightening world of Disney, a process they call "inversion." In this stock-in-trade feature of the plots of Disney comics, the youngsters (in Donald Duck cartoons, his nephews) "invariably" step in to right abuses of power and betrayals of accepted values and restore the "old hierarchy of domination." In Dorfman and Mattelart's understanding of the process of inversion lies the core idea of their whole analysis of the meaning of the Disney comic.

> Since the child identifies with his counterpart in the magazine, he contributes to his own colonization. The rebellion of the little folk in the comics is sensed as a model for the child's own real rebellion against injustice; but by rebelling in the name of adult values, the readers are in fact internalizing them. (p. 36)

Is there no escape from this pervasive "struggle for vertical subordination and obsessive propagation of the system?" the authors ask themselves. "Indeed there is. There is horizontal movement and it is always present" (p. 37). In this way the authors anticipate their explanation of the other major (and complementary) feature of the Disney plot—the race, the contest, the search for gold in which the "dominated" incessantly compete with each other.

The authors end their treatment of the biological features of Disney society with a discussion of their gendered and sexual meanings. Women never change roles in the "dominated–dominator" relationship. With few exceptions they are stereotypically cast as "humble servant or constantly courted beauty queen; in either case subordinate to the male . . . . [The woman's] only power is the traditional one of seductress, which she exercises in the form of coquetry" (pp. 37–8). By "suppressing true sexual contact," the authors conclude, Disney creates "another aberration: an asexual sexuated world." The sexual innuendo, however, is "more evident in the drawing, than in the dialogue itself" (p. 39).

In chapters 2 and 3, "From the Child to the Noble Savage," and "From the Noble Savage to the Third World," Dorfman and Mattelart attempt to show how the ideological mechanisms they have discovered in the workings of the domestic Disney family relate to the Third World. This is no small, peripheral matter: nearly half of the hundred magazines they examined showed the Disney characters "confronting beings from other continents and races," (p. 43) usually in some stereotyped part of Asia, Africa, or Latin America. These beings are primitive. They come in all colors except white. They are generally "enormous, gigantic, gross, tough, pure raw matter, and pure muscle." And they are like children: "[f]riendly, carefree, naive, trustful and happy" (p. 44). But unlike the domestic urban child-adults of Duckburg (a place that resembles a small town in the United States), the foreign natives lack "intelligence, cunning, discipline, encyclopedic knowledge and technical skills" (p. 46).

The dynamics of these encounters go something like this. The ducks flee the city, which is often depicted as noisy, polluted, and conflictual, in search of hidden treasure—gold, diamonds, jewelry. Treasure is what the natives of the rural domains they head for have in abundance. But it is useless to them, its market value unappreciated. The natives gladly exchange their treasure for the technological wonders borne by the ducks—things like watches and detergent. Sometimes the ducks help revamp the politics and economies of the primitive societies they visit, dethroning rulers, changing cultural attitudes, introducing market-based economic exchange (pp. 50–51).

Many of the comics thus parallel the history of Western "imperialist plunder and colonial subjugation" (p. 52). Yet this story appears, the authors argue, as a benign and natural process. Disney accomplishes this amazing feat by delinking the treasure the ducks seek from the present-day inhabitants of these backward lands. The treasure is often a product of an ancient, bygone civilization that met with some catastrophe. The current inhabitants are not heirs to it because they have no history. "By depriving them of their past, Disney destroys their historical memory in

124 LABOR AND THE COURSE OF AMERICAN DEMOCRACY

the same way he deprives a child of his parenthood and genealogy, with the same result: the destruction of their ability to see themselves as a product of history" (p. 62).

The rest of the book (chapters 4 through 6) amplifies these concepts and specifies their theoretical and political implications. It is here that the authors develop what they earlier call the "crux" of their whole analysis, the meaning of the Disney comic for labor and the working class.

> The problem is not only Disney's equation of the child with the noble savage, and the noble savage with the underdeveloped peoples. It is also . . . that what is said, referred to, revealed and disguised about all three of them, has, in fact, only one true object: the working class. (pp. 58–9)

How can this be? The authors begin their explanation by showing that the quest of the ducks and other First World characters like them is about gold, or (when the setting is the city) fortune, in the form of money or fame. Yet nowhere is the actual *production* of wealth depicted. Moreover, the world of Disney is a world of consumers. "There is a constant round of buying, selling and consuming, but to all appearances, none of the products involved has required any effort to make" (p. 64). And work, when it is depicted (such as when Donald gets fired from a job for incompetence), happens only in the service sector, to hairdressers, watchmen, salespeople and their likes. "This is the world the bourgeoisie have always dreamed of. One in which a man can amass great wealth, without facing its producer and product: the worker."

> It is a world of pure surplus without the slightest suspicion of a worker demanding the slightest reward. The proletariat . . . sell their labor "freely" to the highest bidder, who transforms the labor into wealth for its own social class. In the Disney world, the proletariat are expelled from the society they created, thus ending all antagonisms, conflicts, class struggle and indeed, the very concept of social class. (pp. 64–5)

"Marx," the authors continue, "had a word—fetishism—for the process which separates the product (accumulated work) from its origin and expresses it as gold, abstracting it from the actual circumstances of production."

> It was Marx who discovered that behind his gold and silver, the capitalist conceals the whole process of accumulation which he achieves at the worker's expense (surplus value). The words "precious metals," "gold," and "silver" are used to hide from the worker the fact that he is being robbed, and that the capitalist is no mere accumulator of wealth, but the appropriator of the product of social production. The transformation of the worker's labor into gold,

fools him into believing that it is gold which is the true generator of wealth and source of production. (p. 65)

The only obstacle to the appropriation of treasure and the accumulation of gold in the Disney comic is the thief. The Beagle Boys, always a threat to the money bin of multibillionaire Scrooge, are the prime example. They are "oversize, dark, ugly, ill-educated, conceited . . . and unscrupulous" (p. 66). But in real life, the authors remind us

> the element which truly challenges the legitimacy and necessity of the monopoly of wealth, and is capable of destroying it, is the working class, whose only means of liberation is to liquidate the economic base of the bourgeoisie and abolish private property. (p. 67)

Disney, like the bourgeoisie in general, tries to weaken the proletariat by portraying its class struggle in the moral terms of good and evil.

Thus, in Disney the working class is split into two groups, criminals in the city and noble savages in the countryside. The rural, or "peasant" sector is harmless, childlike, and static; the bourgeoisie makes it the object of a romanticized popular, or "folk," tradition. The urban sector is "dangerous, dirty, and mobile"; it must be criminalized. The authors contend that this mythical division, old in the West, was reinforced and extended to Africa, Latin America, and Asia as Europe expanded after 1500. It was finally and fully elaborated in the United States, which, by "opening the frontier further and further," developed the myth into a "'Way of Life,' [an] ideology shared by Disney" (p. 59).

But, one might ask, isn't Donald always looking for work and bemoaning his burdens? Doesn't that run counter to the authors' thesis? No, they argue. Donald never works for need—to pay the rent or the food bill. Rather he works to consume, to buy a television or a present for someone. The job Donald wants to find has to be easy, "undemanding of mental and physical effort." "[H]e wants wages without sweating" (p. 71). In the world of Disney there is no chronic unemployment; there are always plenty of jobs. But even the simple ones Donald finds turn out to be too much for him, and he is fired for incompetence. Donald incessantly looks for work and is obsessed with not losing a job when he finds one. But no sooner has he "crossed the employment threshold" than he "becomes the victim of crazy and chaotic commotion." These "absurd paroxysms" of activity generally end in Donald's rest and reward. But sometimes he "cannot escape these apocalyptic gyrations." In either case, the outcome does not depend on Donald. It depends on "fate" (p. 72).

Outside the city, in his rural and foreign adventures in search of treasure, Donald suffers a similar form of "nervous suffering." One accident after another befalls him; the gold he searches for is not "easily attained."

> One has to first suffer *deconcretized labor*: work in the form of adventure . . . . This process symbolizes work, without actually being work. It is a passively consumed form of toil, rather than one which is actively creative and productive. (pp. 72–3)

During the search for treasure, as on the job at home, Donald "does not propel himself, but is propelled by destiny"; he thus learns "the necessity of obeying its designs" (p. 73). How can one go on strike, or demand higher wages, the authors ask, if everything is left to providence?

For Dorfman and Mattelart, then, Duckburg is no fantasy, but the *phantasmagoria* Marx spoke of:

> Donald's "work" is designed to screen off the contradictions in the bosses' mythology of labor, and hide the difference between the value of labor, and the value which labor creates. . . . In his phantasmagorical rhythm of suffering and reward, Donald represents the dominated (mystified) at the same time as he paradoxically lives the life of the dominator (mystifier).

Donald may be "sensed as the true representative of the contemporary worker," but in fact he "is the bastard representative of all workers" (p. 73).

One final dimension of work as portrayed in the Disney comic is central to Dorfman and Mattelart's analysis. That is the relationship between work and the function of the entertainment industry in contemporary capitalist societies. Work, the authors contend, is always defined in Disney "as a function of its contrary, leisure." Work is an "unusual, eccentric phenomenon" segregated from leisure, the normal state to which everyone aspires (p. 73). Just as Disney proposes that "children transcend the concrete reality of their [lives]" and "surrender to the 'magic' and the 'adventure'" of his comic books, "contemporary mass culture . . . is based on the principle that only entertainment can liberate humanity from the social anxiety and conflict in which it is submerged" (p. 76).

Forms of mass entertainment in capitalist culture try to "reconcile everything—work with leisure, the commonplace with the imaginary, the social with the extrasocial, body with soul, production with consumption, city with countryside—while veiling the contradictions arising from their interrelationships." The conflicts of the real world are "molded" in ways "functional" to the class interests of the bourgeoisie, then returned "veneered with innocence" to the mass consumer.

> Once [social reality] is interpreted as a magical, marvelous paradigm of his own common experience, the reader then can consume his own contradictions in whitewashed form. This permits him to continue viewing and living these conflicts with the innocence and helplessness of a child. (p. 76)

When the social conflicts of advanced capitalist society get out of hand, or when the struggles of Third World peoples reach revolutionary proportions, the mass media act to discredit or dilute these phenomena, and isolate them from their systemic origins (pp. 54–8). This happens at all levels of "the system," including the arts. The "artist who shatters the habits of vision imposed by the mass media" is customarily dismissed "as a mere eccentric." "[T]he genius is isolated from real life, and all his attempts to reconcile reality with its aesthetic representation are neutralized" (p. 55).

The mass media complement these strategies by incorporating a species of social criticism into their programming. Dorfman and Mattelart broach this issue indirectly, in the form of a question posed by a hypothetical critic of their argument. Doesn't Disney stigmatize bureaucracy and attack pollution, criticize technological excess and unbridled consumerism, and denounce the excessive concentration of wealth? "[I]sn't the character of Scrooge McDuck a great social satire on the rich . . .?" (p. 92).

The authors reject the notion that Disney's treatment of such themes constitutes meaningful social criticism because it fails to focus on the systemic origins of these evils.

> Disney hopes that by incorporating the weaknesses of the system as well as its strengths, his magazines will acquire an appearance of impartiality. They embody pluralism of motifs and criteria, and liberty of expression, and while promoting sales, creative freedom for writers and artists.

But Disney's challenge to the system "is stereotyped and socially acceptable." It is the

> facade of democratic debate, which while it appears to open up the problems defined by the bourgeoisie as "socially relevant," really conceals the subtle censorship they impose. This "democratic debate" prevents the unmasking of the fallacy of "free" thought and expression. . . . (p. 93)

Disney, the authors conclude, is a threat to Chile because "underdeveloped peoples take the comics, at second hand, as instruction in the way they are supposed to live and relate to the foreign power center." Disney impresses the false utopian dream world of the capitalist bourgeoisie onto the minds of workers; he offers the poor "the only food

they know." Reading Disney is thus "like having one's own exploited condition rammed with honey down one's throat." Disney's "fabrication of a
mass culture built on the backs of the masses" must therefore be challenged; doing so is a prerequisite for cultural liberation.

To those who would criticize them for producing "merely a destructive
study which fails to propose an alternative," Dorfman and Mattelart reply
that "no one is able to 'propose' his individual solution to these problems."

> What happens after Disney will be decided by the social practice of the peoples
> seeking emancipation. It is for the vanguard organized in political parties to
> pick up this experience and allow it to find its full human expression. (p. 99)

In the years following its publication, *How to Read Donald Duck* was
greeted by leftist intellectuals around the world with enthusiasm.
Conservative critics, in contrast, ridiculed and disparaged it. The book
went through several editions in Latin America and was eventually translated into some seventeen languages. Fear of copyright litigation
dissuaded US houses from publishing it, however, denying Dorfman and
Mattelart easy access to the book's largest (and most lucrative) potential
market. And Disney Corporation lawyers alleging copyright infringement
succeeded in severely limiting imports of the English-language edition
into the United States until the middle of 1976. Nevertheless, by 1984,
when a second, enlarged English-language edition appeared, the book
had sold over half a million copies worldwide. Meanwhile, conservatives
in Chile and abroad continued to denounce the book, labelling it an
obscure Marxist diatribe, an indecent assault on wholesome Disney fare.
Following the military coup in Chile in September 1973, *How to Read
Donald Duck*, like many other "Marxist tracts," was publicly burned in
Chile by supporters of the newly installed Pinochet dictatorship.

II

Nowhere in *How to Read Donald Duck* do Dorfman and Mattelart seriously
consider the question of what makes the Disney comic, and the duck
comics in particular, so popular. We are not even apprised in the text of
the magnitude of that popularity in Chile and in Latin America as a
whole, although the authors do tell us that Disney comic strips, translated
into more than thirty languages, appear in some five thousand newspapers world-wide. Only in the translator's introduction to the 1975
English-language edition do we learn that Chilean editions of the Disney

comics, which also serve Peru, Paraguay, and Argentina (and, one sup-
poses, Uruguay as well), sold 800,000 copies of four magazine titles per
month "in a recent year" (p. 15). At that time, there were three other
regional Latin American editions, a Mexican, a Colombian, and a
Brazilian, the last of which was selling over two million copies of five
Disney magazines per month.

These are very high numbers given the degree of poverty in some of
these countries and the size of their populations at the start of the 1970s
when Chile had about 10 million people, Peru some 13 million, Paraguay
more than 2 million, Argentina about 24 million, and Brazil more than
95 million. The degree to which Disney comics penetrated the US market, however, appears to have been much greater, although the numbers
available make systematic comparison impossible. At the apogee of the
Disney comic book's domestic popularity in the early 1950s, a *single* number of an Uncle Scrooge comic book could sell more than 3 million
copies within the United States. At that time the total population of the
United States was about 151 million.

On just three occasions do Dorfman and Mattelart touch upon the
popularity of the Disney comic. In each case the context of their discussion reveals a great deal about the way they think about the question of
popularity. Near the beginning of the book they speculate on the appeal
of comic-book animals to children, but they focus on the way Disney
allegedly uses that appeal to capture the attention of his young readers
and enclose them in his manipulative world (pp. 41–2).

At another point they claim in passing that while the virtuous and disinterested Mickey Mouse is the Disney character who has been most
successful in the United States and Europe, Donald Duck is more popular in Latin America. "We Latin Americans," as they put it, "tend to
identify more readily with the imperfect Donald, [who is] at the mercy of
fate or a superior authority, than with Mickey, the boss in this world, and
Disney's personal undercover agent" (p. 91). (In fact, as we shall see
below, this assertion is misleading; beginning in the early 1940s Donald
Duck films and comic books became far more popular in the United
States than those of Mickey Mouse.)

The other reference to popularity comes at the end of the book, at the
point when the authors are trying to establish the threat posed to Chile
by the Disney comic. " Why," they ask, do these comics "exert such influence and acquire such popularity in the underdeveloped countries?"
Their answer merits close attention.

The primary reason is that [Disney's] products, necessitated and facilitated by
a huge industrial capitalist empire, are imported together with so many other

consumer objects into the dependent country, which is dependent precisely because it *depends* on commodities arising economically and intellectually in the power center's totally alien (foreign) conditions.

"[W]e send copper," they go on, "and they send machines to extract copper, and, of course, Coca Cola. . . . Behind the Coca Cola stands a whole structure of expectations and models of behavior" (p. 97). "[O]ur intellectuals" have reacted to this cultural dependence using "alien forms" to express in "warped, but very often revealing and accurate ways" the reality of their situation. In contrast, the "great majority" of people "have passively to accept" the cultural dependence that infuses their daily lives (p. 98). In other words, Disney comics are "popular" in Chile and the rest of the underdeveloped world not because of any special merit or attractiveness of their own, but because they are part and parcel of a material and cultural complex uncritically imported from the developed world.

As these examples indicate, Dorfman and Mattelart are not really interested in what makes Disney popular in Chile or in the rest of Latin America. They do not frame the problem in those terms. The creators of popular culture, Dorfman and Mattelart imply, use their enormous capital resources and their control over channels of commercial distribution to place their technologically sophisticated cultural products before the "masses." In their view, Chilean consumers, especially those who are not intellectuals, do not choose the cultural products they import from the United States and other parts of the developed world. Passive recipients of these cultural forms, they are manipulated by a structure of dependency that serves the ideological and material interests of the Chilean bourgeoisie and the foreign capitalists allied with them.

According to Dorfman and Mattelart, then, Chilean readers of the Disney comic are exploited and mystified in a double sense, both as workers and as Third Worlders. As workers they are beguiled by the fraudulent bourgeois vision of social reality projected through these comics. As Third Worlders they internalize the self-denigrating notion that they are backward because they lack the modern values and the white skin of First Worlders.

Although Dorfman and Mattelart do not do so explicitly, their argument can be readily extended and applied to consumers of the Disney comic outside Chile, including those in the United States itself. If Donald is the "bastard representative of all workers," then the bourgeois dream that readers are forced to consume affects all workers, including those in the homeland of the Disney comic. Ironically, however, their analysis seems to illuminate the history of US workers better than it does that of the Chilean workers it takes as its primary concern.

Dorfman and Mattelart seem to forget, or at least fail to acknowledge, that the dual exploitation to which the Chilean working class was subjected fostered not relative passivity but revolutionary consciousness and potential. Historically, as suggested in chapter 3, it was in the sectors of the Chilean economy most dominated by foreign and US capital, nitrate and copper export production in particular, that powerful organizations of workers emerged to challenge the interests of foreign capitalists and the capitalist system itself. Efforts by these workers to improve and better control their lives could be understood—by themselves, and by Chileans in other walks of life as well—as a patriotic struggle to liberate the nation from foreign capitalist oppression. Class and national perceptions of exploitation coincided in Chile, and they fostered the development of a class-conscious, anti-imperialist labor movement that became a powerful political and cultural force in the nation. Contrary to what Dorfman and Mattelart say, it was precisely *because* Chile exported copper that many Chileans came to Marxist consciousness.

In the United States, in contrast, as suggested in chapter 2, workers' consciousness of their exploitation as a class was undermined by the assumption (projected through the Disney comic and in a thousand other ways) that, like their bosses, they were culturally and racially superior to the darker, underdeveloped foreigners of the colonial world. Exploited as workers, they participated as "Americans" in the life, in the "way of life," of an imperialist capitalist power. Unlike that of their Chilean counterparts, their struggle seemed to have nothing to do with the liberation of the nation. It appeared instead to many as a subversive, "unAmerican" threat to the glory of the nation. Thinking about the struggles of US workers in this way helps us to understand the relative ideological weakness of a labor movement that, over time, came to assume as its own the pro-capitalist, pro-imperialist stance of the nation as a whole.

But the class dynamics of the racial and cultural assumptions imbedded in the Disney comic help us to understand much more than the different trajectories of the US and Chilean (and Latin American) labor movements. They also help us to explain the relative lack of consciousness of class among US creators, readers, and critics of the Disney comic. In a word, they help us to understand how it is that the United States sent Latin America Donald Duck, and got back, in return, *How to Read Donald Duck*.

Dorfman and Mattelart do not acknowledge a debt to Chilean workers in their book. Yet ironically their own ability to "see" class and racial oppression in the Disney comic necessarily reflects the long cultural struggle of Chilean workers that culminated in the Allende regime.

Understanding by many Chilean workers of their class position in Chile's capitalist society, and of Chile's dependent position in a hierarchy of capitalist nations, created the political conditions that made the very writing of *How to Read Donald Duck* possible. Yet the working people responsible for bringing the revolutionary Chilean regime to power are cast by Dorfman and Mattelart in the role of passive, unquestioning, "masses"—childlike consumers of a product that reinforces their own exploitation and mystification.

This is why the issue of the popular is so important to studies of so-called "mass" culture. And it is why studies of popular culture, in turn, can help us think about democratic politics in the world today. Because Dorfman and Mattelart ignore the popular dimensions of Disney's appeal, they miss the democratic content and implications of his comics.

III

Demonstrating the validity of these assertions will not be easy. Nor can such an exercise be conclusive. Texts, as noted earlier, are subject to a range of interpretations. And it may be that the more "open" they are to multiple meanings, the more intriguing and popular they become—if only because more individuals and groups of people, in the aggregate, find significant (albeit different) meanings in them. Moreover, it is one thing to interpret a text in a logical or theoretically consistent way and illustrate one's argument through persuasive textual evidence. (That is what, for the most part, Dorfman and Mattelart succeed in doing in their book.) It is quite another to demonstrate that others, or a majority of people, "read" the text in that way.

Works of popular culture, like all human cultural artifacts (literary "classics" for example), are subject to manifold—and often conflicting—interpretations. But very few studies of culture, popular or otherwise, move from interpreting the "text" to trying to gauge or measure what people actually "see" in it, or remember from it. Precious little evidence exists on the question of what people take away from the world of Disney. But by analyzing what we know about the creators of the Disney ducks, by examining aspects of the content of these comics during their golden era in the United States, and by focusing our attention on what might have made the ducks so popular we can rethink Dorfman and Mattelart's interpretation in important, and, I will argue, democratic ways.

The argument that follows is based on a reading of Donald Duck cartoons that appeared in the flagship of Disney comics, *Walt Disney's Comics and Stories*, during the era when the comic book, and the Disney comic book in particular, reached its apogee in the United States, the period from roughly 1943 to 1953. This period, as we shall see in more detail in chapter 5, is of pivotal importance in the history of US labor and in the history of the United States and Latin America as a whole. It frames the era when US industrialists and an organized labor movement grown strong during more than a decade of depression and war were forced to compromise on the fundamental issues that historically had divided them. This compromise, mediated and enforced by the government, proved to be the linchpin in a new set of social arrangements (a new structure of accumulation, to employ Gordon, Eduards, and Reich's term, discussed in chapter 2) which facilitated the extraordinary economic growth of the United States and the expansion of US economic interests around the globe in the postwar era. The domestic compromise with labor, like the world-wide US economic expansion that followed, was predicated on an ideology of anti-Communism and a politics of confrontation with the Soviet Union.

These Cold War issues, which largely defined world politics until our own time, are reflected only obliquely in the formally "apolitical" Disney comic. Nevertheless, the history of the Disney Corporation and that of its comic books in particular closely parallels these postwar ideological and economic trends. Labor relations at Disney illustrate the role of anti-Communism in weakening the power of US labor, while the global expansion of Disney's interests prefigures the rise of the US-based multinational manufacturing corporation in the postwar era. And although outright political positions are rare in the Disney comic books, the basic cultural assumptions imbedded in them, as Dorfman and Mattelart's critique has already suggested, rationalized and reinforced the expansion of US capitalism. In fact, as we shall see at the end of this chapter, the cultural assumptions of the Disney comic are the same ones enshrined in formal social science theory and US policy in the decades after World War II.

All of the Donald Duck comics in the ten-year sample I reviewed (110 stories in all) were written and illustrated by one man, Carl Barks. Barks developed the animated Donald Duck of the Disney film of the 1930s into the personality we recognize today. He had a hand in creating Donald's nephews, who became, after 1943, Donald's main companions and antagonists. And he created, in 1947, Uncle Scrooge, a character whose popularity came to rival that of Donald Duck himself.

By the late 1940s Barks was recognized by his employers, his cartoonist colleagues at Disney, and his US readers (who "voted" by spending their dimes at comic stands around the nation) as one of the "best" in the business. These early indicators of his popularity and mastery of the genre have subsequently been echoed by US critics and commentators on the comic arts, and confirmed in the sales of reprints of his comics. Readers abroad seem to have agreed with these assessments. By 1954, a single magazine, *Walt Disney's Comics and Stories* (to which Barks was contributing all the Donald Duck and Uncle Scrooge stories), was selling 30 million copies a month worldwide.

Despite the popularity of his work, Barks himself remained in obscurity throughout most of his career. Under the terms of his contract, he relinquished all rights over his artistic production. His publishers did not forward him most of the fan mail directed to him, although they used occasional complaints from readers to limit his creativity. Only in the early 1960s, near the end of his career, did some of his most dedicated fans manage to establish contact with him. And only after the death of Walt Disney, and Barks's retirement in 1966, did the Disney Corporation elevate him from obscurity and publicly acknowledge his artistry and commercial success.

In recent years publishers licensed by Disney have reprinted Barks's work in lavish multi-volume editions. Those collections are now out of print, and like Barks's original comics, they have become very expensive collector's items. Currently, Gladstone Press, under contract from Disney, is publishing a paperback edition of Barks's comics that appeared in *Walt Disney's Comics and Stories* between 1943 and 1966. That collection, *The Carl Barks Library of Walt Disney's Comics and Stories* (Prescott, AZ, 1992–96), is comprised of fifty-one volumes (references below, preceded by the abbreviation *CBL*, are to these undated, unpaginated volumes). The collection reproduces, along with Barks's comics, some of his correspondence and portions of interviews done with him. The most detailed information on the man and his work, however, appears in a study by one of his most dedicated and knowledgeable fans, Michael Barrier's *Carl Barks and the Art of the Comic Book*. Thanks to these sources, aspects of Barks's life and career with the Disney ducks have now become public knowledge. Imbedded in this information are clues to a democratic reading of his comics and an explanation of their extraordinary popularity.

Carl Barks was born in 1901 on a ranch near the little town of Merrill, Oregon, a couple of miles north of the California border. His father, a farmhand and sometime blacksmith, acquired the ranch as a homestead in the late nineteenth century, cleared the land, and eventually prospered raising wheat. By the time Barks was born, his father had bought out some of his neighbors and established a feed lot at the railhead in nearby Midland, Oregon. Barks helped his father on the ranch and the feed lot, and came to know the cowboys who herded cattle in from eastern Oregon and bunked at his father's place. They were tough fellows,

Barks recalled, with names like Skeeter Robbins and Windneck Mitchell. Their talk made a big impression on him, especially its profanity.

Barks managed to finish eight years of schooling before he began to earn his living as a wage worker. During World War I, he recalled, he made "fantastic wages" as a farmhand, and with the money he saved he left the ranch for San Francisco to try his luck as a cartoonist. He had long been fascinated by cartoons and for a short time had taken correspondence lessons in drawing. He was unable to sell his cartoons to newspaper publishers in San Francisco, however, and worked for a year and a half in a small printshop in the city before returning to Oregon. There he married in 1923 and took a job as a logger. Some time later he and his wife returned to California to search for work in the oilfields. He didn't like the "looks of the oilfields," he later said, and ended up working for the Pacific Fruit Company in a railroad repair shop near Sacramento. There he labored for more than six years. "I worked in the heavy steel section," Barks remembered, "which mostly repaired the steel underframes and wheel 'trucks.'"

> I started out just swinging a sledge hammer, and common labor, and got put on to heating rivets on a riveting gang, and that was piece work. I was on that for five and a half years or so. God, was I getting sick of that. (Barrier, p. 8)

In 1929 he quit that job and returned to the logging camps of his native Oregon. He eventually got taken on at a box factory, but soon lost his job as the Depression deepened. At about this time he and his wife filed for divorce, a move biographer Barrier attributes to her lack of interest in his cartooning career, which by then was consuming virtually all his free time.

The coming of the Depression coincided with a major turning point in Barks's life. From 1930 on he would earn his livelihood as a cartoonist. He had already begun to sell his art to the *Eye-Opener*, a risqué humor magazine in Minneapolis, and in 1930 he was offered the position of head cartoonist on its small staff. Five years later he applied to the Disney studio in Burbank, California, and was offered a provisional position in the animation unit.

Barks began at Disney doing "fill-in" animation for Donald Duck films. He did well at his job, and was promoted to storyman within a short time. But he was never really happy in the medium of film animation. He chafed under the limitations of an operation over which he had little artistic control. His dissatisfaction came to a head during 1942 as he watched the Disney studio being turned into a war plant to produce films for the military. "I couldn't see myself getting tied up with that sort of thing," he later said.

I had seen one generation of young men marched off to war—World War I—
and I was stupid enough that I wanted to get into it, but I was just a little too
young. And then here comes this Second World War, and I had learned my lesson in the meantime. When I saw how little we had accomplished with World
War I, I thought, why in the devil kill off another whole generation of young
men to accomplish the same result. (Barrier, p. 28)

In November 1942 Barks quit his job at Disney and moved with his second wife to San Jacinto, a small town east of Los Angeles, where they set
up a chicken farm.

It was not long after Barks left the Disney studios, however, that he got
taken on at Western Publishers, a firm that produced comics under contract with Disney. There, in short order, he came into his own as the
principal creator of Donald Duck comic books.

Barks never made much money doing his duck comics, but he enjoyed
the freedom of his new job. He gradually withdrew from frequent contact
with his employers, preferring to work at home in San Jacinto and deal
with them through the mail. Many of his colleagues either wrote or illustrated comics, but Barks, although he often illustrated other people's
scripts to make extra money, preferred to create and execute every aspect
of his stories. He quickly established a reputation for turning out a finished product his editors and colleagues could only admire. He was paid
on a piece-rate basis, and although he faced deadlines for completion of
his stories, he could work at his own pace to meet them.

Barks was rarely asked by his editors at Western to make changes in his
comics, at least during the 1940s. By the 1950s, however, he had to contend with what Barrier calls a "growing thicket of taboos." Domestic critics
charged that the comic-book industry contributed to a variety of social
ills, including violence and juvenile delinquency. And although Disney
comics were considered "clean" and avoided most of this criticism, Barks
himself later acknowledged that he modified fundamental aspects of his
Donald Duck and Scrooge comics in the 1950s in response to reactions by
readers and the criticism of his editors.

For the most part, according to Barrier, Barks experienced censorship
"of the self-imposed variety" during this period (p. 81). Barrier notes, for
example, that the crude racial caricatures that appeared in Barks's comics
in the 1940s could never have gotten by his editors by the mid-1950s.
Barrier believes that the quality of US comic books in general, and
Barks's comics in particular, declined in the 1950s and 1960s. In his view,
the innovative and creative quality of the comic arts in the freewheeling
1940s was stifled by the increased bureaucratic control of editors in later
years (p. 82). Barks, for one, shared Barrier's evaluation of the declining
quality of his art. He confided to a correspondent in early 1962 that he

had recently spent an evening reading the twelve monthly issues of *Walt Disney's Comics and Stories* for 1952 and comparing them to his current production. "The difference is alarming," he wrote. "I went to bed in a cold sweat" (*CBL*, Volume 13).

What is certain is that the extraordinary popularity of Barks's comics declined as the 1950s wore on. By the early 1960s, an installment of *Walt Disney's Comics and Stories* was selling only a million copies domestically, whereas a decade earlier sales of more than three million were the rule. (In 1954 the Disney magazine ranked third in national circulation, behind only *Life* and the *Saturday Evening Post*.) By 1966, Barks noted in a letter to a fan, Scrooge installments were selling 350,000 copies, whereas at one time, in the early 1950s, they sold ten times that number.

Some of this decline may have been a result of increased competition from other comics and increased television viewing by Disney comic-book readers. Animated cartoons and Disney programming were among the mainstays of that industry, whose explosive growth during the 1950s made it the most popular of all the US entertainment media. Barks himself once attributed the decline to a lack of "pizzaz" in his more recent comics. By that he meant, at least on that occasion, that they lacked some of the violent action, the ingenious slapstick "sight gags," of his earlier work (*CBL*, Volume 15). But some of the decline must also have reflected the changes he made in Donald Duck plots and the character of Scrooge, which stripped his comics of much of what can properly be termed their democratic content.

Barks himself understood that the popularity of Donald Duck comics was related in part to plots that pitted Donald and his nephews against each other. When his editors endorsed a complaint about such stories from the mother of one of his young readers in 1956, Barks fired back a sarcastic response that indicates what he thought made Donald Duck popular and at the same time reveals his resignation before the authority of his employers. He began by declaring that he would avoid any more stories using "conflict or rivalry between Don and the kids." He said he had bought a number of Tom and Jerry, Porky Pig, and Chester Chipmunk comics and that he would "confine plots and gags to 'switches'" on the material he found in those "*safe* family journals." He recalled, however, that when he worked in the Disney duck unit

the basic theme in a great number of the Donald Duck shorts was rivalry between the kids and Donald. Certainly the main body of the public didn't object to this theme, for during those years, Donald and his nephews overtook and passed Mickey Mouse and his nephews in box office popularity.

Barks went on to stress that he had liberally used rivalry plots in his early years doing Donald Duck comics and noted that "the magazine didn't seem to go broke." (In fact, by the mid-1940s sales were climbing by as much as 100,000 copies a month.)

> Now comes a neurotic female with a cramped, fault-finding mind and a cry-baby son, and proves all of those millions (well, dozens, at least) of boys and girls who have bought and read Disney comics over the years were and are sadists, masochists, murderers, lechers and *worse!* I agree with her.
> From now on you will see changed stories coming from this former breeding place of vice.

In a postscript Barks added: "All of this letter except the first paragraph is so much jousting with windmills." Barrier, who cites the letter, affirms that Barks did step away from stories in which Donald and the nephews were in open conflict. He concludes that, as a result, Barks's stories "took another step down" (p. 82).

Giving up the rivalry and conflict plots between Donald and his nephews seems to have compromised the popular appeal of Barks's comics. These plots—and a variation on them, in which the nephews show their superiority to Donald by "saving" or rescuing him—all embody the mechanism Dorfman and Mattelart call "inversion." That is, the nephews oppose Donald, or help him, in the name of "adult" values. Either way, these values are vindicated in the end. Dorfman and Mattelart curiously elide the question of what these values are, however. In fact, they include honesty, integrity, courage, kindness, boldness, inventive-ness, persistence, generosity, resourcefulness, loyalty, common sense, valor, and, occasionally, caution in the face of overwhelming odds. These are admirable values, viewed from any angle. Are they not, for example, precisely the ones any good Marxist would like to see embodied in the organized working class? In the hands of Huey, Dewey, and Louie, more-over, these values are often turned to the cause of *rebellion against authority*. The nephews struggle constantly against the authority of their stronger uncle. Their combativeness persists even in the face of Donald's continual threats to use physical coercion (spankings, in plain English) to bring them into line.

Barks used this kind of plot often, and in fact allowed the nephews to become more and more rebellious as the 1940s wore on. He pushed the limits of their rebellion when he treated the theme of truancy. When the kids played hookey from school their challenge to authority overflowed the bounds of the private sphere of the family into the public arena. Barks felt he had to resolve this kind of rebelliousness by ultimately allow-ing Donald, disguised as a truant officer, to capture and punish them. "I would have used the theme oftener," he confessed, "if it weren't for the fact that the kids had to be shown as lawbreakers" (*CBL*, Volume 14).

As often happens with Barks, however, there is a final, ironic twist to the story of his use of the "inversion" technique in his rivalry plots. For he often subverted his own carefully crafted inversions, undermining the very adult values his stories showed the nephews internalizing.

A fine example is "Days at the Lazy K," originally published in August 1945 (*CBL*, Volume 6). The story begins when Donald and his nephews leave the dude ranch they are visiting to catch a movie in town. The film they watch depicts a boy taming a wild horse "by *kindness* alone." The kids are impressed. "The colt has learned to love him," they exclaim in unison. Leaving the theater, Donald announces with typical bluster that he could tame a horse like that even faster than the boy in the movie. "You!" the kids respond. "That boy was always *patient!* You'd have *blown up* the first time the colt disobeyed you!" Donald sets out to make good his boast. He gets a cowboy to capture him a wild pony from a herd up in the mountains. "I'll give him every chance to *express* himself," Donald resolves. But his best efforts to win the colt's friendship meet with kicks, bites, and worse. At several points Donald loses his temper and the kids have to step in, reminding him to be patient. After another series of increasingly violent rebuffs by the colt (and ever more angry threats by Donald to sell him for glue), Donald tries to hypnotize him. Instead, the colt hypnotizes Donald, making him believe he's a wild horse, and causing him to almost trample the nephews.

At that point, the kids tie Donald up ("If you're going to *act* like a horse, we'll *treat* you like a horse") and proceed to deal with the colt ("[H]is meanness is too deep down to feel a whipping! Only *one thing* will *touch* his kind of cussedness . . . *CASTOR OIL!*"). They tie up the colt and force-feed him the oil—not once, but twice. Only as they threaten to use it on him a third time does the colt, sweating blood, give in. "He has *reformed*," they affirm. "Gee! He's a *swell* little guy now." They run to tell Donald, hoping he'll let them keep the colt. Once untied, however, Donald ridicules the idea that the colt has reformed and reaffirms his decision to sell him to the glue works "first thing in the morning." That night, the nephews hear the whinnies of the colt and his mother, who has come down from the hills to search for him. They resolve to set the colt free ("He will *love* us for it!"). They open the gate and the colt gallops toward his mother, then stops and looks back at the nephews. "He knows he *owes* us something!" they exclaim. The colt runs back toward the nephews. "He's coming back to *pay* us his *thanks!*" they conclude. Instead, the colt kicks the three of them so hard they sail into a water trough. "Remind me in the morning," says one, "that we owe Unca' Donald three bottles of *glue!*"

How are we to interpret a story like this? As a spoof on the inevitable hypocrisy of the "enlightened" child-rearing habits of modern parents? As a vindication of the use of old-fashioned, patriarchal physical restraint and corporal punishment to tame the rebelliousness of the young? The old fashioned means (castor oil) of purging rebelliousness goes so "deep" that any reader who has ever had to ingest that ghastly substance instinctively flinches at the prospect. But is the other, modern method really any better? Does its professed means (love) justify the end (domination)?

This funny, and seemingly simple, short story contains much more than initially meets the eye. It is a marvelously compressed, complex, and critical exploration of the perverse and hypocritical means through which social hierarchies are enforced. It even includes a swipe at the role of the mass media (the movie about the boy and the pony that precipitates the action) in this process. I read the story as a celebration of resistance to domination.

This example of Barks's subversion of generally accepted social hierarchies is by no means an isolated case. His comics frequently call into question accepted social norms and patterns of behavior. He often presents social stereotypes only to undercut them. This technique extends even to the realm of patriarchy, in ways that even Barks's most devoted fans and critics (not to mention Dorfman and Mattelart) fail to appreciate.

Barks would seem an unlikely critic of sexist values. His cartoons for the *Eye-Opener* included lots of sexual innuendo and often depicted curvy, scantily clad women. For a time in the late 1940s he aspired to launch a comic strip of his own and fulfill his aspiration to draw human figures (mainly sexy women, judging from his trial sketches) and be free of the constraints of the ducks and Disney. The women in his duck comics seem to be of two types, the coy coquette represented by Daisy, or the ugly, fat, old "battleaxes" that were standard fare in US comic books of the era.

Nevertheless, perhaps in part because he helped raise two daughters, Barks could challenge traditional gender stereotypes. "Kite Weather" (March 1944; *CBL*, Volume 3), for example, subverts the myth of female physical and technical incompetence by showing that girls (albeit with heavy lisps) can fly kites better than the nephews (although Donald, the adult male, finally wins this children's contest disguised as a girl). He could spoof the ideal of chivalry, through which the females of Duckburg internalize their traditional roles as women, and simultaneously ridicule Donald and his cousin Gladstone for their incessant, boorish, male competitiveness and inability to act in polite, civilized, and cooperative ways ("Knightly Rivals," May 1951; *CBL*, Volume 18). And he could satirize Donald's anxiety over women and his fear of appearing to be feminine ("Donald Duck's Worst Nightmare," February 1949; *CBL*, Volume 14).

The other major change Barks made in his comics in the 1950s concerns the character of Scrooge, the multibillionaire uncle of Donald, "the richest man in the world." Scrooge was Barks's most original contribution to the world of Disney and by far his most popular and controversial one. Created and developed by Barks at the height of his powers, roughly the period 1947 to 1953, Scrooge has confused and confounded his critics—fans of Barks and detractors of Disney, liberals and Marxists alike. Barks himself seems at times to be in two (or more) minds about him, alternatively casting him as the ultimate capitalist exploiter (as in "Billions to Sneeze At," January 1951; *CBL*, Volume 17) and calling him "the greatest enemy capitalism ever had" (in an interview quoted more extensively below).

Part of the problem for the interpreters is that Scrooge changed over time. A trading card featuring Scrooge distributed with Volume 15 of the *Carl Barks Library* in 1992 described the change this way.

> Barks created Scrooge in 1947, but it was two years before McDuck acquired his trademark top hat. Originally a mean-spirited miser, he became sympathetic after receiving his own comic [in 1953], Barks giving him a background that made his frugality seem heroic.

This description, which encapsulates the official story of the Disney Corporation on the matter, confuses the essence of the change in Scrooge even as it seems to explain it. Barks's early Scrooge was more than a "mean-spirited miser." In the "Billions to Sneeze At" story cited above, for example, Scrooge is revealed as a capitalist who accumulates wealth through foreclosures. "Let's see!" he muses as he scrutinizes a massive ledger in his office, "How many mortgages are due today?" Among his victims that day is a poor working-class woman in tattered clothing who earns her living as a laundress. Unable to pay the last nickel on the installment loan for her washing machine, the woman pleads with Scrooge to give her until the next day to make the payment. "It's due *today*," says Scrooge, and instructs Donald (who is working for Scrooge to avoid foreclosure on a loan of his own) to "take the machine away." (Fortunately, a nickel falls out of the washing machine as Donald is reluctantly pushing it away; Donald gives it to the woman, and her washing machine is saved.)

In these early years Barks sometimes depicts Scrooge as the owner of the means of production. His early Scrooge could also threaten to use his wealth to bend politics and the judicial system to his liking. In the first issue of Disney's *Christmas Parade*, for example, Scrooge tells a judge about to throw the book at him: "Be careful, bub! I'm Scrooge McDuck and, if I don't like what you say, I'll buy this *whole* city and *fire* you" (the scene is reproduced in Barrier, p. 46).

It is true, however, that in subsequent years, Barks fabricated a more "heroic" explanation for Scrooge's phenomenal wealth. We are told that Scrooge originally struck it rich in the Klondike gold rush. And we learn that he builds his wealth through entrepreneurial foresight and legendary frugality.

It is this later Scrooge who is the subject of Dorfman and Mattelart's analysis, which dismisses the idea that Scrooge could be "a great social satire on the rich." They view Scrooge's wealth as a "decoy" (p. 78) designed to lead critics astray. They focus not on Scrooge's urge to accumulate, but on what they call his "fundamental" trait, his "solitude." "Outside his tyrannical relationship with his nephews and grand nephews, he has no one else." His "money cannot buy him power." "Stripped of its power to acquire productive forces, money is unable to defend itself or resolve any problem whatsoever." This is why Scrooge is "vulnerable," they assert, and his vulnerability creates "an aura of compassion" for him (p. 78).

Dorfman and Mattelart believe that feeling compassion toward Scrooge prepares the reader to assimilate the central myths of capitalism. Scrooge exemplifies the Horatio Alger rags-to-riches myth that deludes workers about the possibility for advancement in the system. And he dramatizes the myth that capitalists earn and conserve their wealth through entrepreneurship and frugality. Since Scrooge never turns his money to production, he cannot be identified as the source of social exploitation. Like Donald, the bogus worker, Scrooge is a capitalist without substance. His solitude and the sterility of his money make him the object of our compassion not the cause of our misery.

Dorfman and Mattelart are not alone in interpreting the Scrooge who had emerged by the 1960s as a vehicle for the celebration of capitalism and the capitalist entrepreneur. In 1961 students in the Business School at Harvard University adopted Scrooge as their mascot and requested a picture of their hero from the comic's publisher. Informed of their request, Barks was happy to oblige. He drew them a sketch of Scrooge with a motto in Latin that said, "Fortune Favors the Bold." In his covering letter he said that he thought the motto was "appropriate to many of Scrooge's profitable adventures . . . [and to those of] today's young capitalists in battling for profits in an economy overrun by clamoring freeloaders" (*CBL*, Volume 8).

But other Barks comments on Scrooge complicate this simple, procapitalist interpretation. In a 1975 interview Barks was asked if he agreed with readers who accused Scrooge of being "the arch-capitalist." No, he responded, he is a complete enemy of the capitalist system; he would destroy it in one year's time. The faster money is spent, the more prosperity everyone has. But Scrooge would freeze onto all the stuff that keeps capitalism going. He would never spend anything, so everybody would progressively grow poorer as he accumulated more of their money, and in time nobody would have any money but him. That would be the end of capitalism. (*CBL*, Volume 3)

The most revealing thing Barks ever said about Scrooge, however, came in response to a pointed critique of his work made by Michael Barrier. In a letter to Barks, dated February 11, 1966, Barrier complained about the change he perceived in Scrooge. "Uncle Scrooge isn't the wonderfully greedy, egotistical old bastard he used to be; he's younger, certainly, and more the stock adventure hero." Barks seems to have wanted to avoid the issue and initially provided only a vague, slightly defensive response in a postscript to a letter to Barrier of March 27, 1966.

P.S. About my more recent Scrooge stories. I know he's gotten younger or something, but in the desperate grind of keeping up a flow of stories year after year the old thinker gets to slipping its gears. Besides, I get hedged in by taboos and the ever-diminishing supply of interesting locales and plot gimmicks.

But the issue seems to have nagged at Barks and in a letter to Barrier dated June 9, 1966 he was more direct and forthright, if somewhat cryptic:

Mellowing of Uncle Scrooge's personality came about gradually, but was partly deliberate. Some fan letters that I saw about that time [1949] made me feel that capitalists were not too well loved. (*CBL*, Volume 15)

With these words Barks acknowledged that after 1949 he deliberately sought to close off anti-capitalist readings of Scrooge by his fans. Whether he was pressured by his employers to effect the change remains unresolved in Barks's statement. Pressured or not, as the years went by, he made Scrooge into a character his corporate bosses could read as "sympathetic" and "heroic." During those same years, as we have seen, Scrooge's popularity fell off dramatically.

All this is not to argue that Barks was somehow anti-capitalist when he created and first developed Scrooge. Nor is it to contend that he had anything like the Marxist consciousness of class that Dorfman and Mattelart would like to see in authors of comics aimed at a mass public. No. All the evidence from Barks's published letters and interviews, which date from the early 1960s on, reveal him to be a very conservative man who believed that, despite its faults, the US political and economic system was the best alternative available. And after he retired from doing the duck comics he continued to resist anti-capitalist interpretations of Scrooge. In 1968, for example, he wrote an interviewer who was interested in the social content of his comics that he expected to approve his article before it was published. The piece was to appear in a fledgling national magazine called *Cheetah*. "*Cheetah* doesn't *seem* to be advocating the violent overthrow of Democracy (and money bins)," wrote Barks, "so I'm assuming the editor won't insist on limning Uncle Scrooge in hateful adjectives" (*CBL*, Volume 22).

Nor is there any evidence that Barks was much more radical, in a formal ideological or political sense, when he was younger. He apparently was a Disney loyalist, or at least remained on the sidelines, during the bitter strike that pitted a union of Disney animators against their boss in 1941. (That strike ended in bitter recriminations and charges by Disney, then a privileged secret informer for the FBI, that the union leaders were Communist sympathizers.) And on the one occasion in his published correspondence when Barks comments on unions and strikers (a reference to a printers' strike at the *Cleveland Press* in 1962–63) he had negative things to say about their demands (*CBL*, Volume 13).

That said, however, it is no less true that meditations on the nature of work and of capital, and of the relationship between the two, suffuse the comics of Carl Barks. His two primary characters, Donald (inherited from Disney) and Scrooge (his own invention) embody the two fundamental classes in capitalist society. Contention between Donald (the worker) and Scrooge (capitalist and financier) is the central feature of the relationship between them.

Barks always insisted that the reason for the popularity of his comics was their fidelity to the real problems people have in everyday life. He thought of the ducks as humans with complex personalities, and he tried to show them, he said, solving serious problems by funny means. He wanted them to "meet their problems with the everyday weapons that we have in our lives" (*CBL*, Volume 3). He never could understand, he said, the appeal of superheroes.

Barks's treatment of Donald as worker and Scrooge as capitalist, however, is always ambivalent and ambiguous. It never fully conforms to, or is fully consistent with, either standard Marxist or liberal expectations about the values and behavior of members of the working and capitalist classes. Donald's fundamental trait is hatred of work. Whether he hates it because he is lazy and incompetent (the typical capitalist perception) or because his work is boring, he has no control over it, and the product of his labor goes to the boss (a Marxist reading), is a question always open to interpretation in Barks's comics. After 1953 Barks developed the issues of competence and control on the job in a series of stories his admirers call his "mastery" stories. In each of these, as Geoffrey Blum, the associate editor of the *Carl Barks Library* puts it, "Donald becomes exceptionally proficient at a particular job, until a crucial blunder or character flaw precipitates his ruin" (Volume 12). Even in these stories, however, Donald's fate is open to a range of interpretations.

Scrooge's fundamental trait is the desire to accumulate money. In doing so, does he embody the great virtue of capitalism, its capacity (unique in human history) to foster long-term economic growth and industrial transformation? Or does Scrooge's accumulation reveal capitalism's fundamental defect, the creation of social inequality and periodic crises when capitalists fear that workers have become too poor to buy enough for them to make a profit, and they refuse to invest in productive activities?

The fact that Scrooge accumulates money for its own sake, never spending a dime of it or engaging in productive investment, lends support to the Marxist interpretation that Scrooge embodies capitalism's fundamental flaw. Yet Barks's latter-day Scrooge is never shown accumulating wealth by appropriating it from workers. Instead, we are told, he "earned" it the "old-fashioned" entrepreneurial way. These aspects of Scrooge seem to support a pro-capitalist reading.

The ambiguity of reading Scrooge is compounded by Barks's celebrated symbols of his wealth—the famous money bins that grow in scale and exquisite detail as the early 1950s progress—and by Scrooge's extraordinary behavior in and around them. In "Billions to Sneeze At" (January 1951; *CBL*, Volume 17) Scrooge pilots a bulldozer to aerate the tons of coin and currency in his immense "Money Barn No. 68." In "A Financial Fable," (March 1951; *CBL*, Volume 18) Scrooge stores money in a crib of gargantuan proportions on a farm he owns. "Everybody thinks it's full of *corn*, so thieves never bother to look inside," he assures himself. Scrooge loves to cavort in his pools and barns and cribs of money. "I *love* the stuff!" he shouts as he dives into the *"three cubic acres"* of cash in his money corn crib. "I love to dive around in it like a porpoise! And burrow through it like a gopher! And toss it up and let it hit me on the head!"

Scrooge's bizarre behavior toward his money amounts to what can only be termed fetishism. Yet Scrooge himself, unlike Donald the worker, is clear that "money isn't worth *anything*! It's just a lot of paper and metal." Thus does Barks treat the subject that Marxists identify as the fundamental mechanism capitalists use to mystify workers about their exploitation.

All of these ambiguous themes are powerfully illustrated in "A Financial Fable," the 1951 comic cited above, which features Donald and his nephews as hired hands on a farm owned by Scrooge. In the course of the story a cyclone dips into Scrooge's immense money crib, sucks out all his cash, and eventually scatters the money into the hands of grateful workers (including Donald) "all over the country." Newly minted millionaires, Donald and all the other beneficiaries promptly quit work and set out "to see the world." Meanwhile, Scrooge is strangely unconcerned by the loss and redistribution of his billions. He tells Huey, Dewey, and Louie, who have remained loyally on the job, that he'll get it back if he tends to his "beans and pumpkins."

Scrooge knows what he is talking about. Donald finds out that with no one working, he is unable to get gas for his car, buy food in a restaurant, or even buy hiking boots to see the world on foot. "Hiking boots?" a dispirited fellow worker-millionaire tells Donald outside the closed shoe store. "Haw! Nobody even *makes* boots anymore." Soon Donald is back asking Scrooge for work. "Sure you can have your job back!" says Scrooge. "But if you want breakfast, the eggs are a million dollars apiece." Because work has not stopped on Scrooge's farm he has the only stock of food in the country. He has armed workers Huey, Dewey, and Louie with guns to protect his piles of eggs and wool, and is charging the multitude of people in line outside his gate astronomical prices for food ($4 billion for hams, $2 million for cabbages, $4 billion for an ounce of wool, and so on). In short order, he has re-accumulated his mountain of wealth.

Donald painfully learns in the course of the story the necessity of productive labor, whose joys and benefits the nephews cheerfully accept and commonsensically understand from the beginning. The opening pages show Donald grumbling about his work while the nephews happily shear sheep and gather eggs. "That boy [Donald] is too young to understand things," they observe. "If you're gonna wear warm wool jackets, you gotta *work* to get the wool . . . And if you're gonna eat poached eggs en casserole, you gotta *work* to get the eggs." Donald also learns the power of the market. Its iron laws of supply and demand determine his ability to put food on the table and finally force him back to work. Donald initially covets money so he won't have to labor. He ends up coveting work which is the source of all value.

But Donald never fully understands the role of Scrooge's money in all this, nor does he understand the enigma of Scrooge's attitude toward it. "You claim that money is *worthless*," he exclaims at the end of the story. "Yet you've cornered that whole mountain of it! How come?" "You wouldn't understand, nephew!" a smug and enigmatic Scrooge informs him, then dives once again into his money and begins to recite his porpoise and gopher refrain. Donald simply can't fathom his uncle's behavior. But he takes up his hoe and begins to work. "Disgusting!" he says in the last panel of the story, as he hoes his row and the sun sets behind him.

The story from which I have taken these highlights can be read as a basic introduction to classical liberal and Marxist economics. It validates the labor theory of value on which both systems of thought initially rested. It serves as a reminder of just how far modern liberal economics (the "science" taught in US universities today) has strayed from the commonsensical principle that all wealth derives from labor. In the story Barks also shows Scrooge as the owner of the means of production who rewards and disciplines his labor force with raises (for the industrious kids) and kicks in the rear (for a recalcitrant Donald). But already in this 1951 comic Scrooge is an owner-producer, who works alongside his nephews. Clearly, Scrooge's sale of the product of labor on his farm, the food and the other agricultural commodities for which he charges astronomical prices, allows him to re-accumulate wealth in the form of money. But why Scrooge worships money for its own sake is never clear to Donald (or to the reader). And Scrooge won't tell him (or us). Donald is disgusted by what he experiences and observes as a worker. But the only thing he knows (has learned) for sure in the story is that he must labor until sunset in order to survive.

Barks, of course, did not fancy himself an economist or social theorist, and it is unlikely that he consciously intended this story as more than an object lesson for the young in the virtue of work. In fact, he sometimes resisted the idea that he intended anything but fun in most of his stories. He felt uncomfortable with the literary and social critics who admired his comics and found complex philosophical meanings in them. On occasion he claimed that his comics were simply a form of escapist literature (*CBL*, Volume 13).

Yet Barks also insisted that his comics dealt with serious problems that people face in everyday life. And issues of work preoccupied him throughout his life, as we shall see in more detail below. It thus seems only natural that he would explore these concerns (turn them over in his mind) in his work as a symbolic artist and that his readers would do the same. Creating or reading comic books, like making or consuming other forms of popular entertainment (films or television, for example), is a process akin to dreaming, or better, daydreaming. It allows us to escape from our daily routines and entertain ourselves by engaging our fears and hopes in vicarious, safe, imaginative, and thus pleasurable or "fun" ways.

Barks's talent, like that of other popular artists, lay in his ability to create an aesthetically and technically pleasing product that appealed to large numbers of people because it dealt in meaningful, imaginary ways with issues and problems that concerned them. The subjects of authority and work held special meaning for the children and teenagers who formed the bulk of his audience. But Barks's understanding of those problems was necessarily that of an adult who had lived through childhood, practiced parenting, and, what most concerns us here, labored as a wage worker throughout his life.

Carl Barks's work experience began in childhood and spanned the whole range of productive endeavors. He worked in agriculture and in timber extraction (in what economists call the primary sector of the economy), in metal shops and other manufacturing industries (the secondary sector), and finally in the service (or tertiary) sector, producing popular art for the entertainment industry. We know the most about his experience with work, and his attitudes toward it, in the Disney organization, where he labored for more than thirty years before he retired in 1966. But the comic art he produced there reflected his experiences during his formative years and early manhood.

It is apparent from his published correspondence and interviews that Barks was acutely aware of his position and status as a wage worker in the Disney operation. This attitude comes across even though Barks was extremely cautious about what he said and wrote for "outsiders," fearful as he was of the possible repercussions his statements could have for his job. He refers to himself, nevertheless, as an anonymous "sharecropper on old Marse Disney's animal farm," and, urged by an interviewer, admits that he regrets that his best work appeared unsigned (*CBL*, Volume 6). He complains often about what he calls on one occasion his "pitifully" low wages (*CBL*, Volume 13). He reveals that when the idea came along that Donald Duck should have three nephews, he initially opposed it.

> I thought, "Oh my God! We're going to have all these little kids to draw and think up things for . . . ." But I was working for wages, so I had to go along with the idea. (*CBL*, Volume 3)

When Barks quit his job at Disney Studios in 1942 he apparently thought that being his own boss as a chicken farmer was better than doing a clean, white-collar job for military ends under Disney's direct control. He cherished his autonomy after he began to do the duck comics for Western, although he confessed that sometimes he would feel Disney's hand on his shoulder and become "tooth-chatteringly careful" (*CBL*, Volume 6). He also admitted that there were times when he felt like telling his publisher to "take their comic books and shove them you-know-where" (*CBL*, Volume 4). He worked hard at his new job, seven days a week (in "fits and starts"), and never took a vacation or traveled abroad (*CBL*, Volume 6). He was highly productive, but despite the low page-rates that determined his pay, he valued the quality and integrity of his work over its quantity. He criticized colleagues who "hack[ed] it out," padding their work and putting out material just "good enough to get a paycheck" (*CBL*, Volume 1). He attributed the success and popularity of his comics not to "unusual talent" on his part, but to sweat, patience, and "a large wastebasket"(Volume 8).

Barks's work experience suggests a different interpretation of Donald Duck as worker from the one advanced by Mattelart and Dorfman. *Nobody* likes to work when the boss, or the supervisor, or the way production is set up is the sole arbiter of how, and how fast, things should be done. It is hard for any of us to commit to work when we have no claim on the product of our labor. When Barks has Donald express his hatred of work, when he exaggerates his loss of control over his work or shows him messing up on the job, he dramatizes feelings and experiences shared by all of us who labor for wages.

In this interpretive light, the stock-in-trade treasure hunts of Donald and the other ducks in the comics of the 1960s analyzed by Dorfman and Mattelart speak to universal aspirations shared by working people in two ways. Treasure promises freedom from wage labor. And the search for it allows the ducks (usually at the expense of their primitive Third World hosts) to *control* their own actions as they ingeniously overcome the obstacles "fate" places in their way. Freedom from alienating, run-of-the-mill work helps explain how even Donald can become so extraordinarily competent, innovative, and productive during the search for gold.

These Third World escapades become frequent only from the mid-1950s on. They are virtually absent from Barks's production during the 1940s and early 1950s. (The only time Barks takes Donald abroad in the ten-year sample I reviewed happens in "The Tramp Steamer," a story published in February 1945; *CBL*, Volume 5; it concerns a trading voyage to Mexico, not a search for hidden treasure.) Their timing thus mirrors, as we shall see in chapter 5, the expansion of US-based manufacturing corporations into Latin America (and other parts of the world), a process that began in earnest a decade after the end of World War II.

Treasure hunts among the primitives in exotic climes provided Barks with an easy, formulaic solution to his artistic problem of turning out a never-ending stream of Donald Duck and Scrooge adventures. (Barks said he found inspiration in the pages of *National Geographic*, another immensely popular magazine which stepped up its coverage of Third World areas in these years and which often played on the theme of the encounter between traditional societies and modern ones.) But this solution also enabled him to avoid the delicate and sensitive issues of work and its relationship to wealth at home, which in the early 1950s he was confronting, however ambiguously and inconclusively, in powerful symbolic terms. Barks's artistic solution to his own repetitive and increasingly supervised tasks thus uncannily mirrors the strategies of US capitalists and organized labor during the same period. Forced into a major compromise with labor at home, US manufacturers sought to protect their profit margins through foreign expansion. Organized labor endorsed that strategy until it realized, some decades later, that expansionism involved more than broader foreign markets, and that it included wholesale transfer of manufacturing jobs abroad as well.

Barks's experience put him in touch with the deepest concerns and aspirations of working people. But he never identified with workers in a collective sense. He believed the problems facing workers could be solved through individual effort. Ultimately, he blamed himself for not achieving more in terms of material and psychological rewards for his labor. When Michael Barrier read him a passage of David Kunzel's draft introduction to the English-language edition of *How to Read Donald Duck* that emphasized the exploitative conditions of his work on the Disney comics, Barks (who apparently never read Dorfman and Mattelart's book) laughed out loud: "[T]hat's too true to be funny." But when Barrier asked him point-blank if he didn't blame his employers or the "economic system" for his failure to move beyond his long hours and poorly paid labor as a duck cartoonist and realize his aspiration to start a comic strip of his own, Barks responded this way:

> No, the economic system is such that a guy that has any ability can make something of that ability, and I just didn't have the ability, so I was where I was. I accepted that and that was it.(Barrier, p. 86)

Thus did the man whose tireless labor and mastery of comic book artistry helped earn the Disney Corporation untold millions come to terms with his fate as a worker.

Sensitive to the problems experienced by workers, and ambivalent toward the power of wealth, Barks never challenged the individualist values and property relations that legitimize capitalist organization of society. His personal politics thus mirrored the public politics of the majority of working people in all capitalist societies during this century. In every capitalist nation Marxist-inspired, anti-capitalist political parties have generally failed to attract the support of more than a fraction of the working population. Even Chile, where worker-supported Marxist political parties in control of roughly a third of the national electorate managed to win control of the presidency in 1970, is not an exception to this generalization.

But that does not mean that democratic visions of the meaning of work and capital are absent from Barks's comics. Contrary to what Dorfman and Mattelart say, it is the democratic side of Barks's Donald and the nephews, and the anti-capitalist side of Scrooge and the symbols of his wealth, that seem best to explain the extraordinary popular appeal of the early Disney duck comics. The point is not that Disney readers would have used these terms to explain their attraction to the Disney duck comics. But those terms encompass the subversive attitudes toward social hierarchy and authority and toward wealth and work that Barks explored in his comics. Despite censorship both overt and subtle, despite the ambiguity of Barks's own attitudes, democratic visions born of his own work experience illuminate his best comic art.

IV

In ignoring the popular appeal of the Disney comic Dorfman and Mattelart miss its democratic content and implications. Like many early students of popular culture (in particular those influenced by the leftist "Frankfurt School" of German cultural critics of the 1920s), they assume a pro-systemic conspiracy on the part of the creators of popular culture and the corporations that market it. They view Disney's "mass" working-class audience as passive victims, forced to consume alien, pro-capitalist understandings of the social world around them. For them, the world of Disney systematically "mystifies" the people, protecting and perpetuating an exploitative social order.

At best, this kind of analysis is a half-truth, and it can easily become elitist, manipulative, and undemocratic. No democrat can deny the vital importance of alternative means of communication and interpretation. But if the "masses" are judged to be wholly "mystified" and passive in their encounter with mainstream culture, they must be taught to appreciate their "real" interests by a counter-elite armed with the appropriate cultural means to "enlighten" them. In Chile those means were to be provided in part by the state publishing house, Quimantú. In addition to commissioning and publishing *How to Read Donald Duck*, it launched a comic strip called "Cabro Chico" ("Little Kid"), on which Dorfman collaborated, whose properly revolutionary class values were to supplant those propagated by Disney. Making this rival comic strip popular, however, proved not an easy task.

Quite apart from political considerations like these, the assumptions imbedded in Dorfman and Mattelart's analysis of Donald Duck are difficult to square with what we now know about Disney and his comics. The genesis of the strange masculine animal world of uncles and nephews that Dorfman and Mattelart posit as the foundation of the manipulative world of Disney is a good example. The many biographies of Disney,

critical and adulatory alike, make clear that the animated world he created was largely the response of an ambitious man to a particularly
unhappy childhood. And if his comics are suffused with the values of a
dog-eat-dog capitalist world, they reflect in part Disney's own desperate
struggle to succeed in the animated film industry.

Walt Disney's boyhood seems to have been an unending round of
farm chores and child labor under the oppressive eye of an overbearing
(some accounts say brutal) father. Disney spent his early manhood in the
1920s living on a shoestring in a desperate attempt to turn his limited
drawing ability into success in the novel and ruthlessly competitive world
of film animation. The immediate and universal appeal of his first major
cartoon character, the consistently altruistic Mickey Mouse (who hit the
theaters at the start of the Great Depression), catapulted Disney's small
enterprise into the forefront of the animated cartoon industry in the
1930s. But Disney, like most creators of popular culture, seems to have
had no clear idea of what made his cartoons popular. Although his ambition to stay at the cutting edge of film animation was all-consuming, his
feature films often flopped at the box office. True, his operation grew in
size and technical sophistication. Yet he stayed just a step ahead of his
banker creditors during most of the 1930s and 1940s. Only in the 1950s
did the Disney enterprise enter a period of sustained financial security.
That stage was reached when income from his tried-and-true Mickey
Mouse and Donald Duck films and comics was supplemented by a range
of new endeavors connected with them. These included sales of an
astounding variety of paraphernalia depicting his comic characters, successful ventures into the new medium of television, and, most
importantly, the establishment of an immensely popular and lucrative
amusement park in California.

The creation of Donald Duck in the late 1930s (along with military
contracts in the early 1940s) helped sustain the Disney enterprise during
the difficult period before the 1950s. The predictably disinterested
Mickey, who existed far above the competitive, commodified world of
Disney's audience, had placed severe limits on the kinds of plots available
to his creators. Donald opened up a greater range of human motivations
and problems for the creative energies of Disney animators. In the hands
of people like Barks, Donald, the imperfect, came to represent "everyman." "There isn't a person in the United States who couldn't identify
with him," Barks asserted in 1975, and he admitted that he himself identified more with Donald, the tragic victim of circumstances partly of his
own making, than with any other of his characters (CBL, Volume 21).

The peculiar shape of the world of Disney, like the history of Barks's
Disney ducks that I have reviewed in this essay, does not support the

impossibly simplistic notion of a corporate conspiracy somehow consciously in league with the conservative designs of a capitalist ruling class. That naive and undemocratic rendering of the meaning of contemporary popular culture is a caricature of the complex process I have examined. The popularity of the mature world of Disney undoubtedly owed not a little to the power and resources of the Disney Corporation to mold public tastes and expectations. And surely the ideological messages encoded in Disney comics, as even the most democratic of Carl Barks's Donald and Scrooge stories reveal, have reinforced generally accepted notions about the meaning of the social world around us.

Yet the ideological conservatism of the Disney comic seems primarily to reflect, not to engender, the mainstream attitudes of the larger society in which it is imbedded. The artistic creations of people like Disney and Barks—abstract, symbolic, autobiographical expressions of their own personal traumas, hopes, aspirations, and fears—appeal to many people because they dramatize, in compelling ways, sentiments and problems experienced by millions of people over the course of their lives.

What is instructive about the evidence I have reviewed is not this simple, commonsensical general explanation of the wide appeal of the Disney comics. Rather, it is the specific notion that subversive democratic readings of these texts help account for their phenomenal popularity. Even Mickey Mouse—who, as Disney was fond of pointing out, counted Franklin D. Roosevelt and Adolf Hitler among his fans—lends himself to anti-capitalist readings. Mickey appeals to a utopian, non-materialistic, selflessness in all of us. His disinterested motivations and heroic actions are totally at odds with the base material calculus that permeates our daily lives in capitalist society. Barks's Donald and Scrooge, in contrast to Mickey, live in *this* world, where every human motivation and relationship is entered in a capitalist ledger of profit and loss. (Small wonder that for a time the official Soviet line on the Disney comic was that it was a *parody* of capitalist social relations.) Barks's duck comics undoubtedly appealed to readers on many levels, including their aesthetic qualities as humorous, complex, tightly conceived, and masterfully crafted verbal and visual stories. But they achieved their greatest popularity when they were most open to democratic interpretations. Barks brought that dimension to his work not by design, but because his own life experience invested him with certain democratic sensibilities.

In recent years, students of popular culture have begun to challenge the elitist and conspiratorial assumptions of early academic studies on popular culture. This new work, some of the best of which is listed in the suggested readings for this chapter, views the terrain of popular culture as a battleground in the struggle for cultural meaning. The "mass" media, which appear as highly centralized, highly capitalized, overwhelmingly powerful tools of elite cultural domination, turn out to have feet of clay, or at least Achilles' heels. Their vast audience, which may appear to be composed of passive recipients of manipulative messages, is in fact made up of active interlocutors. Their attention and reactions to the cultural product beamed at them determine its commercial success.

To be sure, the obvious boundaries of this cultural struggle are defined beforehand by the property-owning elite in capitalist societies. We should not expect to find in Disney an overworked Donald losing a hand to an unsafe machine or organizing fellow industrial workers against the boss.

But on a symbolic level, the potential of democratic readings of popular texts is far greater than is generally realized. When Scrooge sends Donald back to work with a kick on his behind (as he does in "A Financial Fable") he encapsulates in a single dramatic gesture the essence of an entire world of labor relations. Workers and employers intimately experience that world in infinite variation on a daily basis. But the participants in this daily drama know, like the specialized scholars who analyze and document their interactions, that "labor discipline" (the capitalist term) and "worker dignity" (labor's term) constitute *the* central issue in production. Similarly, when in that story Scrooge brings Donald to his knees through manipulation of the market, the two are re-enacting the fundamental feature that *defines* capitalism as a social system. They are dramatizing the issue that unionized workers have bent their best efforts over two centuries to modify or change.

Such interpretations involve active, creative reading by consumers of popular texts. And precisely for that reason these readings are potentially much richer and more inclusive, more passionate and emotive, and, finally, more pleasurable and fun, than those of workers targeted by the blatantly manipulative, condescending propaganda of "proletarian art" and "socialist realism" sanctioned historically by Marxist political parties and socialist regimes.

We still do not know very much about what people "see" when they consume forms of popular culture. What we do know, however, is that some products aimed at a popular audience are successful while others are not. If the corporate magnates and artists who finance and fashion these products in capitalist society knew for sure what makes something popular, we would not witness the frequent box office flops of movies despite the expenditure of millions of dollars to promote them. Nor would we contemplate the failures of lavishly produced television series in the United States every year. The television and film industries seem so at sea about the question of the popular that when they hit on something that really does have wide appeal, their best efforts are harnessed to successfully clone it.

For the most part, the links between the democratic and the popular continue to elude the creators of popular culture as well as their academic critics. A good example is media and critical reaction to *Dallas*, the most popular television series ever. Nowhere in the voluminous commentary on *Dallas* is its openness to democratic, anti-capitalist readings explicitly acknowledged and systematically explored. Yet the show, whose extraordinary appeal abroad in the early 1980s matched its phenomenal success at home, was about a Texas family that owned a chunk of the oil industry, the most powerful sector of the capitalist world economy. Its protagonist, J.R. Ewing, was a capitalist whose predatory instincts make anti-capitalist readings of Barks's early Scrooge pale by comparison. J.R. began as a secondary male character, who shared the limelight with his patriarchal father and his humane and considerate capitalist brother. But father and brother (like Mickey Mouse in Disney) soon became secondary characters, as viewer reaction made J.R.—the "man you love to hate"—into the centerpiece of the show. When J.R. was mysteriously shot and apparently dead, the episode that promised to answer "Who Shot J.R.?" became the single most watched hour on television ever. What made the suspense so intriguing was that virtually *everyone* who had ever appeared in the drama had a motive to kill J.R. All had seen aspects of their lives ruined by a man whose ruthless pursuit of wealth and power commodified every human relationship and destroyed every generous aspect of community.

Academics have analyzed *Dallas* from a bewildering range of angles and spun elaborate (often convoluted) theories to explain its success. No one among the critics of the series has emphasized its obvious openness to anti-capitalist readings. Perhaps the person who came closest to describing the show's democratic appeal was Larry Hagman, the consummate actor who played J.R. and made him into a household word world-wide. In May, 1991, on the eve of the showing of the last episode of the series' thirteen-year run, he told a *TV Guide* interviewer that

> J.R. came along at the perfect time. TV audiences wanted to see some raw, rich people who made it with their own gumption and guts and just kicked ass and had some fun. People couldn't go out much because there was a recession, and so we all had fun on Friday nights.

The "gumption and guts" Hagman referred to were not the virtuous entrepreneurial qualities the Disney Corporation found in Barks's later-day Scrooge. "I knew all those back-stabbing oil men in Texas—I grew up with them," Hagman said. "I knew exactly what direction the show should take."

V

The lasting achievement of Dorfman and Mattelart's *How to Read Donald Duck* is not its one-dimensional treatment of capitalist ideology in the Disney comic. Rather, as the book's subtitle accurately suggests, its great contribution to the literature on popular culture is its analysis of *imperialist* ideology in the Disney comics of the 1960s. Dorfman and Mattelart showed how Barks's duck comics projected cultural assumptions—particularly the division of the world into "modern" and "traditional" societies—that legitimized the entire history of Western and US expansionism.

In accomplishing that task, Dorfman and Mattelart's work illustrates much broader intellectual trends in the post-World War II era. For the cultural assumptions that separate the Disney comics from their Latin American critics are the same ones that divided US and Latin American social scientists and humanists in the postwar period. Review of the recent intellectual history of the hemisphere—particularly the debate between US "modernization" and Latin American "dependency" theorists—thus poses a final question for those who would dismiss the importance of popular culture. To what extent is postwar US academic scholarship on development simply an elaborate, obtuse rendering of what Donald and his creators already know?

As suggested in chapter 1, the challenge Dorfman and Mattelart posed to Disney was part of a broad cultural offensive emanating from Europe's one-time colonies in the post-World War II era. The offensive had its roots in the nationalism that burst forth in Asia, Africa, and Latin America during the interwar period. It reflected the momentous process of decolonization that followed World War II. In Latin America, where Europe's former colonies had won formal political independence over a century earlier, the terms of this offensive focused not on political liberation but on the issue of economic development and the promise of increased national autonomy it seemed to hold.

During the postwar decades US scholars responded to these challenges with a systematic explanation of development they called "modernization theory." This body of thought was progressive and democratic in the sense that it abandoned the racial underpinnings that had historically rationalized Western and US expansionism. But modernization theorists simply replaced overtly racial explanations with a sophisticated elaboration of the cultural assumptions traditionally allied with them. They argued that the division of the modern world into a small group of rich industrialized nations and a large group of poor underdeveloped ones was a function of the triumph of "modern" values.

"Traditional" values inhibited the development of the societies of Latin America, Africa, and Asia. Modernization theorists advocated the diffusion of capital, knowhow, and institutions from the developed to the underdeveloped world through the liberal mechanisms of a global capitalist marketplace. They thus rationalized the informal empire forged by postwar US expansionism.

Meanwhile, Latin American thinkers were forging their own understanding of the development of the modern world. Eventually dubbed "dependency theory" (although most practitioners preferred the less pretentious and precise terms "dependency approach" or "dependency thinking"), their thought was much more radical and democratic than that of their US counterparts. Like Eric Williams before them, they saw development and underdevelopment as two sides of the same coin, structurally related products of an evolving world capitalist system. For them, the impediments to Latin American development were primarily economic not cultural. These obstacles could be overcome through nationalist policies aimed at restructuring the ties of economic dependency that bound Latin America to the advanced capitalist nations of the North Atlantic.

Some dependency thinkers were in reality social conservatives, nationalists who sought to preserve the capitalist organization of their societies by invigorating it. Others sought socialist transformation as the only hope for democratic development. Both groups, however, argued that concerted measures by the state could counteract the inequalities among nations created by the international capitalist marketplace. By stimulating Latin American industrialization and fostering social reform, the state could insure greater political and cultural autonomy among the nations of the region.

Dorfman and Mattelart's critique of imperialist ideology in the Disney comic extended the democratic challenge of Latin American dependency thought to the cultural foundation on which the whole edifice of modernization theory rested. Yet in its failure to appreciate the popular dimensions of the Disney comic, it also reveals fatal flaws in dependency thinking. Latin American dependency thinkers virtually ignored the role of popular struggle in their analysis of historical change. They were also fundamentally elitist in their vision of how dependency could be overcome. The nationalist capitalist reformers among them placed their faith in a cadre of technocratic bureaucrats, the Marxists in vanguard political parties. Both groups exalted the role of state power and neglected the idea that truly democratic organization of society must emanate from participatory institutions in the workplace and the local community. For all its democratic insights, today dependency thought is bankrupt politically. In contrast, the liberal precepts of modernization theory undergird the US-led "new world order" which all Latin American governments (save embattled Cuba) are scrambling to be a part of.

The failures of dependency thinking, however, should not obscure its democratic contributions to understanding the nature of the world we live in. Nor should the current vogue for neo-liberal ideology blind us to the growing international and domestic inequalities world capitalism will continue to foster. The trick is to link the democratic insights of thinkers like Dorfman and Mattelart with the aspirations of the working people who enjoy the forms of popular culture academics like them criticize so roundly. Labor history, chapter 5 argues, suggests promising ways to begin to do just that.

Further Reading

Ang, Ien, *Watching Dallas: Soap Opera and the Melodramatic Imagination*, London 1985.

Barrier, J. Michael, *Carl Barks and the Art of the Comic Book*, New York 1981.

Beezley, William H., Cheryl E. Martin and William E. French, eds., *Rituals of Rule, Rituals of Resistance*, Wilmington, DE, 1994.

Bergquist, Charles, *Alternative Approaches to the Problem of Development*, Durham, NC, 1978.

Finch, Christopher, *The Art of Walt Disney*, New York 1973.

Denning, Michael, *Mechanic Accents: Dime Novels and Working-Class Culture in America*, London 1987.

Dorfman, Ariel, and Armand Mattelart, *How to Read Donald Duck: Imperialist Ideology in the Disney Comic*, Valparaíso, Chile, 1971; Eng. trans. by David Kunzle, New York 1975.

Dorfman, Ariel, *The Empire's Old Clothes*, New York 1983.

Eliot, Marc, *Walt Disney: Hollywood's Dark Prince*, New York 1993.

Jameson, Fredric, "Reification and Utopia in Mass Culture," *Social Text*, vol. 1, no. 1 (winter 1979), pp. 130–48.

Kubey, Robert, and Mihaly Csikszentmihalyi, *Television and the Quality of Life: How Viewing Shapes Everyday Experience*, Hillsdale, NJ, 1990.

Lutz, Catherine A., and Jane L. Collins, *Reading National Geographic*, Chicago 1993.

Liebes, Tamar, and Elihu Katz, *The Export of Meaning. Cross-Cultural Readings of DALLAS*, New York 1990.

Miller, Diane Disney, as told to Pete Martin, *The Story of Walt Disney*, New York 1956.

Potter, David, *People of Plenty*, Chicago 1954.

Radway, Janice A., *Reading the Romance: Women, Patriarchy, and Popular Literature*, Chapel Hill, NC, 1984.

Sklar, Robert, and Charles Musser, eds., *Resisting Images: Essays on Cinema and History*, Philadelphia 1990.

Thomas, Bob, *Walt Disney. An American Original*, New York 1976.

Willis, Susan, *A Primer for Daily Life*, London 1991.

Two views of the labor mobilization of the mid-1930s that succeeded, by the end of World War II, in organizing the industrial core of the world economy. Above, workers battle police during the San Francisco General Strike of 1934. Below, strikers occupy a General Motors plant during the Flint Sit-down Strike of 1937. These momentous union victories had unforeseen paradoxical consequences for the course of American democracy.

5

Envisioning a History and
a Politics Democratic

What do these labor perspectives on the course of American democracy have to say about democratic politics in the here and now? And what, in turn, are the demands and expectations that democratic politics place on the work of historians?

This chapter approaches these questions in three parts. The first involves making sense of the contemporary era. Understanding the very special circumstances in which labor finds itself today, I argue, can help us think about the role it can play in democratic politics in the future. The second part reviews what people who study the history of labor have been saying in recent decades. Curiously, while the general public and most historians have been learning to dismiss the subject of labor as old-fashioned or inconsequential, labor historians have been (re)discovering its centrality in modern history and its relevance to major problems we face today. The third part of the chapter addresses the most important challenge facing contemporary labor historians, the fact that only a handful of specialists read their work. Like the book as a whole, this chapter challenges what is taken for common sense these days by the many in the general public and most academics alike. It argues that labor and its history are important.

I

The defining features of the contemporary era were cemented into place in the aftermath of World War II. Yet despite their seeming durability, they have come completely unstuck in our own time. In international political terms the outline of this era is clear enough. It begins with the falling-out between the capitalist and Communist victors in World War II and the escalating ideological and military confrontation between the

United States and the Soviet Union after 1947, known as the Cold War. It ends with the collapse of the Soviet bloc and the disintegration of the Soviet Union itself in the years around 1990.

In economic terms, the fifty-year period since 1945 seems to fit the pattern of the "long waves" discussed in chapter 2. The period began with spectacular expansion of the US and world economies until about 1970. There followed a long period of sluggish growth and frequent recession in the United States, the leading capitalist nation, outright retrogression by the 1980s in Latin America and much of the Third World, and finally, the virtual economic collapse of the Soviet bloc. There were important and revealing exceptions to this pattern, in particular the economies of Japan and West Germany and those of a handful of small East Asian nations, which continued to grow rapidly throughout the 1970s and 1980s. And economic trends in the Soviet bloc, although tied to the fortunes of the capitalist world economy, reflected the escalating crisis of its own peculiar authoritarian social order. But the general pattern of approximately twenty-five years of rapid economic expansion followed by a period of similar length when fitful growth, stagnation, or decline set in seems to describe the behavior of the world economy as a whole over the last fifty years.

In chapter 2 we saw how in the late nineteenth century, the expansive potential of the US economy was unleashed as the threat of insurgent labor at home helped propel US elites into a policy of imperialism. We also saw how, in the decades after 1898, the growing ideological and organizational weakness of the US labor movement was closely connected to the rapid growth of the economy that accompanied foreign expansion. Finally, we saw how the weakness of organized labor in the United States contributed to the crisis of demand that overwhelmed the US and world economies by the end of the 1920s.

A similar pattern emerges in the fifty-year period since the Second World War. In this period, however, the issues posed for capitalists by insurgent US workers were of a different order. Seemingly less radical in ideological terms, they proved far more formidable in organizational terms. In the decade following 1935, the workers succeeded in organizing the industrial core of the largest economy in the world. Resolution of the issues posed by mobilized workers at the end of World War II involved a momentous compromise between labor leaders and corporate managers that seemed, initially, to favor labor. Over the course of succeeding decades, however, US capitalists eluded their compromise with labor at home, particularly by investing abroad. This policy favored US capitalists as a class and underwrote the tremendous postwar expansion of the global economy. In the end, however, it proved destructive for US labor and for US society as a whole.

In terms of the history of labor in the United States, then, the contemporary era is also well defined. Organized labor emerged in 1945 from the crisis of world Depression and war at the zenith of its power and influence in this century. Workers' long-standing struggle for legally sanctioned union rights and social welfare policies had already found expression in national legislation. Through alliance with the Democratic Party organized workers played an important role in politics and government. In 1945 the US labor movement looked forward to ever wider distribution of wealth and increased participation in decisions about production.

How different are the position and expectations of the labor movement today! Labor has seen its political power gravely eroded and its leverage in the workplace drastically decline. Its vision of itself and its future is confused and defensive. It is often perceived, even by many union members, as corrupt, inefficient, or selfish. Many people in the United States today view organized labor as an impediment to national progress.

The erosion of labor's strength can be measured in physical terms— for example, the declining relative numbers of unionized workers. But at root labor's contemporary crisis is ideological. It reflects the way labor thinks about itself and is perceived by others. In terms of ideas, labor today seems almost as powerless as it was at the start of the industrial era. It seems unable to contest the vision of a market-centered liberal capitalist order. More than two centuries of collective struggle by working people to create a social order able to protect them from market forces seems to have ended in virtual ideological surrender. Today the market-driven principles of a reconstructed liberal economic order dominate political discourse and the policy agendas of most of the nations of the globe. Competition, productivity, free trade, and increased material consumption are the watchwords of the day. Governments are expected to scale down the regulation of private economic enterprise and their support for social welfare programs. They are to reconcentrate their activities on the classical liberal goals of protecting private property and facilitating commerce.

Contrary to much current belief and public discourse, however, it was not until recent times that this liberal capitalist agenda and vision of the future began to dominate the way most of us think about the world we live in. Historically, workers have always directly opposed the free play of market forces in the organization of production in capitalist society. Their collective actions had precisely the opposite goal. Workers fought to raise wages, better control their work environment, and protect themselves on the job and off by establishing unions under their own control to *monopolize* the market in labor. Analysis of the contemporary era reveals how organized labor lost the long-term ideological struggle to justify this historical goal. Paradoxically, as we shall see, it lost the battle to justify unions precisely because it succeeded in unionizing the core of the world economy in the years following World War II.

Labor historians have shown that the strange turnabout in labor's position in the contemporary period is a consequence, largely unforeseen, of historic compromises made by capitalists and organized workers at the end of World War II. Most people are unaware of the momentous nature of these compromises and the way they have affected our attitudes toward labor today. To appreciate the importance of these compromises it is necessary to place them in a very broad historical context. Doing so reveals their novelty in the history of workers' relationship with capitalists in the industrial era. It also highlights the difference between workers' position in capitalist and socialist organization of production in this century. Once the historical context of the compromises is made clear, we will be in a position to trace their extraordinary implications for the fate of labor in the United States and elsewhere today.

The momentous compromises worked out between capitalists, organized workers, and the state at the end of World War II in the United States and other capitalist nations reflected the strength of democratic forces unleashed by the two world wars and the great economic crisis of the 1930s. The liberal capitalist powers—Britain, France, and the United States—mobilized their peoples and their international allies and colonies by justifying both world wars as a struggle for democracy. The wars defeated the expansionist and imperialist designs of newly industrialized capitalist competitors, Germany in World War I and the fascist triad of Germany, Japan, and Italy in World War II.

Victory in World War II depended, however, on alliance with the Soviet Union, a huge and rapidly modernizing anti-capitalist state born of the dislocation and democratic ferment of the World War I era. The Soviet Union's formal commitment to democracy differed from the political and individual rights championed by the liberal capitalist powers. Soviet Communists defined democracy in Marxist terms. They called for the end of social inequality. To achieve that goal they abolished capitalist organization of society and empowered the state, guided by the Communist Party, to organize production and distribution.

These rival liberal and Marxist visions of a democratic order inspired people around the world from World War I onwards. They galvanized the twentieth-century struggle for political and economic independence in Europe's former colonies in Asia, Africa, and Latin America. They legitimated, during the great economic crisis of the 1930s, the struggle for social reform and labor rights in the capitalist world. And in the

Communist world, much broadened after World War II by Soviet power and the initial appeal and success of its social system, they were used to justify socialist organization of society.

Ironically, it was this same democratic vision that ultimately totally discredited and transformed the Soviet regime and its client states in Eastern Europe in the late 1980s. The collapse of the Soviet bloc was a result of its failure to realize in practice either of the democratic visions that have mobilized people to democratic struggle in this century. On the one hand, despite an elaborate democratic institutional and legal façade, the reality of Soviet politics was always authoritarian. On the other, despite much rhetoric about "worker states" and industrial democracy, the Soviets early adopted a despotic, state-directed managerial regime in the workplace.

Paradoxically, Soviet organization of the workplace mirrored the authoritarian private organization of production in capitalist societies in the early twentieth century, with two essential differences. The first is well known and generally accepted as decisive in the collapse of the Soviet bloc. The abolition of capitalist property relations and market incentives effectively eliminated competition between firms and sectors in the Soviet economy. Over time Soviet managers failed to innovate technologically and rationalize production as efficiently as their capitalist rivals. This is the explanation of Soviet economic failure preferred by capitalists and their apologists. It points to the tremendous capacity of capitalist organization of production to promote economic growth and technological development over time.

The other explanation for Soviet economic failure is less widely appreciated, but it is of great concern and importance to labor. Like their early-twentieth-century capitalist counterparts, the Soviets sought to destroy independent organization among workers and institute Taylorist principles of scientific management to break workers' control of the labor process. But unlike their counterparts, the Soviets also virtually eliminated unemployment. And they developed social programs that gave all workers and their families access to food, housing, medical care, and education.

In capitalist economies, except where effective unions and social welfare programs are in place, worker discipline and efficiency on the job are insured by the threat of being fired or unemployed. Being out of work means finding oneself naked in the capitalist marketplace, unable to purchase the basics of subsistence. In Soviet-style economies none of these market sanctions applies. Workers who hate their jobs often get away with working less, or working less efficiently. Aside from pay incentives (which despite Communist theory were widely used), and changes in the productive process itself (for example, the introduction of more labor-saving machinery), labor discipline and productivity had to be improved through appeals to political or moral values or through coercion.

Historically, workers' organizations in capitalist societies succeeded in different places and different times in limiting the authoritarianism of their workplace environment and the social inequalities of capitalist organization of society. It is important to stress again, however, that they did so by directly challenging the liberal logic of the free market system. Since the dawn of the industrial era, workers have struggled collectively against the principle, vital to capitalist organization of production, of a free market in labor. They fought to improve wages, influence the way work was organized, and protect themselves on the job by controlling the supply of labor through organizations of their own.

The labor movement has also sought to curb the power of free market forces in society at large. It has done so, for example, by building political coalitions able to institute social welfare measures (such as unemployment and retirement insurance) administered by the state. Such measures sought to protect working people from the social inequalities fostered by the capitalist marketplace. They helped to sustain workers and protect their health during their productive years and provide for them once their working lives were over.

Precisely because the historical goals of working people contravene the free market principles of capitalist social organization, they have always been resisted by capitalists. As a result, implementation of labor's historic goals has been highly selective and fragile in all capitalist societies. This is true even in the rich, highly industrialized economies of the twentieth century. In the United States, for example, before the great organizational victories of the decade after 1935, only a small fraction of industrial workers, most of them skilled, enjoyed the benefits of effective, independent union organization. And in recent years the relative power that industrial unions enjoyed for a few short decades following World War II has been drastically undermined. Similarly, the limited social welfare benefits won in the United States during the Great Depression and ratified after World War II covered only a portion of the workforce, and since the 1980s even they have come increasingly under attack. The concessions made to labor in capitalist societies have been won not because capitalists willingly concede these principles, but because they have had to compromise on them in the face of workers' organizational power.

The democratic surge in union organization during the Great Depression and World War II left the labor movements of the allied liberal nations (including those of Latin America) in an unprecedented position of influence and power at the end of the war. But capitalists in these nations (unlike those in the defeated fascist nations) also emerged from the war strengthened by the wartime economic boom and emboldened by the defeat of their fascist rivals. Nowhere were both capitalists and organized labor stronger than in the United States. In the context of the United States' extraordinary economic and political power at the end of the war, the concessions US capitalists and organized workers forced on each other in the immediate postwar period had repercussions far beyond US society. In important respects they defined the direction of the whole postwar era.

The principles of the postwar compromise between capital and labor in the United States and other capitalist nations were deceptively simple. Organized labor forced capitalists and the government to accept the legal right of workers to organize, to bargain collectively, and to strike for higher returns for their labor. Capitalists, for their part, forced organized labor to recognize management's exclusive prerogative to make decisions about the way work was done.

These principles, however, are so basic that neither side could afford to adhere to them for long without compromising its fundamental interests. Just as workers, since the advent of the industrial era, have struggled collectively to protect themselves against the workings of a free market in labor and to maximize their control over the way work is organized, capitalists, for their part, have always fought labor organization tenaciously. They have done so because their survival depends on their ability to hire and fire workers at will and organize labor and machines in the way most likely to enhance their profits. Under the terms of the compromise, US industrial workers won their long struggle to establish effective unions in the workplace. But they did so by formally abandoning their historic struggle to influence the way work was organized. Capitalists, for their part, won labor's formal recognition of their exclusive right to manage production. But they did so at the expense of formally giving up their historical opposition to effective unionization.

In the years following the war each side sought to enlist the government and public opinion in a concerted effort to turn these concessions to its own maximum advantage. Management and organized labor each pressed for what it believed were natural, logical corollaries of the concessions it had won from its adversary. At the same time each side sought to limit the damage to its own fundamental interests that making such basic concessions to its historic antagonist entailed. The process of give and take that resulted often led in surprising directions, which compromised each side's fundamental interests in ways neither had fully foreseen.

That concessions on such fundamental principles were made at all reflected, as noted above, the relative strength of organized labor and the extraordinary position the United States found itself in at the end of the war. The United States emerged from the fighting with its huge industrial infrastructure unscathed, its human resources largely intact, its enormous military power inflated by a monopoly on atomic weapons, and its confidence in the future unbounded. Its fascist capitalist rivals had been devastated by the war, its liberal capitalist allies exhausted by it. Only the Soviet Union, the Communist ally most responsible for the defeat of Germany in Europe, stood in the way of the establishment of a "new empire" of truly global proportions underwritten by US economic power, military might, and the prestige of its liberal economic and political institutions. Under these conditions the future for US capitalists and organized workers seemed unlimited. They could afford, it seemed, to give ground on fundamental principles in order to realize its promise.

To be sure, the balance of power had already shifted toward capital by the end of the war, whereas it had decisively favored labor in the mid-1930s. During the depth of the Great Depression capitalists were widely held responsible for the disaster that had befallen the nation. With fully a third of the nation's workforce unemployed in 1933, and others working at reduced hours or below their skill level, the rights of labor and the appeal of radical blueprints for national recovery acquired a legitimacy among US citizens unknown since the end of the nineteenth century. Socialists, Communists, and syndicalists, small but growing minorities within the labor movement, advanced a variety of Marxist explanations and socialist solutions to the crisis. Much more influential among workers, however, were the ideas of laborites associated with the American Federation of Labor.

The AFL officially responded to the crisis in 1930 by calling for full employment through a reduction of the workweek to thirty hours. In 1933 an AFL-supported proposal to establish a federally mandated thirty-hour workweek passed the Senate and almost became law. At its 1934 national convention in San Francisco the AFL threatened a general strike if the law were not enacted and a series of basic labor rights protected by law. This was no idle threat. By 1934 large-scale strikes by transport and maritime workers in different parts of the country signalled a new militancy among US workers and in San Francisco a key organizational strike by West Coast longshoremen resulted in the violent general strike depicted in the photograph at the beginning of this chapter.

Advocates of the AFL's work-sharing solution to the crisis stressed its human goals and its principle of social justice. But even many conservative labor leaders were also aware of its radical, transformative potential.

Full employment and legal protection for labor's organizational rights would decisively shift the balance of power in favor of unions and enhance the prospects for social democracy.

Perhaps because the Roosevelt administration belatedly realized the radical implications of the thirty-hour bill, it withdrew its support for it at the eleventh hour and the initiative never became law. Thereafter, although the government did not abandon programs to redistribute income and lessen unemployment, the primary thrust of Roosevelt's "New Deal" focused on state support for expanded production in the private sector.

But in order to win labor support for its program of national recovery the Roosevelt administration took the unprecedented step of recognizing labor's legal right to strike and bargain collectively. These rights were endorsed in principle in the famous Section 7a of the Industrial Recovery Act of 1934, then specified and given institutional force in the landmark Wagner Act of 1935. Legal support for labor organizing, coupled with a resurgence of economic growth by 1935, triggered an explosion of labor militancy in subsequent years.

Spearheading labor's organizational drive was a new and dynamic union entity, the Congress of Industrial Organizations. The CIO rejected the AFL's organizational philosophy based on the unionization of skilled workers along craft lines. It championed an industrial unionism that sought to organize skilled and unskilled workers alike in mass-production industries like steel, automobiles, rubber, electrical equipment, and meat-packing. These were the industries in which Taylorist principles designed to speed production and eliminate highly skilled workers by breaking the labor process into a series of simple tasks had gone furthest in the decades since the 1890s. They were also among the industries that had been most successful in resisting effective labor organization. With the support of the CIO, many of whose grass-roots leaders were affiliated with the Communist Party, workers now took advantage of the vulnerability of such mass-production industries to job actions by a minority of committed workers. If a key part of their integrated operations could be shut down, the whole assembly process could be halted.

Workers also developed a revolutionary tactic that outflanked legal restrictions on their traditional reliance on pickets to keep strikebreakers out of the plants they shut down. Instead of walking out, they sat down on the job. Now employers were faced with the delicate problem of ejecting workers from their plants. To that task many government officials in the 1930s proved resistent. This was especially true of authorities at the local and state levels who owed their elections to people sympathetic to labor's cause.

The sit-down strikes that enveloped firms across the nation in the mid-1930s reached a climax at the huge General Motors operation in Flint, Michigan, in 1937 (see the illustration on page 160). Precipitated by rank-and-file militants, that hard-fought and ultimately successful strike catapulted the newly formed United Automobile Workers (UAW) union of the CIO to the forefront of the US labor movement. In rapid succession the UAW won contracts with other major automakers and the CIO won acquiescence to union contracts from the nation's giant steel corporations.

Labor's organizational momentum was slowed during the severe depression of 1937, when unemployment once again reached dramatic proportions. The new crisis seemed to expose the failure of a recovery policy based on government stimulation of private production, rather than on the full employment, redistributive formula first endorsed by the AFL. Those sympathetic to capitalists, for their part, used the "Roosevelt depression" to discredit the policies of the administration in general, including its support for labor rights. The question of economic recovery lost urgency, however, with the boost to economic production provided by the outbreak of war in Europe.

The war itself revitalized the US economy and the labor movement. Despite a decision by the Supreme Court that outlawed sit-down strikes, and government policies that gave executives on loan from major corporations an overwhelming voice in federal agencies charged with mobilizing the nation's economy and its labor force for war, union organization continued to expand. Government policies also sought to discourage strikes and hold back workers' demands in the interest of maximum production. Nevertheless, tight wartime labor markets fostered the growth of AFL and CIO unions, many of which enrolled unprecedented numbers of female and non-white males during the course of the war. Pent-up labor demands and price inflation unleashed a wave of strikes in the immediate postwar period comparable in scope and intensity to the labor mobilization that followed World War I. Unlike what happened then, however, capitalist forces in the late 1940s succeeded only in limiting the advance of labor and in circumscribing the union rights won by workers during the Great Depression and World War II.

The enhanced power of capitalists in relation to organized workers at the end of the war was revealed in the Taft-Hartley labor legislation of 1947. Taft-Hartley sharply curtailed the advantages accorded labor by the Wagner Act of 1935. The Wagner Act had not only legalized the rights of workers to form unions, and to strike, picket, and boycott. It had also defined as unfair such time-honored employer tactics as organizing company unions, arbitrarily firing and blacklisting labor activists, and employing labor spies. Taft-Hartley, in contrast, made sympathy strikes and boycotts more difficult. It deprived foremen of the protection accorded union activists in the Wagner Act. And it allowed state governments to ban the "closed shop" (an arrangement, already typical in many northern industrial states, whereby a union elected by a majority of workers in a plant could require all workers to become members). Taft-Hartley also required union leaders to declare they were not members of the Communist Party. And it empowered the government to require large unions to postpone for eighty days any strike the president deemed a "national emergency," a power the national executive used frequently in ensuing years. By eliminating the element of surprise in strikes, that measure blunted the most powerful weapon available to workers in large industries.

Taft-Hartley codified elements of the compromise worked out between capitalists, organized labor, and the government during the war and in the years immediately following it. It established the basic legal framework for US industrial relations in the whole postwar era. Although it was denounced by many union leaders as a "slave labor bill," in fact it validated, while limiting, the fundamental victories that organized workers had won in previous years. Taft-Hartley helped confine organized labor to the industrial sector, helped defeat labor's ambitious postwar plan to organize the South, helped foster the division in the labor movement over the issue of Communism, and decisively favored management by eliminating the crucial element of surprise in big industrial strikes. But unlike the rollback of labor's organizational gains after World War I, Taft-Hartley left intact labor's great organizational victories of the preceding decade. Henceforth, management in basic industry would have to contend legally with the powerful industrial unions in place in its plants.

Even more revealing of the stakes involved in the postwar compromise than this formal legislation was the outcome of struggles between corporation managers and organized industrial workers in the workplace. The most significant of these struggles (as David Brody shows so convincingly in *Workers in Industrial America*) involved the largest corporation in the world at the time, General Motors, and the most powerful of the new CIO unions, the United Automobile Workers. The struggle began with a momentous strike called by the UAW at the end of 1945. The terms of the settlement between the two sides were revealed in the collective contract they signed in 1948. That contract set the pattern for US industrial relations in the postwar era.

UAW officials, like many progressive US labor leaders at the time, sought nothing less than a strong labor role in the management of the

US economy and its largest corporations. This position was reflected in the union's justification of its demand of a 30 percent wage increase when it went on strike in late 1945. The union claimed that the increase could be met by General Motors with no increase in the cost of its products to consumers. It challenged the company to "open its books" to prove its point.

The company interpreted this union demand as a wedge that would eventually lead to co-management of the firm. It walked out of negotiations with the union when a government-appointed fact-finding board ruled that ability to pay was a valid consideration in reaching a settlement. The company then endured a 113-day strike and losses in the tens of millions of dollars to resist the union's demand. In the end, the union capitulated on the issue of management rights and gave up its strategy for redistributing company profits to consumers and its members. In return it eventually won a handsome wage and benefits package. The 1948 collective contract between the union and the corporation contained management rights clauses that gave the company wide powers to dictate the organization of work. Wage and benefits increases were linked to rises in the cost of living and to gains in productivity.

Contracts like this had devastating long-term implications for the democratic vocation of the labor movement and for the vitality of US capitalism itself. The formal acceptance by union leaders of exalted versions of management rights meant abandoning workers' historic struggle to control aspects of the productive process on the shop floor. That many workers rejected and resisted the abdication by their union leaders of workers' vital interest in control issues is revealed in the frequency of unauthorized work stoppages (called "wildcat" strikes) supported by rank-and-file workers in the postwar era. One-third of all strikes in the 1950s were wildcat stoppages that typically arose in response to management efforts to speed up production or undermine established workplace rights.

By the terms of most collective contracts, wildcat strikes were illegal, and wildcat strikers were often subject to union discipline. From the perspective of the union leaders who negotiated these contracts, those who advocated unauthorized work stoppages and broader visions of worker control had to be prevented from influencing co-workers. The implications for free discussion at union meetings and in the union press were quickly manifest. Many union leaders stifled dissent, sacrificing internal democracy in their effort to live up to the terms of the contract. Management quickly recognized the advantage of union-enforced labor discipline and sought ever-longer terms for the collective contracts it signed.

The abandonment by unions of the effort to influence corporate decisions about investment and pricing also gravely limited labor's postwar goal of influencing national industrial policy. More, it implicitly endorsed the principle of the geographic mobility of firms. Unions made these concessions in the expectation that union jobs would not be lost, and that increased wages and benefits, indexed to inflation and productivity gains, would be forthcoming.

For decades big unionized US corporations fulfilled all these expectations. Their perennial search for production sites where costs, especially wages, were low, and labor organization feeble, did not entirely cease even in the early postwar decades. But manufacturers could not lightly abandon existing production facilities. And they could afford to pay high wages, expanded fringe benefits, and rising local taxes as long as their products remained competitive in national and international markets. Payment of escalating wages and benefits was also facilitated by industry-wide union organizations. The fact that agreements on wages and benefits in one corporation were often quickly generalized to whole industries worked to limit competition over labor costs between large oligopolist firms (such as the Big Three automakers) that sold primarily in the huge domestic US market. Such corporations could view the rising wages of their employees (which they passed on in higher prices to consumers) as guaranteeing a steadily expanding market among unionized workers for their products.

The basis of these understandings, indeed of the whole postwar "partnership" between big labor and big corporations, depended, however, on the weakness of foreign competitors. As long as sales (and even production) abroad fattened corporate profits, and foreign manufacturers did not seriously challenge domestic US producers, above all in their home market, the postwar compromise seemed to work quite well. During the early postwar period many US manufacturing corporations did locate production facilities abroad, in Latin America, for example, and especially in Europe. But these moves were conceived primarily as a way to gain better access to foreign markets. Only as Western European and Japanese competitors began to compete more successfully with US manufacturers in the world and US markets did the issue of labor costs begin to assume the central importance it has today in corporate decisions on locating plants abroad.

The growing competitiveness of the main industrial economies outside the United States was a result of factors intimately connected to the Cold War. Under US guidance, and thanks in part to US assistance, Japan and the nations of Western Europe, particularly West Germany, rebuilt their industrial plants in the postwar period. US government support for this endeavor, which included efforts to establish US-style industrial relations systems and the elimination of Communist influence in unions, was part of a global US strategy to contain the advance of Soviet Communism.

Unlike the United States, nations like Japan and West Germany were not burdened by the massive, and largely unproductive, military expenditures of the Cold War. Nor, in the early postwar period, did these nations engage, as did the United States, in large-scale direct and indirect investments abroad. Under these conditions, the relative strength and ideological autonomy of organized industrial workers in postwar Japan and West Germany also contributed to the rising productivity of firms. Because capitalists were discredited by their links to the failed fascist military regimes of the past, and socialist aspirations among workers (despite US and domestic government hostility to them) remained strong, management was forced to adopt strategies for increased productivity that involved relatively greater participation of workers and unions in production. For all these reasons rates of capital investment and productivity gains in manufacturing were higher in these societies than in the United States.

Since labor's role in this outcome is rarely stressed or viewed in comparative terms, even by labor historians, it bears some elaboration. To state the matter differently, it was precisely because of the relative ideological and political strength of the organized labor movements of Japan and West Germany in the immediate postwar period—significant sectors of the union movement in both countries, for example, continued under Socialist and Communist leadership and labor enjoyed important political and legislative support from those political parties and from their social democratic rivals—that the concessions organized labor made to management and the state in the postwar period were more likely than in the United States to preserve elements of worker control and participation. Conversely, in the United States, capitalists were ideologically and politically stronger than their counterparts in West Germany and Japan, a position reflected in the purge of leftist union leaders in the United States and the failure of the US labor movement to launch a political party of its own. The great strength of US industrial unions at war's end was economic, and it was reflected in wage rates, which were initially much higher than those in West Germany and Japan. And increasing wages was an area in which US capitalists, unlike their German and Japanese counterparts, could easily grant concessions. That was true because of the postwar command of US manufactures over the capitalist world market and the support the US state (state support of a kind unavailable to German and Japanese capitalists) gave to the expansion of US investment and commerce in the immediate postwar decades.

Over the long term, then, the different kinds of compromises US, West German and Japanese capitalists were forced to make with organized labor, and the different investment strategies that flowed from these compromises, favored more rapid growth and productivity gains in the manufacturing sectors of the national economies of West Germany and Japan than they did in the United States. Gradually, as the volume and competitiveness of manufactures from these nations increased, they began to capture ever larger shares of their own as well as world and US markets. By the 1970s, Japanese and West German firms were locating manufacturing plants abroad, sometimes in the United States itself.

The decline in the competitive position of US manufactures in world markets as the postwar period proceeded led US capitalists increasingly to elude their compromise with high-cost unionized labor at home. Managers used a variety of strategies to achieve this goal, including efforts to weaken the protection for labor organizing and unions in the federal labor legislation we have already surveyed. Employers also took advantage of federal immigration laws and enforcement policies. These failed to stop the flow of millions of illegal migrant workers into the United States, particularly from Mexico and the Caribbean Basin, but they succeeded in criminalizing the civil status of such workers. US immigration policy effectively guaranteed a large pool of low-wage workers for agriculture, manufacturing, and service industries. It undercut efforts at union organization among immigrant workers. And it provided a convenient scapegoat for conservative, racist elements within the labor movement, who could blame the growing problems of US workers on the existence of large numbers of dark-skinned foreign migrants willing to work for less.

The most important strategy available to US firms facing high labor costs and powerful unions, however, was to locate production in low-wage areas where unions were weak. The southern United States was an attractive early candidate for relocation. There, thanks to the legacy of colonialism discussed in chapter 1, labor was cheaper than in densely unionized northern states, and employers did not face the problems of operating in a different nation-state. By the 1970s, however, the search to reduce costs—wages, but also taxes and the expense of growing environmental regulation—had led large numbers of US manufacturers into productive investments far beyond the confines of the United States. This process led eventually to the massive global restructuring of production that is familiar to us all today.

The development of global networks of production and distribution is often explained as a natural, inevitable process, a byproduct of technical progress, particularly the revolution in communications based on computer technology. "Global sourcing," where components of a finished industrial product may be produced in one set of nations, assembled in others, and sold in still others, has clearly been facilitated by these new forms of communication. But its fundamental cause is the difference in national wage levels and union power in the world economy. In a real sense, the driving force behind the global restructuring we know today lies in the emergence, a half-century ago, of powerful organizations of industrial workers in the US core of the world economy.

The implications of the postwar compromise between US capitalists and organized workers were not confined to the economic sphere, however. They had long-term domestic and foreign political consequences as well. Acceptance by mainstream US labor leaders of capital's exclusive right to manage implied no less than an uncritical endorsement of capitalism as a whole. Those within the labor movement who aspired to fundamental reform of the capitalist system of production thus became suspect and potentially dangerous. Communist activists bore the brunt of the purges within the labor movement mandated by national labor legislation and encouraged by capitalists and conservative labor leaders. Conservative US union leaders had long been committed to the ostensibly "apolitical," "bread-and-butter" unionism that lay at the heart of the historic compromise between capital, labor, and the state at the end of the war. Subsequently they used every means at their disposal to eliminate Communists, many of whom were among their most effective labor organizers, from union ranks. But Communists were not the only victims of such attitudes. Union activists committed to visions of co-management and social democracy, or simply to effective democratic procedures in union affairs, could become suspect as well.

By the 1950s uncritical acceptance of capitalism—and of its corollaries, virulent anti-Communism and total support of US foreign policy—became official policy of both the AFL and the CIO. Their growing philosophical and political convergence was reflected in the merger of the two organizations in 1955. When the Cuban Revolution brought Cold War concerns into the very heart of the hemisphere, the leadership of the AFL-CIO joined with prominent US investors in Latin America and the US government to found the American Institute for Free Labor Development. That organization, which served as a model for organizations dealing with other world regions, has since trained thousands of Latin American labor leaders and funneled millions of dollars into programs to benefit Latin American labor organizations which share the AFL-CIO's anti-Communism and philosophy of "bread-and-butter" unionism. First through the AFL, then through the CIO, and finally and most systematically through AIFLD, the leadership of US labor threw its considerable weight behind US policy to defeat the efforts at fundamental reform in Latin America we surveyed in chapter 3.

Viewed from the perspective of what it gave up in the postwar compromise, then, the long-term consequences for labor were decidedly negative. Labor's decision to abdicate the struggle for a voice in the management of the firm and to capitulate on the issue of control over the labor process ultimately eroded both its own strength and that of the US industrial economy as a whole. It also undermined labor's democratic political influence within the nation and democratic institutions within the union movement itself.

Unfortunately, the long-term balance sheet is hardly more positive when looked at from the perspective of what labor gained in the postwar compromise. We have already explored some of the consequences of the high wages and benefits organized workers won in the decades after 1945. Over time they led capitalists increasingly to invest abroad. Yet winning higher material returns for their labor was a victory justly celebrated by unionized workers. Many had suffered through the Depression and seen their wartime and early postwar earnings eaten up by inflation. Moreover, given the way work was organized in big industrial plants, and the nature of most industrial workers' jobs, these material gains were tangible compensation for the conditions workers endured and the sacrifices they made.

As we have seen, however, these gains were made in the context of union abdication of the struggle for a voice in the way work was organized. And that trade-off had serious psychological and political ramifications for unionized workers. Under its terms the speed-up and simplification of tasks proceeded under the relentless, management-dictated logic of increased efficiency. Increasingly alienated from work on the job, workers found relief and satisfaction in their time away from the factory. They spent part of their rising wages, learned new skills, and realized their aspiration to engage in purposeful activity under their own direction in ambitious home-improvement projects, recreational activities, and hobbies. The increasingly absolute division between hateful formal work and pleasurable leisure-time activities had obvious benefits for individual workers off the job. But it had serious consequences for the quality of their lives on the job and for the quality of the things they produced there. And it led workers away from collective efforts to improve and control their formal work lives into the atomized, individualized world of private activity and consumption.

More obvious and direct were the negative consequences that flowed from labor's celebrated victory on the issue of the legal right to organize collectively and to strike. It is important to emphasize again that this labor victory was of no small moment. Up to that point, employer recognition of independent unions in the United States was the exception not the rule, especially in the largest and most important industrial firms. Government recognition of the rights of workers to form unions, moreover, initially proved a great boon to labor organizing.

Nevertheless, as US labor historians like Nelson Lichtenstein and Melvyn Dubofsky have shown, acceptance by unions of the jurisdiction of the state over labor organization had serious negative long-term consequences in the United States (as it did elsewhere). First of all (as already revealed in the contrast between the Wagner Act and Taft-Hartley), the government could change the rules, or its interpretation and implementation of them, to the detriment of labor. Second, labor's acceptance of the state-imposed legal framework that regulated union activities forced unions into intricate, time-consuming, and costly legal battles to protect their rights.

Acceptance by the state and employers of labor's legal right to organize and strike implied for many workers and their leaders a "closed shop." By that, as we have seen, they meant that once a majority of workers voted for a union, all workers in its jurisdiction should be represented by that union and be members of it. Once that principle was won, it was then a small step to expand and broaden agreements sanctioned during the war by the government, which made employers themselves collect union dues from the paychecks of employees and turn them over to the union. This procedure, called "dues checkoff," became standard in labor's collective contracts with big industrial employers in the postwar era.

Dues checkoff was also a historic victory for organized labor. It enabled unions to establish large strike funds to sustain members during walkouts, and gave them the wherewithal to offset the massive resources of corporations, not only in the costly legal arena that increasingly enveloped labor's struggles but in the broader effort to influence public opinion and politics. Theoretically, these funds could finance efforts to unionize sectors of the labor force still unorganized and to influence the political process in favor of working people generally.

But the closed shop and dues checkoff proved to be serious threats to the health of internal union democracy. And in the end they threatened the very legitimacy of unions themselves. Mandatory membership of all workers in the shop and the guaranteed flow of funds into the union distanced officials from the demands of the rank and file. It also made less imperative the task of convincing members on a day-to-day basis that the union in fact protected their vital shop-floor interests. Instead, union leaders increasingly based their legitimacy on the one thing they could deliver, increased wages and benefits. That seemed to be enough for many union members in the early postwar decades. But how was union legitimacy to be sustained once collective bargaining with employers turned into a question, as it did by the 1980s, of how much labor would give back, not how much it would gain?

Moreover, as management tried to make the best of a bad situation that forced it to recognize independent collective organizations of workers, it insisted all the more on its right to manage and it demanded that union officials enforce the terms of the contracts they signed. In order to insure uninterrupted production, management sought to channel worker complaints into routinized, hierarchical grievance procedures that were stipulated ahead of time in the contract and enforced by union officials. And, as we have seen, it also sought to minimize industrial conflict and enhance its ability to calculate long-term costs by pushing for contracts that covered long periods of time. Union officials acceded to these principles because they solidified their own institutional power and because they enhanced their ability to extract better wages and benefits from management. As a result, however, many unions turned into contract police while the most fundamental and daily concerns of rank-and-file members were ignored, bogged down in red tape, or shunted aside.

Many union leaders thus began to find that their own positions depended more on their ability to deal with management and manipulate the legal system and the contract than they did on their responsiveness to issues that were vital to members on the shop floor. As dealings between management and union leaders became highly technical affairs that involved professional union staffs, unions became more bureaucratic. Decisions were made at the top to preserve and enhance the interests of the organization itself. To insure the conformity of a rank and file deemed ignorant of legal and technical fine points, union leaders often limited and manipulated the information available to members. They enforced the terms of the long contracts they signed with management by stifling internal dissent and punishing nonconformity. Union leaders often sought to perpetuate themselves and their cronies in power and arrogated to themselves and their dependent professional staffs the distribution of union funds. For the most part labor leaders left off efforts to organize the unorganized.

Labor's enemies made much of the high salaries of union officials and the corrupt, illegal, and "shady" deals some union leaders engaged in. But the greatest cost of winning the closed shop and dues checkoff was the toll these victories eventually took on the attitudes of existing and potential union members. The way many unions functioned alienated their captive rank and file and gave unionism a bad name among unorganized workers. As unions lost the spirit if not the form of democracy in running their affairs, they became their own worst enemies.

In these and other ways the historic organizational victories of US industrial workers turned sour in the decades following World War II. And as this internal labor dialectic was unfolding, public opinion and the government turned steadily against labor. Already in the 1950s the FBI was moving from the harassment of alleged Communists in the labor movement to the pursuit of "racketeering" in major unions. Meanwhile, liberal forces from within the Democratic Party staged "show trials" of corrupt union leaders, notably Jimmy Hoffa of the Teamsters. In subsequent years the courts and government agencies charged with implementing national labor legislation, particularly the National Labor Relations Board, made union organizing and legal certification of unions ever more difficult. During the 1980s Republican administrations, whose elections organized labor proved unable to prevent, turned the prestige and power of the presidency squarely against labor, providing full support for the growing employer practice of hiring "permanent replacement workers" to take the jobs of striking workers. (Wide public acceptance of this euphemism for strikebreakers, or, as US unionists call them, "scabs," is itself a telling index of labor's declining legitimacy and power.) Meanwhile, labor's traditional influence within the Democratic party was displaced and fragmented by new constituencies advocating democratic reforms to favor the rights of ethnic minorities, women, and gays.

Finally, in 1993, organized labor lost its battle against congressional approval of the North American Free Trade Agreement (NAFTA). This pact, signed between the United States, Canada, and Mexico, promised both to facilitate the movement of capital and commodities within the hemisphere and to undercut national legislation designed to protect labor and the environment. NAFTA, which is discussed in more detail in the next section, was a major defeat for organized US labor. It not only seemed certain to stimulate the flow of investment in manufacturing production into low-wage Mexico, eliminating jobs in unionized US industries. It also symbolized the growing legitimacy of a liberal capitalist agenda for the future of the Americas in which unions and their historic democratic goals have no theoretical or practical place.

Understanding what went wrong for labor in the historical era just ended, however, does not necessarily imply that the collective democratic struggle by working people in the United States and elsewhere has effectively ended. Capitalists may think (or hope) so. Academics hostile to labor or ignorant of the paradoxes of its postwar history may wittingly or unwittingly reinforce the view that organized labor is out of date or inconsequential. And even many working people may today seem resigned to the way things are, while others place their faith in movements that speak to their concerns and democratic aspirations as women or environmentalists or as ethnic or sexual minorities.

But labor historians who take the long view of these things are not so pessimistic about the future of labor. After all, whatever our differences—of nationality, gender, ethnicity, and so on—most of us continue to work for wages in a highly unequal social system that denies us meaningful work and a decent return for our labor. That simple fact defines a set of common interests of immense democratic potential. To be sure, those interests have never been articulated very well by either of the great social philosophies, liberalism and Marxism, that have structured our political understandings of the world around us. Yet as labor's fortunes have declined in the postwar era, labor historians have been busy rethinking those political philosophies and the role of labor within them. The next section reviews their work and assesses the contributions it can make to revitalizing the labor movement and democratic politics generally.

II

If labor's postwar fate involves one paradox—of victory turned into defeat, of strength made into weakness—scholarship about labor reveals another. For as the labor movement in much of the industrialized world has declined in recent decades to what is arguably its lowest ebb this century, students of labor history have been producing some of the most vigorous and innovative social scholarship of our times.

The crisis in which US labor finds itself today, which I discussed in some detail in the previous section, is symptomatic of much wider trends. Rates of unionization provide an important index of what has been happening. In the United States, the proportion of non-agricultural workers belonging to unions is only 16 percent today, half the all-time high reached in 1953. In Japan, where rates of unionization were much higher than in the United States in the early postwar period, the relative decline is virtually the same. The unionized portion of all employed Japanese workers has fallen from a high of 53 percent in 1949 to about 26 percent today. This trend is all the more remarkable since, unlike what has happened in the United States, Japanese economic growth has been extraordinary in recent decades. Rates of unionization have declined less rapidly in most European nations but even more severely in many Latin American ones.

In ideological terms, however, the crisis of labor abroad is even more severe than it is in the United States. In most of the nations of Western

Europe and Latin America, for example, Marxists played a much larger role in the leadership of the labor movement in the postwar period than they did in the United States. The collapse of the so-called "workers' states" of Eastern Europe, especially the disintegration of the Soviet Union itself, has placed the nominally socialist goals and Marxist philosophies of left-wing parties and trade unions in these countries decidedly on the defensive. For more than a century Marxist socialism inspired much of the world labor movement and deeply influenced scholarship on labor, especially in the field of labor history. Now, however, neo-liberalism, not Marxism, is the philosophy that is sweeping the globe. In the "new world order" of free trade and privatization, market forces are to unleash the productive potential of all human beings and sweep away the inefficiencies of the bureaucratic, interventionist, social-welfare state. In this new world, unions, the subject of traditional labor history, have no theoretical or practical place.

Nevertheless, as this extraordinary historical transformation has been unfolding, Western scholars, Marxists preeminent among them, have been fashioning a large body of innovative work on labor that ranks among the best scholarship of recent decades. Most historians and social scientists, regardless of specialization, are aware of the contributions of British labor historian E.P. Thompson. His *The Making of the English Working Class*, published in 1963, was in some sense a response to growing recognition on the left of the abuses committed in the name of Marxism and socialism by the Stalinist regime in the Soviet Union. Thompson's work inspired a new generation of Western social and labor historians. Over the last thirty years they have collectively transformed the writing of labor history.

"Old" labor history focused on economic change and the political and institutional history of unions. The "new" labor history shifted its attention to the social and cultural spheres. It emphasized the experience of unorganized as well as organized workers. It incorporated study of workers' private, family, and community life into the story of labor's public activities. And it complicated, and greatly enriched, the traditional preoccupation of labor historians with issues of class by emphasizing ethnic and gender perspectives. The quantity and quality of this new labor history show no signs of declining. Recent studies in US labor history, for example, have been showered with prizes by the historical profession. And in my own field, Latin America, labor history has been judged to have "come of age," its conceptual and methodological contributions worthy of emulation by historians working in otherwise far more developed fields.

The new work in labor history, like Thompson's itself, reflected a growing sense among labor scholars that the progressive democratic gains made by working people during the nineteenth and early twentieth centuries had somehow gone awry since World War II. By the 1960s their traditional optimism over labor's inevitable progress had given way to a growing recognition of the ways past advances were being distorted and even subverted in capitalist and so-called socialist societies alike. In recent decades, labor historians have turned their attention to questions of "what went wrong," "what might have been," or "what still could be." As they have done so, they have challenged traditional labor history in ways that have implications far beyond that field. It can be argued, in fact, that these challenges contain within them clues to a new, post-Cold War democratic politics, one capable of confronting the ideology of neo-liberalism and its claim that the interests of capitalists are co-terminous with the interests of humanity.

Generally speaking, however, the new labor history has not had this political effect. True, its concern with the working majority in society and its efforts to write history "from the bottom up" have broadened and deepened the range of inquiry of historians and the kinds of sources they use. These trends are graphically revealed in the mainstream liberal US college textbooks I examined to develop the argument in chapter 2. They are full of information on the daily life of working people and take special pains to convey the experience of ethnic minorities and women.

But the most fundamental democratic challenges posed by the new labor history have been ignored by mainstream historians and are virtually unknown to the general public. Each of the four I survey here—I will call them the challenges of control, gender, globalism, and postmodernism—is understood primarily by a small number of labor specialists. And although in democratic terms these challenges are interrelated and mutually reinforcing, even those who specialize in one or another of them may not fully appreciate their essential unity and joint implications. Taken together, these challenges invite us to rethink not only the specialized field of labor history but our broader understanding of modern world history.

Control

This challenge emphasizes the centrality of the struggle between capitalists and workers over control of the labor process. Its impact on contemporary labor studies owes much to the influential book by Harry Braverman, *Labor and Monopoly Capitalism*, published in 1974. Following Marx, Braverman argued that the ability to do purposeful, meaningful

work is what defines us as human beings. Capitalist organization of production, he claimed, progressively shatters the unity of conceptualizing
tasks and executing them, the unity of mind and hand. It then subdivides
tasks into their simplest components, substituting cheap, unskilled labor
for skilled. Braverman argued that this dehumanizing process, inherent
in capitalism, was no less characteristic of the Soviet organization of production, which had incorporated these principles in its effort to match
Western standards of productivity.

Historians have used the concept of control to fundamentally revise
our understanding of labor history. Worker protest in nineteenth-century
Europe provides one example. It now appears more as resistance to proletarianization and loss of control over the labor process than it does, as
orthodox Marxists would have it, a consequence of either.

Focus on the issue of control has also led to a radical recasting of the
meaning of workers' struggles in the United States, most notably in the
book by David Montgomery I discussed in chapter 2. In that chapter we
saw how worker resistance to managerial initiatives to break their control
of the labor process contributed to the scale of industrial conflict at the
end of the nineteenth century. We also saw how these initiatives, often
called Taylorism or scientific management, contributed both to the
tremendous expansion of the US economy and to the weakness of labor
organization in big industrial firms during the first three decades of the
twentieth century. Then, in the first section of this chapter, we saw how
US workers developed tactics during the Great Depression to organize
the very industries where Taylorist practices were most advanced. We
also saw how industrial workers relinquished their historic goal of influencing the productive process in their post-World War II settlement with
management.

Emphasis on the issue of control also has been used, beginning with
Braverman, and most tellingly in the works by Michael Burawoy cited at
the end of this chapter, to demonstrate the similarities between the organization of production in capitalist and socialist societies. Burawoy, a
sociologist who has actually labored in comparable metalworking plants
in the United States and Eastern Europe, has also probed the ways
authoritarian factory regimes in both systems induce worker consent.

Yet the full revisionist potential of the issue of control for labor studies
is far from realized. Focus on workers' struggle for control over the way
they work blurs the conceptual categories that have customarily defined
labor studies. Following Marx, labor history has traditionally defined its
subject as the industrial proletariat, propertyless wage workers in manufacturing industry. Control issues force us to question the supreme utility
of this definition. They ask us to rethink the usefulness of defining labor

history as the study of free but not coerced workers, urban but not rural workers, industrial but not agricultural workers. The drive for control links motives and goals of artisans, so-called "peasants," small producers, and blue- and white-collar workers alike. It helps to make political sense, for example, of the remarkable unity of landed and landless rural workers documented by Lawrence Goodwyn in his study of Populism in the United States, which I discussed in chapter 2.

Students of so-called "peasant" movements in Latin America have likewise documented the unity of rural workers, propertied and propertyless alike, in struggles for land. But, like students of "peasant" society generally, they have often failed to appreciate the importance of control issues in explaining the motivations of rural workers. Fixated on the issue of property relations, Marxists especially have ignored the democratic implications of control in their own philosophical tradition.

Emphasis on the issue of control thus has far-reaching implications. It subverts the bias against rural, pre-industrial, so-called "traditional" workers or "peasants" that informs so much liberal and Marxist labor history. It provides, as noted in the first section of this chapter, a democratic labor perspective on the crisis and demise of socialist regimes in recent times. And, as we shall see below, it suggests ways to recast current debates, dominated by neo-liberal assumptions, over productivity and international competitiveness. For all these reasons, control issues suggest ways labor can redefine itself and its democratic goals and begin to build political coalitions that stretch far beyond the traditional concerns of industrial workers in a single nation.

Gender

This challenge questions the emphasis in traditional labor history on production over reproduction and the public over the private. In focusing almost exclusively on work in the formal economy of patriarchal societies, and on the public expressions of workers' experience, consciousness, and action, traditional labor history effectively defined itself as men's history.

By thus marginalizing women, labor history virtually eliminated half of its subject matter and deprived itself of crucial tools for analyzing some of its most important—and vexing—problems. These tools center on the role of households and families in structuring and giving meaning to the experience of individuals. Families coordinate the work, both paid and unpaid, of their members. They influence the decisions individual members make about marriage and bearing and raising children. Families, and the communities they help build and sustain, provide role models and inculcate basic values in the young. Families decide, for example, whether to send their children to Protestant Sunday school, or, as many did in the stockyard communities of Chicago in the 1930s, to Communist "catechism" class. In contemporary Latin America families may urge their members to join progressive Catholic Christian base communities, or, as is increasingly likely among the poor, Pentecostal religious sects. Families may influence the young to read classic children's stories, allow them to buy Donald Duck comics, or try to prohibit them from playing violent video games, or not. Families and local communities, and the women who have traditionally played such prominent roles within them, invest the daily experience of individuals with collective and transcendent meaning.

Gender perspectives, most notably in the work of Joan Wallach Scott, have revealed how male bias distorts understanding of labor's past. Such bias appears in celebrated accounts of labor's public heroes (including those of E.P. Thompson himself), the iconography, culture, and organizational tactics of unions, and even the collection and analysis of "hard" statistical data on workers by government agencies. Gender perspectives have also shown how the standard periods of labor history often do not capture the most important ways economic, technological, and cultural change affects women, wage workers and unpaid home workers alike. The promise of gender analysis in labor history has been easier to articulate than to practice, however, and it is revealing that, for the most part, application of these ideas has been the work of women.

Gender perspectives are particularly important to the labor movement today. While many labor organizations are still dominated by male leaders and male perspectives, the feminization of waged work is proceeding rapidly in developed and underdeveloped economies alike. Gains in the numbers of unionized women workers in the US labor force, especially public employees, have partially offset the drastic decline in unionization in many industries where men have traditionally predominated. Women also constitute the vast majority of workers in many of the US industries that in recent years have moved production to export processing platforms in free trade zones abroad. This is particularly true of the *maquiladora* assembly industry developed in recent decades along the northern border of Mexico. NAFTA now promises to extend the low-wage, non-union, free-trade principles that made the *maquiladora* program so attractive to US corporations to the whole of Mexico.

Perhaps the most dramatic illustration of the power of gender perspectives in addressing the traditional concerns of labor history—and providing clues to a democratic politics for the future—are studies of the intersection of workplace and community mobilization. It is just this link between shop floor organizing around wages and work conditions and community mobilization to demand public services like housing, transportation, and sanitation that has helped make the contemporary labor movement in Brazil one of the few bright spots in the grim world of labor politics today.

Globalism

This term refers to the interconnectedness of labor and its struggles within the world capitalist system. This perspective, derived from the postwar Latin American development thinking I discussed in chapters 1 and 4, has inspired much of the analysis in this book. It questions the definition of labor history as solely the experience of workers in manufacturing since the advent of industrial capitalism. It posits instead a definition that encompasses the experience of workers since the beginning of the capitalist transformation of the whole modern era (1500 to the present). It thus challenges the definition of labor history as a simple story of free wage workers who emerged first in Europe, arguing instead that their history is inextricably bound up with the broader history of coerced labor in Europe's colonies.

As detailed in chapter 1, this perspective challenges the ethnocentric cultural assumptions (and covert racism) that pervade much scholarly and popular understanding of American history. It argues that the legacy of coerced versus free labor best explains the divergent development of the European colonies of this hemisphere and helps clarify the debate over the relative importance of "internal" versus "external" factors in the industrialization of Europe itself. In this hemisphere, since virtually everything was influenced by colonialism, external factors predominated. The one part of the Americas that industrialized did so as it avoided the coercive labor systems of the rest of the hemisphere, and began, early on, to participate in world trade as though it were a Western European nation.

In the era of industrial capitalism this perspective questions the idea of a labor history focused on the industrial working class in geographical regions like Latin America whose primary function in the global economy was to produce primary agricultural and mineral commodities for export. In the late nineteenth century and the first half of the twentieth, workers in export production decisively influenced the making of labor movements in Latin America. As revealed in chapter 3, they played a pivotal role in the Latin American social revolutions of this century.

The promise of this approach to labor history is far from realization, however. More than two decades ago, for example, Arghiri Emmanuel advanced a cogent theoretical case for the idea that in a world of relative capital mobility and labor immobility, trade between high- and low-wage economies is inherently unequal. His work challenged the basic assumptions of both classical liberal and Marxist development theory and is particularly pertinent to evaluating agreements like NAFTA today. Yet, like other labor-based theories of global economic development, it has yet to be tested through empirical research and comparative historical analysis.

Unfortunately, few labor historians have ventured beyond the confines of study of a single nation. For reasons discussed in the next section, the national perspective of historians is deeply ingrained in our methods. Yet the integration of world manufacturing production under the aegis of multinational corporations demands more than ever that historians internationalize their work. Like the labor movement itself, students of labor must develop analytical concepts, and informational and organizational networks, that transcend their traditional focus on the nation-state.

In this book I have tried to suggest the democratic interpretive and political potential of a labor history that looks at the whole of American history in global context. Engaging in this kind of analysis, I have argued, is more than an exercize in how well one can explain the historical information on the table, or how closely one can approximate historical reality or "truth." Such analysis, I have attempted to show, can also work to undercut the nationalism, cultural chauvinism, and racism that continue to divide world labor.

Postmodernism

"Historical truth" is a notion discordant with the postmodern assumptions that today challenge traditional labor history—and widely accepted notions about the production of knowledge itself. Postmodern thought emanates from post-World War II Europe and reflects the disillusionment of intellectuals from that continent with the optimism of the early industrial era. From the vantage point of their "postmodern" world, the promise of eighteenth-century reason and nineteenth-century industrial technology, the optimism about human progress imbedded in liberal and Marxist thought, now appears naive and dangerous. For these thinkers the human and material destruction of the two world wars that emanated from the cradle of European "civilization," the environmental degradation of industrialism itself, the social and political pathologies of both capitalist and socialist organization of society (including the fates of their respective labor movements) call for a reassessment of intellectual inquiry itself. Postmodernism takes apart discourse to reveal the historically contingent, the contextual, the constructed, indeed, the autobiographical nature of all knowledge. For historians, these are not new ideas in themselves. In fact, as argued in the next section, they lie at the core of the historical method. But many postmodernists carry these ideas to the point of denying the possibility of knowing in any universal sense. More specifically, they deny the assumption of progress, including democratic progress, imbedded in what they call the "master narratives" of the modern era, liberalism and Marxism. Not surprisingly, most labor historians, whose field is at the centre of these social philosophies, have been extremely chary of postmodernism and its implications.

It is clear, however, that postmodernism can be turned to democratic purpose. Its emphasis on the way we construct reality through discourse can reveal repressive social bias in what we take as common sense. It can legitimize understandings of the past generated by groups of the socially oppressed—workers, women, non-Westerners, ethnic and religious minorities, gays, and so on. Postmodernism provides a healthy justification for pluralism, for the respect of diversity of opinion and interest that is vital to democratic organization of society. But when postmodernists deny the possibility that some stories about the past might be "better" or "truer" than others, they create difficult problems for democratic politics. The relativism of postmodernism seems to lead to a politics and to understandings of history governed by unmediated, selfish individual and group interest.

In a world in which power is concentrated in the hands of a privileged few, postmodernism seems to sanction (as in the United States today) both official endorsement of a vague and divisive multiculturalism and a popular politics of cultural exclusivity and frustration. Meanwhile, capitalist interests have used their power to universalize a vision of a post-Cold War order in which the collective ideals of working people are excluded from consideration. As is true for the labor movement today, the practical problem facing postmodernists (many of whom think of themselves as democrats) is articulating a democratic politics able to appeal to the majority. It is just such a politics, justified by universal notions of democratic progress, that accounts for the real if limited democratization that defines the modern era.

That some stories about the past prove to be "better" or "truer" over time than others may be clearer to historians of Europe's underdeveloped former colonies than it is to historians in the developed West. The experience of the oppressed reveals more clearly the reality of exploitative social relations than does the experience of their oppressors. Whose story about slavery proved, over time, to be accepted by all of us as truer? That of the slave or the slaveowner? Whose story about European colonialism? In this sense, the history of the modern world is one of democratic progress. Will the fate of women's story about patriarchy be different? Or that of labor's story about capitalism or about the socialism we have known?

All of the challenges I have described work to democratize traditional labor history by exposing its urban, male, Eurocentric bias. In thus "decentering" labor history and challenging the "binary opposites" (urban/rural, industrial/agricultural, free/unfree, public/private, male/female) that have been used to define it, they are compatible with postmodern precepts. (The terms in quotations are postmodern and typify the rarified discourse in which postmodern scholars customarily talk with one another.) But the labor history described here need not renounce the idea of democratic progress in the modern world. In fact, as we have seen, it can provide essential elements for the renewal of labor's democratic project.

Of these challenges, it is the issue of control that is the least appreciated by organized labor and by the left in general today. Feminists have forced labor organizations to become more aware of the needs and goals of women in the labor force and in unions in recent years. Unions are also more alive to the global nature of the problems they face than they have been in the past. And although most unionists, like most people outside academia, probably have no clear idea of what postmodernists themselves are about, they are surely aware of the importance today of the politics of cultural identity. The growing ethnic diversity of the US workforce and the initiatives of company managers and public educators to increase our "multicultural sensitivity" have made them aware of that.

Issues of control are another matter. They are ignored by a postwar labor leadership that formally abdicated responsibility for them. They are neglected by a left that trusted in the state to resolve labor's problems. Paradoxically, however, issues of control may contribute more than any of the challenges we have surveyed to extricating labor and the left from the ideological and political crisis in which they find themselves today.

We can address these questions through discussion of two of the most important processes currently affecting working people in this hemisphere. The first involves what scholars call the "informal sector" of Latin American economies. The second pertains to NAFTA.

The term "informal sector" refers to the activities of the large numbers of people (some estimates go as high as half of the active labor force in big Latin American cities), many of whom work for themselves, who provide goods and services outside the legal channels of the formal economy that is sanctioned and regulated by the state. These people fill the streets of Latin American cities, selling food, clothing, and other manufactures. They are the owners of small repair shops for automotive vehicles and household appliances. They run food-processing, construction, transportation, and even manufacturing operations out of their homes. Some informal economic activity is tied directly to the formal manufacturing sector. Some multinational firms which manufacture clothing for export, for example, depend on intricate systems of "putting out" work to local household producers. People in the informal sector have no formal access to credit institutions and are systematically discriminated against or harassed by the police and regulatory arms of the state. Yet, as virtually all studies of them demonstrate, they are highly resourceful and productive. Their productivity is all the more remarkable given their meager resources and the political odds arrayed against them.

Marxists have traditionally ignored or denigrated the economic and political potential of such people, classifying them (as they do rural small farmers or "peasants") as reactionary "petty commodity" producers destined to disappear as capitalist development proceeds. To the extent leftists have paid attention to the burgeoning informal sector of recent decades they have called for greater state involvement in its activities. The state, they contend, should provide people in the informal sector with better access to credit. It should regulate the exploitative, dangerous labor conditions often found there. Leftist scholars have often justified such regulation on the grounds that the cheap labor of the informal sector subsidizes production (and reproduction of the labor force) in the formal sector, including its transnational dimension.

It is apologists for the capitalist order, not scholars on the left, who have seized on the evidence of the inventiveness and productivity of people in the informal sector to advance their political agenda. Neo-liberals have celebrated the "entrepreneurial" values of people in the informal sector in their efforts to promote privatization and advance their broader program of limiting the regulatory and social welfare activity of the state. The most notorious example is the study *The Other Path*, published in English in 1989 by the Peruvian corporate executive Hernando De Soto. The book, which was promoted by private capitalist organizations and US agencies for international development, became a best-seller in Latin America and the United States. It won accolades from people like President George Bush (in a speech to the annual meeting of the World Bank and the International Monetary Fund), Richard Nixon, and leading US and Latin American intellectuals, such as the Peruvian novelist and liberal politician Mario Vargas Llosa. De Soto argued that the informal sector had already proven itself a much more efficient provider of housing and transportation than the Peruvian government. Freed from the stifling, corrupt, and inefficient burden of state regulation, he claimed, the informal sector promised to contribute extensively to economic growth and development in Peru and elsewhere.

De Soto found the origins of the legendary inefficiency of the contemporary Latin American state in the legacy of Spanish colonialism. But the problem of the inefficient, overbearing state today affects capitalist and socialist societies alike. Today only the statist left and a dwindling minority of liberal reformers refuse to recognize what most people in all these societies have been expressing for some time. If many citizens of socialist regimes have come to despise the modern bureaucratic state, most of us in capitalist societies are wary of big government as well—except, of course, when its programs benefit us directly. We fear its impersonal power and its growing impositions on our lives. We resent its costs, despair of its "red tape," and marvel at its inefficiencies. These are feelings we can experience when, even as law-abiding citizens, we file our income-tax returns, cross a border, or try to license a car.

Ironically, however, it is capitalists and the wealthy, the people who benefit most from government policies and state activity, who in recent decades have become most adept at denouncing the state. In contrast, in the postwar era the left and labor unions have watched the state turn progressively against their interests. Yet they continue to advocate statist solutions to our problems while we ourselves have become ever more suspicious of them.

The urban informal sector thus presents the left and the labor movement in Latin America and elsewhere with an important opportunity to rethink its understanding of the ownership of property, control of the labor process, and the role of the state in achieving the democratic objectives of working people. As in their analysis of rural workers' struggles for land, Marxists have fixed their attention on the fact that many in the impoverished informal sector own their means of production. Most view such people as "petty capitalists." They have neglected the fact that these same people also control the way they work and the products of their labor. The evidence researchers have uncovered about the resourcefulness and productivity of workers in the informal sector, and the tenacity with which they struggle to preserve and improve their position, seems to validate the importance of control in their lives. That should not be surprising. Labor historians have shown that these are the same concerns that have inspired workers in manufacturing industry the world over.

If the left and organized labor thought more about control and less about property relations they might see the informal sector less as a school for petty capitalists and more as an extension of the working class. They might think less about government regulation and government programs to aid the informal sector—important as the goals of such programs may be—and more about how negative experience at the hands of the capitalist state validates the democratic suspicions of big government most people share. Finally, they might contest the ideological mileage capitalist apologists make in interpreting the informal sector. They might learn how to understand the experience of people in a huge, grossly exploited segment of the Latin American labor force in ways commensurate with the experience and goals of working people generally.

Envisioning a program that responds to the democratic needs and aspirations of the vast numbers of people in the urban informal sector of Latin American societies (and beyond) will not be easy. But like the problem of coming to terms with the democratic aspirations of rural laborers, sharecroppers, tenants, and smallholders, the left and labor can be sure that traditional collectivist and statist proposals will not appeal. For those in the informal sector, as for the rest of us who labor, control issues provide the firmest place to stand as we contest the neo-liberal order before us.

The question of control has likewise been absent in the debate over NAFTA. As in the case of the informal sector, focus on this issue offers an important way to reassess labor's current political agenda. It also suggests a way to confront the capitalist vision of the future and undermine the terms liberals have imposed for discussion of it. That vision, symbolized and operationalized in this hemisphere by the passage of NAFTA, hinges on the principle of economic growth. Growth is to be achieved through the greater productivity that international market competition under free trade will provide.

Opposition to this liberal agenda, and to NAFTA itself, has been spearheaded in the United States by organized labor, seconded by environmental groups. For the most part, however, this was a marriage of convenience, in which both parties agreed on a common enemy. It did not involve mutual recognition of basic principles that could unify their separate understandings of the problems posed by NAFTA.

Although the opposition to NAFTA put up a good fight, and succeeded in modifying aspects of the agreement, including addenda that address labor and environmental issues, it did not succeed in modifying the agreement's basic thrust. Passage of the agreement was assured when proponents of NAFTA mollified many environmental groups by promising a side agreement that gave more protection against abuses than labor got and an enforcement procedure with more teeth than the one pro-vided to labor.

The US labor opponents of NAFTA argued that the agreement would facilitate and intensify the relocation of US manufacturing industry in Mexico and lead to an overall loss of jobs for the US economy. The great-est losses would occur among high-paying industrial, often unionized, jobs. Labor advocates argued that such relocations, as the *maquiladora* industry had already demonstrated, would not appreciably raise Mexican wages. Nor, they claimed, would the relocation of manufacturing indus-try foster the development of effective democratic unions in Mexico. To support their case labor advocates pointed to the history of union control by the corrupt and authoritarian Mexican state, and to evidence of gov-ernment and official labor support for the repression of fledgling independent unions in foreign-owned industries like auto plants. They joined environmentalists in decrying the lowering of environmental stan-dards, including conditions in the workplace, that NAFTA seemed certain to foster. They pointed again to the sorry environmental record of the *maquiladora* program to support this contention.

Many of these arguments are valid and persuasive. But in the overall context of the agreement's promise to promote growth—a promise all liv-ing US presidents and Nobel Prize-winners in economics assured the American public was real—such arguments sounded hollow or self-serv-ing to many people outside unions. Viewed from the perspective of Latin American labor history, moreover, the long-term effects of large-scale US investment in Mexico may prove less negative than the opposition to NAFTA has contended. They may actually strengthen labor as a force for democratic change. The last time foreign capitalists invested massively in Mexico, during the dictatorship of Porfirio Díaz (1877–1910), they helped precipitate the social revolution I discussed in chapter 3. A more recent illustration of what may happen comes from Brazil. There, in the decades following the military coup of 1964, labor responded to large-scale foreign investment in manufacturing industry by breaking loose of state control and becoming a powerful force for democratization. In 1989 Brazilians almost elected as president of the nation a metalworker running on the ticket of the Workers' Party.

Whatever the validity of the specific arguments made against NAFTA, what is certain is that US labor's opposition to the agreement, like that of most environmentalists, did not challenge the basic liberal principles on which it rests. Labor did not really question the goal of free trade and the principle of international competitiveness. It questioned only the way free trade was being implemented and international competitiveness achieved under the agreement. Nor did labor question the goal of increased productivity and the growing consumption of cheaper goods that it will foster, although some labor voices wondered how, with the loss of ever greater numbers of high-paying unionized jobs, many people could pay for them. In the end, the proponents of NAFTA used the liberal principles of growth through expanded production and free trade to win the battle to influence the political process in favor of adoption of the agreement. Appealing to us as consumers, their arguments ultimately cajoled the US general public, initially opposed to NAFTA, into acceptance if not support of it.

Agreements like NAFTA seem inevitable and will be almost certainly deepened and broadened as long as labor, environmentalists, and the public at large do not begin to question the liberal economic principles which undergird them. These principles, of course, underlie the whole "free enterprise" economic system that continues to transform the world we live in. At some point, those of us who work for a living need to begin to ask ourselves, "Productivity for what?" "Productivity for whom?" "Productivity at what human and environmental cost?"

Such questions do not seem unreasonable at a time when US working people are laboring longer hours than they did a generation ago, yet their share of national income continues to decline. The growing inequality of income distribution in the United States is directly fostered by the globalization of manufacturing production, although public discussion rarely hints at the connection. Freer international trade is fast creating a society in the United States that looks more and more like the historical ones of Latin America. In it a dwindling percentage of skilled industrial workers and a static or slowly growing number of relatively high-wage technical and professional workers stand in opposition not only to a grossly enriched capitalist plutocracy, but also to a large and growing underclass of low-wage service workers, the marginally employed, and the unemployed. The breakdown of the family, widespread criminality, incarceration rates that are the highest in the world, and rampant illegal drug use in the United States are all closely related to the higher stage of world capitalism that liberalization of trade is meant to foster. Yet these serious social problems are addressed in individualistic moral terms by conservative Republicans and in paternalistic statist terms by Democrats, the best of whom engage in rear-guard efforts to provide more worker training and protect declining social welfare programs.

Meanwhile, on a global level, the quality of the air we breathe, the water we drink, the whole physical world we depend on, continues rapidly to deteriorate. Temporary progress to reverse this destruction in places like the United States is currently under assault by the same capitalist interests that promote the globalization of production and freer trade. We all contribute to this process of ecological destruction as we fill our lives with more and more material things. We consume these things in a desperate attempt to compensate ourselves for working harder and faster and longer at jobs that compromise our health and psychological well-being and provide us with less and less satisfaction.

Control issues speak tellingly to all of these destructive trends. There is considerable scholarly and historical evidence that demonstrates that people in control of their work are more efficient and productive—and happier—than those who are not. It comes from studies of small-scale rural producers and the urban informal sector in Latin America and elsewhere and from worker participation experiments in factories and offices in the industrialized world. It is confirmed in this book in the biography of Carl Barks, who carved out a niche of creativity and control in the Disney empire and produced a huge volume of work that is considered among the best popular art of our time. Management itself is acutely aware these days of the possibilities of tapping into the issues of worker participation and control to increase productivity, quality control, and "worker commitment" to the firm. Many workers rightly understand that these initiatives invariably preserve the principle of authoritarian management control. But their own union organizations have generally failed to take the lead in placing control issues, historically at the core of workers' struggles, at the forefront of labor's current concerns.

Most of us do not need scholarly studies and historical evidence to validate and understand the revolutionary potential of control issues. We experience their liberating impact every time we engage in projects that allow us to conceive and execute tasks under our own direction. This happens when we go fishing, for example, or join with others in cooking a good meal. It happens when we garden, re-roof a house, or invite our friends to help us move into a new apartment. We experience what it is like to control how we work when we make or draw or write something we are proud of. We may think of some of these tasks more as "fun" or more as "work." But we know that they are qualitatively different from what we do most of the time at our formal places of employment.

People in control of their work may often be more productive than those who are not. But thinking about the virtues and satisfactions of controlling the way we work can also lead us to question the whole notion of production at any cost and the ideas of unlimited economic growth and consumption that are closely tied to it. Efforts by organized labor to defeat agreements like NAFTA—indeed labor's ability to achieve its broader democratic goals or even to maintain its current organizational strength—seem destined to failure unless we begin to question the idea of unlimited economic growth itself. That notion of human progress, deeply imbedded in liberal and Marxist philosophy inherited from the nineteenth century, no longer seems viable. Capitalism's great historical virtue, its awesome capacity to expand economic production and consumption, is proving now to be its great defect. Capitalism's health depends on expansion. But economic expansion (which, for all its human benefits, has always entailed great social and environmental costs) now obviously threatens our collective health, and that of the planet itself. Clearly, the issues of production and consumption have different meanings for the developed and underdeveloped societies of the world and for the privileged and underprivileged classes within them. Equitable distribution, not unlimited production, is the crucial problem we face today. But as long as levels of wages and benefits and the quality of working conditions are predicated solely on the logic of economic productivity, and we continue to define human progress as ever greater consumption of material things, struggles for greater social equity and responsible environmental policy in a world of infinite capital mobility seem certain to fail.

The history of workers' struggle for control over the way they work is replete with clues to a different, more democratic and sustainable, vision of human progress. Historically, workers have mixed labor and leisure and have resisted the fragmentation of production and speed-ups that capitalists pursue in the name of productivity and competitiveness. They have aspired to do a "fair day's work for a fair day's pay"—enough of each to allow them to enjoy and control other aspects of their lives. They have found satisfaction in the fruits of their labor and in doing a job "right." For too long labor historians associated these attitudes with free, white, wage-earning men. Today we can recognize their democratic significance for the politics of all working people.

III

Unfortunately, the new work on labor history is virtually unknown to the public at large. Yet it is precisely the interests of the general public—the vast majority of people who work for a living—that the new labor history seeks to address. For this paradoxical state of affairs academic historians themselves are largely responsible. Close examination of the way historians actually do their work reveals methods that are surprisingly democratic in principle yet undemocratic in practice. It shows, moreover, how the strengths of the historical method, developed as historians enlisted in the cause of nineteenth-century European nationalism, compromise the ability of labor historians to respond to the global concerns of working people today.

Those of us who earn our livings as labor historians thus find ourselves in a professional crisis that parallels the current ideological and political crisis of the wider labor movement. Labor historians have long argued that workers' democratic aspirations emerge in part from their experience at the point of production. It is fitting, therefore, to end these labor perspectives on the history of US–Latin American relations with a critique of the working methods of the historians who endeavor to write that history. In this section I argue that until historians learn better how to realize the democratic promise in our methods, our histories will remain on the sidelines of the ongoing struggle by working people to democratize the world we live in.

It is not easy to identify exactly what "the historical method" is, or to understand exactly why professional historians work the way they do. In contrast to social scientists, for example, historians have not been very concerned with explaining to themselves and to others why they do what they do. They think they know "good" history when they see it and evince little concern with theory in their methods. They even debate whether theirs is a "method" or a "craft." Following sound and tested practices, not mastering theory, is the way professional historians learn their trade.

I believe, nonetheless, that there is a logic behind the activities of historians. To discover it I have borrowed from the methods of the new labor historians. Labor historians have had to surmount the fact that throughout most of history working people had neither the time, the cultural tradition, nor the skill of literacy to enable them to leave behind the written documents historians depend upon to interpret human experience. Lacking such documents, historians have tried to discover what working people thought by carefully reconstructing what they did. When one looks at professional historians in this way—examining, for example, how they conduct their research, praise and criticize their colleagues, and train new historians—a certain logic appears in their methods.

The distinctiveness of the way historians work emerges with special clarity when their activities are contrasted with those of other social scientists, political scientists, for example, or sociologists or economists. In recent decades, more and more social scientists have turned their attention to historical subjects in efforts to expand the universe of "cases" for their theoretical studies, or because they recognize the importance of understanding the past in addressing the problems of the present. Meanwhile, many historians have been attempting to incorporate social science theory and methods into their work, tendencies that reflect historians' dissatisfaction with the relative lack of theory and method-ological rigor in their own disciplinary tradition.

As a result, it is often assumed that the traditional disciplinary bound-aries between the social sciences and history are being dismantled. But the curious fact remains that even the most celebrated historical writing by social scientists is often received coolly by historians—and vice versa. Historians often grumble that history written by social scientists is "forced" or inattentive to "context." They complain that such history often fails to incorporate archival work with "primary sources," is filled with "jargon," or distorts historical "reality" in its efforts to "model" or "theorize." Social scientists, for their part, often find work by historians "too descriptive," "unsystematic," or insufficiently "analytical." They are frequently frustrated by historians' failure to situate their work in com-parative or theoretical contexts.

These judgments, as we shall see, reflect different assumptions about the most appropriate and productive ways to engage in the study of social change. And those assumptions, in turn, generate particular disciplinary strengths and weaknesses, qualities that are often interrelated. Writing history in one tradition or the other thus involves fundamental intellec-tual trade-offs. Improved mutual understanding of what is gained and what is lost can help historians and social scientists better appreciate each other's disciplinary strengths and better address their own discipli-nary weaknesses. Social science methods, for example, can help historians correct their manifest inability to engage in cross-national com-parison and the study of global processes that affect more than one national society or cultural region of the world.

Perhaps the most important differences in the methods of historians and social scientists, however, have to do with their implications for demo-cratic scholarship. I will argue that, in terms of its internal logic, the discipline of history is generally more democratic than its social science counterparts. But if that is true in theory, it is not equally true in practice. Comparison of the ways historians and social scientists do their work serves to remind historians of the democratic promise of their methods. That is a revelation of special import to the labor historians among them.

Many historians, perhaps the majority, would disagree with elements of the logic I describe here, especially the notion that it contains inherent democratic tendencies (however unfulfilled in actual practice). Such critics must either deny that any logic informs what historians do or else find a more persuasive way of explaining why historians, despite all their other differences (of area, temporal, and thematic specialization and of philosophical and political commitment), exhibit in their procedures such remarkable fidelity to the disciplinary canons described below.

Critics in the social sciences will undoubtedly find the contrast I draw between their methods and those of historians deficient on other grounds. As a generalization, it fails to appreciate the scope and subtleties of their own debates about methods, and lumps together disciplines that actually diverge on many of the issues emphasized here. In response, I can only insist that for purposes of distinguishing between the ways that social scientists and historians write history—as revealed in the ways they define problems, prepare themselves for research, evaluate scholarship, decide on expository strategies, and train new professionals in their fields—the methodological differences I examine are important. Clarifying these differences may contribute to more meaningful dialogue between historians and social scientists. It may also alert them to the different ways their methods inhibit their ability to contribute to the democratic project both often claim is integral to their professional callings.

Close analysis of the way historians work reveals three essential pillars of their method. The first is their insistence on mastery of the *historiography* on a place and time as a prerequisite for all research. (This and the following terms are defined and explained below.) The second is insistence on the critical use of *primary sources* in generating new historical understanding. The third is emphasis on the *interconnectedness* of all aspects of social change. These interlocking concepts form what I call the "logic" of the discipline of history. Social scientists who engage in study of the past typically ignore or violate each of these three principles in pursuit of their different theoretical assumptions and methodological goals.

Historiography

Historians aspire to command what is known about the history of the place and time they specialize in. Their definition of these specialized fields is revealed in the job descriptions they write for the positions they hold and the body of knowledge they expect graduate students to acquire to qualify for such jobs in the future. Traditionally, the "place" in which historians specialize is a nation-state. And the "time" they focus on is usually a period, defined by major political events, of that nation's history. The definitions of historians' specialties betray the nationalist political origins of the discipline.

By "command" of the knowledge of a place and time historians mean in practice that they try to make themselves familiar with all the published books and articles on its history. Historians call this material the "secondary literature" of their field. By that they mean to distinguish this interpretive published material from the "primary" sources, usually documents located in archives, on which they base their research. Historians believe that mastery of the secondary literature on their field is a prerequisite for primary research. That is why graduate students in history are expected to read everything of importance in the secondary literature on their field of specialization and pass a comprehensive examination on this material before they are allowed to begin dissertation research. (In contrast, budding social scientists are trained first in a branch of social theory, such as rural sociology or macro-economics, and once they are judged to be competent in it, they can engage in "case studies" to test or advance that theory. Their cases may range across the cultural areas of the globe and backward in time.)

Historians call this analysis of the secondary literature on the history of a time and place the practice of historiography, or "the study of the study of history." Historiography is what might be called history's "sociology of knowledge." It insists on explanations of how past observers and schools of thought—each influenced by historical events, by class, gender, ethnic, and national allegiances, by intellectual trends and cultural biases, and by personal inclinations and individual politics—interpreted a given historical reality. Historians believe that mastery of the historiography of a time and place must precede research for several reasons. First, because only by evaluating all that is publicly known about a given social reality can one undertake truly new and productive research. Second, this kind of mastery alerts historians to all preexisting "facts" and alternative interpretations that must be addressed and subsumed, modified, or disarmed in any new interpretation of events. Third, as part of the intellectual history of the object of study, previous work is an element of the interconnected social totality (the third pillar of the historical method, discussed below). Fourth, and most important to this discussion, such mastery should make historians conscious of the fact that they themselves are influenced in their perceptions of the past by the same kinds of social and cultural forces that have affected their predecessors.

For all these reasons, but especially the last, the study of historiography should force historians to come to terms with their own position in the historical process. Ideally, it should lead them to ask themselves (and explain to their readers) why they propose to study a given subject in a certain way, with certain goals, at a certain point in time. However, historians rarely take this last, vitally important, step. Most of those in the liberal mainstream customarily adopt a stance before their audience that implies an objective, academic neutrality. They act as if they, unlike the primary sources and secondary works they depend on, were free of the perceptual bias that colors all understanding. One might think that

Marxist scholars, who in contrast emphasize the class dimensions of all knowledge, would have a better record on this issue. In fact, the orthodox among them adopt the position that theirs is a "scientific" theory of human history which, properly interpreted, can reveal the truth about the past. It is these kinds of historians, liberal and Marxist alike, who must feel most threatened by the assumptions of postmodernism discussed in the previous section.

When historians recognize their own assumptions and are straightforward about communicating them to their readers they do not abdicate the scholarly canons of their discipline. What they do is put them into practice in democratic ways. They warn readers to be on guard against the inevitable bias in their work and ask them to judge it, not simply according to their own predispositions, but in terms of its ability to make better sense than other interpretations of the historical information and analysis on the table. To proceed in this democratic way, moreover, follows logically from the emphasis on critical mastery of the historiography of a time and place. When historians fail to acknowledge their own motivations and assumptions they compromise both their disciplinary and their democratic credentials.

Most social scientists who write history ignore historiography. That does not mean that they do not read significant amounts of the secondary historical literature on the subject they study. In fact, they mine that literature for the kind of information they are seeking to test theory or a model of social change. But they usually do not read this secondary material comprehensively and systematically, do not evaluate it in the rigorous historiographical ways described above, and thus often use the material they glean from it uncritically. Like most historians and other academics, most social scientists fail to make their own assumptions and motivations clear to their readers, hiding instead behind an appeal to objective knowledge and social science theory.

Primary sources

The second pillar of the disciplinary logic of historians, the emphasis on primary sources, often appears to scholars outside the discipline, especially social scientists, to be an irrational disciplinary fetish. For their part, general readers often experience frustration over the volume of detailed references to primary material that fill the pages and footnotes of most professional historical works. To the non-historian, many academics seem more preoccupied with citing and discussing their primary and secondary sources than with advancing their main story in the text.

There is no doubt about the importance that historians attach to primary sources. They require that beginning historians build their doctoral dissertations on primary material, and reserve their highest praise for work that incorporates newly discovered or newly understood primary sources. The first thing many professional historians do when they pick up a new book in their field is to thumb through the footnotes and check the bibliography. They want to see if the author reveals a command of the historiography on the subject and what new primary archival sources have been employed. If the author fails these two initial tests, many historians will not even bother to read the work or, if they do, will proceed with great misgivings.

These attitudes and behaviors are clues to the importance of primary sources to the inner logic of the discipline. Much of historians' training revolves around learning to "read" primary sources, that is, learning how to appreciate their innate distortion of reality. Historians understand that all primary material (like the secondary work scrutinized by their critical historiography) emanates from sources colored by interests of self, group, gender, class, and so on. Ideally, then, for historians there are really no "facts," just bits of information that must be evaluated, corroborated from different angles, or rejected as implausible or unimportant. Historians are also acutely aware of the fact that the same source—a quotation from a letter or a diary, for example—is subject to different, even multiple, interpretations. That is why they insist on detailed citation of the source material they use. That way, in theory at least, anyone who takes the time to find the source can check to see if the author's use of it conforms with their own sense of its context and meaning. Full citation of primary sources thus involves deep disciplinary as well as democratic principles. In contrast to all these procedures, most social scientists either neglect primary sources or use them uncritically, as sources of "facts."

In reality, few readers will ever check a primary source. Yet the possibility of doing so acts as an independent control over the honesty and credibility of the historian. Nevertheless, fixation on primary sources can easily detract from the other goals of the historical method. It can beguile historians into believing that they are simply reporting the "facts," and that the "facts," arranged in chronological order, reveal the way history "really happened." It can lead them to concentrate on the minutiae of the part and leave them blind to the nature of the whole. And it certainly inhibits them from doing comparison, especially across national boundaries into cultures whose languages they do not know. Finally, the sheer volume of primary source material can overwhelm or dismay general readers, whose reading of history competes with other demands on their time.

Interconnectedness

The third principle of the disciplinary logic of historians is the emphasis on the interrelatedness of all aspects of social change. It is this concern with totality that most sharply distinguishes history from the social sciences.

Most of the social sciences base their methods on the idea that it is more meaningful and productive to consider a slice of social reality, the economy, for example, or the polity, or the ideas or actions of social groups. They search for important patterns in this circumscribed reality and measure their dynamics over time. Social scientists are interested in generating or testing universal theory about their narrow thematic domain across time and space.

Historians, in contrast, aspire to understand change in whole societies, usually, as noted above, individual nations or cultural regions in a single period of time. Although historical research is often highly specialized (and has become more so over time), the goal of historians' training and scholarship is mastery of what is known about the past of a given subject, usually a nation-state, during a certain period. That usually entails study of the nation's language (or languages) and its literature, its economy, polity, and social structure, its intellectual life, and, increasingly today, its science, its technology, and its impact on the natural environment. Historians are thus less concerned than their social science colleagues with universal theory and are notorious for failing to engage in the kinds of cross-cultural, cross-national, cross-temporal comparison that social scientists routinely perform. But on their own terrain, historians are uniquely well equipped to deal concretely with the subtle, manifold, and dialectical interconnectedness of a bounded social life during a certain period of time.

Insistence on the interconnectedness of social change means for historians that everything affects, and is in turn affected by, everything else (values, perceptions, ideas, technology, economic and social change, and so forth). Interconnectedness also means that everyone affects historical change and is in turn affected by it. This simple and obvious notion (which social scientists share in some measure with historians but choose to relegate to a lower priority in their pursuit of other disciplinary objectives) has had revolutionary implications for the discipline of history. One index of this process is the way historians have reacted to the democratic demands of popular forces. When historians began to define themselves professionally in the nineteenth century, primary sources were conceived of largely as documents created by the state and by men of affairs. Over time, however, the principle of interconnectedness has allowed historians to respond to democratic social forces by widening and deepening the definition of sources. Since the 1960s, to take a recent example I have already discussed, the discipline has bestowed great prestige on "new social historians" who use sources as mundane as the baptismal records of common people, daily police logs that record what elites define as "criminality," and the popular novels consumed by working people.

Another important—and inherently democratic—effect of the principle of interconnectedness is revealed in the manner in which historians present their research. Traditionally, historians preferred narrative forms, stories, rather than more obviously analytical modes of discourse. And unlike their social science colleagues, most have resisted using or inventing language outside the domain of an audience they define as "the general reading public." These expository strategies reveal deep disciplinary assumptions and have important democratic consequences. If everything affects everything else, as historians stress, then the best way to proceed would seem to be to advance one step at a time, chronologically, assessing the influences of change in one sphere on all others and the impact of the dialectical reverberations that result. And if everyone affects history and is in turn affected by history, then it stands to reason that historians must try to write for the general reading public and listen to its responses.

In recent decades historians have found it harder and harder to sustain their commitment to the principle that all aspects of historical change are connected. They are also abandoning the democratic writing styles related to this principle. Some of the reasons for these changes are more understandable and defensible than others. But all have compromised the appeal of historical studies to a broad general public.

A first reason relates to the principle of interconnectedness itself. If everything is connected to everything else, and everyone affects and is affected by history, how does the historian decide what and who is more important? How are historians to decide what to research and which kinds of sources to use? How are they to unravel the "seamless web" of history and isolate and weigh the most important elements in causing historical change? To tell the truth, many traditional historians invoked the canons of the discipline to justify a subject for study simply because it "had not yet been done" or because a set of primary sources had "not yet been tapped." And they often came up with causal explanations that reflected unexamined personal inclinations as well as the national, class, gender, and other perspectives we have noted. As historians have become more sophisticated about these matters, in large part because of the criticism of their work by other academics, many have realized the opportunities presented by more theoretical approaches to their subjects. As a group they have become more systematic in their choice of research problems and strategies and more formally analytical in their writing. In the process, however, many have also adopted the specialized discourse of their fellow academics, and some have abandoned narrative discourse altogether.

A second reason for the retreat from the principle of interconnectedness has to do with the development of the discipline itself. As the number of historians has grown, and the volume of the secondary literature has expanded, historians have had an increasingly difficult time keeping up with the literature in their fields. They have responded to this problem by steadily subdividing the fields of history into ever narrower geographic, temporal, and thematic compartments. Increasing specialization has greatly enriched and expanded the range and depth of historical study in the aggregate. But it has led historians into narrow fields of specialization and limited their ability to relate the part of history they study to the whole. This process of specialization is driven, professionally, by the demands of the first two canons of the discipline. In order to validate themselves professionally, new generations of historians must engage in new primary research in sources untapped by their predecessors. At the same time, they must demonstrate command of an increasingly voluminous secondary literature in their chosen field. The result has been ever greater specialization in fields that must be subdivided in order to remain manageable. Fidelity to the first two concerns of the discipline, in other words, progressively undercuts attention to the third, the principle of interconnectedness.

As historians become ever more specialized, they talk increasingly not to the general public or even to historians generally, but to fellow specialists, the people who must read this highly specialized work in order to maintain their own professional standing. Making sense of much of this writing depends on knowledge of a highly specialized literature, and often on command of a highly specialized academic language. Specialization, in short, has limited historians' understanding of the interconnectedness of social change and has led them away from addressing a general audience in language widely shared.

This whole process has gone furthest in rich, highly developed places and fields like the United States. In underdeveloped places and fields like Latin America historians are still able to command a wide range of secondary literature and they retain a strong commitment to understanding the interconnected nature of historical change. This is true not only at the level of national history, where most historians still confine their work, but at the international level as well. Given the great disparity of power and development that has resulted from the history of colonialism in this hemisphere, for example, students of Latin American history are far more conscious than their colleagues in US history of the global forces that have influenced the history of the place they study.

To the extent that historians are able to reconcile and balance all three of the mutually supporting pillars of their method they are being true not only to their disciplinary calling, but also to a democratic calling. Insistence on evaluating historiography and primary sources is fundamental to the task of constructing democratic societies. Citizens must learn how to discern bias in existing understandings of their social past. That way, they become more capable of judging how things got to be the way they are and of making intelligent political decisions on how best to improve them. But because all perception is governed by questions of class, gender, ethnicity, and so on, only by diffusing knowledge about the past to the general public can democratic understandings of the past stand a chance of influencing current political practice. Thus the historian's ongoing professional dilemma—the need to cleave to all three disciplinary principles and at the same time reach a general audience—both defines and limits the democratic promise of the historical method.

These considerations provide the formal, disciplinary rationale behind a book like this one, which looks at the history of the Americas, particularly that of the United States, from the perspective of a Latin American labor historian. For the most part, the book is not based on primary research. And although it is vitally concerned with key interpretive issues, it does not deal comprehensively with the historiography of each of these subjects. Its primary concern is to make connections, heretofore largely ignored, between the history of working people and the broader history of democracy in the Americas.

In disciplinary terms, then, the book downplays attention to the first two canons of the historical method in favor of emphasizing the third. It is this third dimension, the one that stresses the interconnectedness of social change, that is least emphasized in the work of contemporary US historians. It is also the principle of the historical method whose democratic implications are most ignored in practice by professional historians today.

I have sought throughout to emphasize the democratic corollaries of each of the three principles of the historical method I have outlined. I have tried to be explicit about my own pro-labor position. That does not mean that I have sacrificed a commitment to scholarship. On the contrary, I have attempted to come to terms with the primary material or "facts" about American history as we know them today. And I have been especially concerned with interpretations of this history at variance with my own, measuring them against the evidence, testing them through the logic of comparative analysis. Finally, I have tried to write a book about the construction of historical meaning in language that is accessible to general readers.

The book has stressed connections between US and Latin American history, between social and diplomatic history, between economic change and cultural understandings, that generally go unperceived by historians and the general public in the Americas. Making these connections illustrates the dialectical nature of democratic progress in the hemisphere. It reveals how struggles by working people in one part of the Americas affect the course of democratic politics and cultural understanding in the other. I have not attempted to provide readers with detailed political prescriptions for the many complex issues facing working people in the hemisphere today. What I have tried to do is outline democratic historical ways to think about them.

Further Reading

Note: On labor, readers may also consult the books by Brody, Dubofsky, Montgomery, and Gordon, Eduards, and Reich cited in chapter 2.

Arrighi, Giovanni, The *Long Twentieth Century*, London 1994.
Braverman, Harry, *Labor and Monopoly Capitalism*, New York 1974.
Burawoy, Michael, *Manufacturing Consent*, Chicago 1982.
—— *The Politics of Production*, London 1985.
Chirot, Daniel, ed., *The Crisis of Leninism and the Decline of the Left*, Seattle 1991.
Cronin, James, *The World the Cold War Made*, London, forthcoming.
Davis, Mike, *Prisoners of the American Dream*, London 1986.
De Soto, Hernando, *The Other Path*, New York 1989.
Emmanuel, Arghiri, *Unequal Exchange*, New York 1972.
Geoghegan, Thomas, *Which Side Are You On?*, New York 1991.
Gordon, Andrew, *The Evolution of Labor Relations in Japan*, Cambridge, MA, 1988.
Honey, Michael, *Southern Labor and Black Civil Rights*, Urbana, IL, 1993.
Hunnicutt, Benjamin Kline, *Work Without End*, Philadelphia 1988.
Keck, Margaret E., *The Workers' Party and Democratization in Brazil*, New Haven, CT, 1992.
Laba, Roman, *The Roots of Solidarity*, Princeton, NJ, 1991.
Lichtenstein, Nelson, *Labor's War at Home*, Cambridge, UK, 1982.

―― *The Most Dangerous Man in Detroit*, New York 1995.

McCormick, Thomas J., *America's Half-Century*, Baltimore 1989.

Maier, Charles, "Two Postwar Eras and the Conditions for Stability in Twentieth-Century Western Europe," *American Historical Review*, vol. 86, no. 2, April 1981, pp. 327–52.

Palmer, Bryan, *Descent into Discourse*, Philadelphia 1990.

Portes, Alejandro, Manuel Castels, and Lauren A. Benton, eds., *The Informal Economy*, Baltimore 1989.

Rakowski, Cathy A., ed., *Contrapunto: The Informal Sector Debate in Latin America*, Albany, NY, 1994.

Reich, Robert B., *The Work of Nations*, New York 1991.

Schor, Juliet, *The Overworked American*, New York 1992.

Scott, Joan Wallach, *Gender and the Politics of History*, New York 1988.

Seidman, Gay Willcox, *Manufacturing Militance*, Berkeley, CA, 1994.

Spalding, Hobart, *Organized Labor in Latin America*, New York 1977.

Thompson, E.P., *The Making of the English Working Class*, New York 1963.

Wilkins, Mira, *The Maturing of Multinational Enterprise*, Cambridge, MA, 1974.